CONGRESS
and the WANING of the NEW DEAL

Kennikat Press
National University Publications
Series in Political Science

DAVID L. PORTER

CONGRESS and the WANING of the NEW DEAL

National University Publications
KENNIKAT PRESS // 1980
Port Washington, N.Y. // London

Manufactured in the United States of America

Published by
Kennikat Press Corp.
Port Washington, N.Y. / London

Library of Congress Cataloging in Publication Data

Porter, David L 1941-
   Congress and the waning of the New Deal.

   (Political science series) (National university publications)
      Bibliography: p.
      Includes index.
      1. United States. Congress—History. 2. United States—Politics and government—1933-1945. 3. United States—Economic policy—1933-1945. I. Title.
   II. Series: Political science series (Port Washington, N.Y.)
JK1059 76th.P67   328.73'09'043   79-19328
ISBN 0-8046-9254-8

CONTENTS

ACKNOWLEDGMENTS

Numerous individuals and groups helped immensely during the research phase of this study. Several members of the Seventy-sixth Congress, including C. Jasper Bell, Clifford R. Hope, Claude Pepper, the late John M. Vorys, and Lindsay C. Warren, kindly gave me permission to examine their congressional correspondence. Relatives and friends of Clarence Cannon, Jr., Rush Dew Holt, Daniel A. Reed, and John Taber generously made their manuscript collections available. Arthur Kogan of the State Department and William S. Coker of the University of West Florida granted me access to the Cordell Hull and Pat Harrison papers, respectively.

Librarians, of course, facilitated the project enormously. The personnel and staff of the National Archives and of the Franklin D. Roosevelt Presidential Library particularly gave me invaluable assistance. I am also indebted to the considerable aid and hospitality afforded by the manuscript divisions and staffs of the Library of Congress, the Washington National Records Center, Georgetown University, Rutgers University, New York Public Library, Dartmouth College, University of Vermont, Cornell University, West Virginia University, Western Reserve Historical Society, Ohio State Historical Society, University of Kentucky, University of Michigan, University of Chicago, Herbert Hoover Presidential Library, University of Iowa, University of Missouri, Harry S. Truman Presidential Library, Kansas State Historical Society, Nebraska State Historical Society, University of Wyoming, University of California, Berkeley, Arizona State University, University of Oklahoma, University of Texas, University of Southern Mississippi, University of Florida, University of North Carolina, Duke University, and University of Virginia. At various stages Miriam Hess of the Pennsylvania State University Library and Marion Rains and staff of the William Penn College Library provided assistance.

Three sources deserve special mention. Financial assistance from the National Science Foundation enabled me to learn more about the application of computers to the social sciences at the University of Michigan. The Inter-University Consortium for Political Research at the University of Michigan graciously afforded me the use of relevant roll call data. I am particularly grateful to the National Endowment for the Humanities for providing me with financial assistance. The NEH grant enabled me to participate in a summer seminar for college teachers at the Hoover Presidential Library. The seminar enhanced considerably my understanding of the nature of reform and the role it played in the Harding, Coolidge, Hoover, and Franklin Roosevelt administrations. In addition, the NEH grant afforded me an opportunity to examine several pertinent manuscript collections both at the Hoover Library and the University of Iowa Library.

I am very grateful to the participants in the NEH seminar for helping to clarify for me the nature of American reform in the 1920's and 1930's. Seminar director Martin L. Fausold of the State University of New York at Geneseo, Ellis W. Hawley and Lawrence E. Gelfand of the University of Iowa, Donald R. Mc Coy of the University of Kansas, George H. Nash of West Branch, Iowa, Richard Lowitt and Richard N. Kottman of Iowa State University, Peter T. Harstad of the State Historical Society of Iowa, and Susan E. Kennedy of Virginia Commonwealth University provided me with enormous background information on the development of American reform. Discussions with seminar participants, including James E. Cebula of Raymond Walters College, Roger W. Corley of Northwest Missouri State University, Larry Grothaus of Concordia Teachers College, David A. Horowitz of Portland State University, Bernard M. Klass of L. A. Pierce College, Carl E. Krog of the University of Wisconsin Center - Marinette, C. Roger Lambert of Arkansas State University, David D. Lee of Western Kentucky University, Nile P. Norton of Our Lady Lake University, William G. Robbins of Oregon State University, and William R. Tanner of Humboldt State University helped clarify my understanding of American reform.

This book has benefited from the help and criticism of several people. I am particularly indebted to Ari Hoogenboom of Brooklyn College, who helped foster my interest in both political history and the Seventy-sixth Congress. Robert James Maddox, Elton Atwater, and Harry Stein of Pennsylvania State University made constructive suggestions on individual chapters. Cornell Jaray, editor in chief of Kennikat Press, provided several helpful suggestions concerning the general format. I dedicate this work to my wife Marilyn, who has been a tremendous source of inspiration to me throughout the study. Justus D. Doenecke of the University of South Florida made numerous perceptive comments and suggestions on the entire manuscript.

PREFACE

Historians originally made several basic assumptions about Congress in the New Deal era. The legislative branch was pictured as being a virtual rubberstamp for President Franklin D. Roosevelt in enacting a wide variety of relief, recovery, and reform measures. Congress, they stressed, approved numerous proposals during the "first hundred days" and then continued the hectic pace for the remainder of Roosevelt's first term. Despite congressional opposition in 1937 to Supreme Court reorganization, the chief executive was depicted as clearly leading and controlling both the Senate and the House.[1] The sharp differences between the White House and the Supreme Court over the constitutionality of New Deal agencies captured great attention from academia. The Republican Party usually was characterized as being very weak numerically and disorganized on legislative roll calls.[2] Historians also argued that New Deal reforms terminated with the Fair Labor Standards Act of 1938, implying that little happened on domestic issues in the 1939–41 period. They paid scant attention to the development of the Republican–conservative Democratic coalition in the legislative branch, concentrating instead on the congressional response to foreign policy and defense measures.[3]

Some traditional assumptions were modified when writers began examining the entire New Deal period. The journalist Samuel Lubell argued that by 1938 conservative southern Democrats in Congress had started clashing with Roosevelt and aligning with Republicans resisting New Deal measures. The southern filibuster against the anti-lynching bill of 1938 and the President's unsuccessful purge of selected conservative Democratic senators the same year further split the majority party. James MacGregor Burns and William E. Leuchtenburg, in penetrating analyses of the New Deal, rejected the rubberstamp concept and described the congressional rebellion from 1937 to 1939 against the President on domestic issues. Roosevelt's attempt to reform the Supreme Court in 1937 undercut his authority with Congress and triggered the alliance of Republicans and conservative Democrats. At the 1938 session the bipartisan coalition gave Roosevelt few legislative victories and waged a successful defensive battle against expansion of New Deal reforms. The President's abortive purge of conservative Democrats in the 1938 primaries backfired, as the anti-Roosevelt bloc gained considerable numerical strength in Congress. According to Burns and Leuchtenburg, the alliance by 1939 seized the offensive from the President and extended legislative controls over the executive branch. Besides conducting investigations of New Deal policies, the coalition exercised authority over the hiring of administrative personnel and sliced funds for bureaucratic agencies. Burns and Leuchtenburg concentrated on the anti–New Deal Democrats in the 1938 period.[4]

Two excellent studies in the late 1960s substantiated the interpretations made by Burns and Leuchtenburg. Richard Polenberg examined how the anti-Roosevelt coalition in Congress rejected the President's legislation to reorganize the executive branch, dampening prospects for the future of the New Deal as a reform movement. Besides analyzing Roosevelt's reorganization program, Polenberg concluded that the Senate and the House held considerable independence by 1938 from the White House. In a perceptive landmark study James T. Patterson provided the most comprehensive and analytical account of Congress and especially of the anti-Roosevelt forces in the 1937–39 period. According to Patterson, the southern Democrats directed the revolt by conservatives within Roosevelt's party. The President's plan to enlarge the Supreme Court marked the major turning point in executive-legislative relations, providing a common issue on which conservative Democrats could unite with Republicans. Senator Arthur H. Vandenberg of Michigan and the midwestern delegations provided the core of Republican opposition to Roosevelt's internal policies. Deflating the rubberstamp theory, Patterson described how the bipartisan coalition seized the initiative from the administration in opposing housing, reorganization, relief, and tax measures. The rapidly growing Republican minority became much more organized and influential on domestic legislation following the 1938 elections. Patterson also stressed that Congress considered a wide variety of New Deal measures after adopting the Fair Labor Standards Act, but he devoted only one chapter to the post-1938 period.[5]

Historians, however, have made no serious effort to determine if traditional assumptions about Congress should be revised for the post-1938 portion of the New Deal. A major gap has remained in historical literature concerning domestic legislation enacted by Congress in the period immediately preceding American entrance into World War 2. Historians have concentrated so assiduously on the response of President Roosevelt and Congress to German expansion in Europe and Japanese movement in Asia that domestic legislation has received scant attention. In an effort to fill the existing void, this historian examines the role of the Seventy-sixth Congress in enacting during 1939 and 1940 several major economic and political measures.

This book likewise challenges several traditional interpretations about Congress in the New Deal era. By mid-1939 the legislative branch clearly had seized the offensive from the Roosevelt administration on economic and political issues. Congress wielded an increased amount of independent power on domestic questions, extending legislative controls over the executive branch. The nature and leadership of the conservative coalition on some economic legislation defies traditional stereotypes. Republican members, although still belonging to a minority party, were organized quite effectively by 1939 and often capitalized on sharp divisions within the Democratic Party.

This book argues that the New Deal entered a third stage after 1938. Historians traditionally have divided the New Deal into two stages, the first covering 1933-34 and the second extending from 1935-38. The First New Deal utilized the federal government to promote business recovery and agricultural relief, as exemplified in the National Recovery and Agricultural Adjustment Acts. The Second New Deal stressed social justice and reform and was much more comprehensive in scope, extending federal assistance to include organized labor and the unemployed. Organized labor benefited from the Wagner National Labor Relations Act and the Fair Labor Standards Act, while the unemployed were hired by the Works Progress Administration and other relief agencies. A more liberal, innovative stage, the Second New Deal markedly increased federal spending for public works projects and relief programs and initiated the social security system. Historians usually stress that the Second New Deal ended with the Fair Labor Standards Act of 1938 and seldom discuss subsequent New Deal reforms.

The third stage of the New Deal, which began in January, 1939, was characterized by a spirited battle between the New Deal Democrats and a bipartisan conservative coalition. During the third stage, Congress increased its power in relation to the executive branch, extended several New Deal programs, enacted a few pioneering domestic measures, and reduced federal spending. Utilizing a case study approach, this book examines the role of Congress in three economic and three political measures enacted in the 1939-40 period. The New Deal economic issues include extension of the presidential power to devalue the dollar and purchase foreign silver, enactment of transportation reform, and continuation of the reciprocal trade agreements program. Works Progress Administration funding, reorganization of executive agencies, and restriction of campaign activities of federal officials are the three political questions scrutinized.

The third stage of the New Deal, like the Republican era from 1921 to 1933, was more reform-minded than previously thought. Traditionally, the Warren Harding, Calvin Coolidge, and Herbert Hoover presidencies have been pictured as periods of relatively little reform following the extensive innovations of the progressive era. Historians increasingly have described the reforms accomplished by the Hoover presidency and, to a lesser extent, by the Harding and Coolidge administrations.[6] This book describes how the New Deal continued on a more restricted basis after 1938 and how Congress continued to enact significant domestic programs.

Although many significant bills were enacted, several considerations influenced this historian to select these six particular legislative issues for closer examination. James T. Patterson briefly summarized the congressional response in 1939 to monetary policies, work relief, and executive reorganization, but the six specific measures studied here have not received extensive analysis in other historical works. Historians have explored very little the nature and impact of legislative action on monetary, transportation, and trade issues. Allan Seymour Everest and Fred L. Israel mentioned the Monetary Act of 1939, featuring the roles of Secretary of the Treasury Henry Morgenthau, Jr., and Senator Key Pittman of Nevada.[7] Ralph L. Dewey, Truman C. Bigham, Robert W. Harbeson, Claude Moore Fuess, and Ari and Olive Hoogenboom analyzed the provisions and impact of the Transportation Act of 1940, stressing the effect upon the Interstate Commerce Commission.[8] The origins and operation of the reciprocal trade program have been investigated by James C. Pearson, Lloyd C. Gardner, Samuel Flagg Bemis, Richard N. Kottman, and others, but the 1940 congressional battle over extending the policy is seldom discussed.[9] Historians have treated political issues slightly more often, but have focused primarily on the pre-1939 period. Searle F. Charles, Donald S. Howard, and Jane DeHart Mathews investigated the influence of the Works Progress Administration, concentrating either on the agency director Harry Hopkins or on the federal theater-arts program.[10] Executive reorganization has been investigated by Barry Dean Karl, Richard Polenberg, and A. J. Wann, who stressed the origins of the controversy and the stormy congressional reception prior to the 1939 session.[11] The Hatch Acts have been referred to often by historians, but the initial legislative battle over their enactment is hardly mentioned.[12]

The six measures provoked lively controversy in the Seventy-sixth

Congress. Senators and representatives, both in public statements and in private correspondence, often phrased their views on these questions in very candid, colorful terminology. These issues, therefore, make excellent examples for testing the various traditional assumptions about the New Deal and for determining the nature of congressional alignments. In addition, they furnish good models for examining whether political party affiliation or sectional considerations had a greater impact on congressional voting behavior, for revealing to what extent the legislative branch actually rebelled against the President, and for showing how much pressure groups influenced congressional action.

Each issue selected profoundly affected major aspects of American economic and political life. The monetary question centered on whether the United States should raise or lower the value of the dollar in relation to gold and continue purchasing foreign silver. In regard to transportation, Congress debated if the federal government should still help the tottering railroads and if inland waterways should be regulated. Concerning trade, the legislative branch argued whether the United States should maintain a low tariff policy encouraging foreigners to undersell American producers or raise duties on imports and discourage foreign competition. On the WPA issue representatives and senators argued over the degree to which the national government should furnish relief for the unemployed and whether the jobless rate still warranted massive federal intervention. Reorganization focused principally on how to create greater efficiency in national government and on deciding how much direct control the President should have over administrative agencies. When considering the Hatch Acts, the legislative branch debated the financing of elections and the extent to which further restrictions should be placed on the activity of government officials in federal and state primaries and elections.

These issues still remain vital. The mass media continually discuss how to improve the status of the dollar in relation to the gold standard. Railroads face numerous problems competing with other forms of transportation and continue receiving substantial federal subsidies. Foreign competitors flood American markets with cheaper goods, provoking protectionist sentiments among some American producers. In the early 1970s unemployment rates soared so much that the federal government again developed public works programs. Several recent presidents have proposed reorganization of the executive branch so as to make the bureaucracy run more efficiently and economically. Following the Watergate-related scandals, Americans pressured Congress to enact major campaign reform legislation limiting political spending and curbing election malpractices.

This book has several basic objectives. It attempts to provide the reader with an increased understanding of the nature of Congress in a period characterized by the decline in prestige of New Deal programs. In order to provide a sharper focus, the origins, committee treatment, floor debates, voting, and impact of the various economic and political issues are examined. This book concentrates on the battle within Congress between the New Dealers and the bipartisan conservative coalition. New Dealers were comprised almost exclusively of Democrats, who supported the growth o executive power and opposed any significant reduction in federal expenditures for domestic programs. They not only favored keeping intact existing New Deal monetary, reciprocal trade, and work relief programs, but backed executive reorganization' and generally rejected the Hatch Acts. On the other hand, the bipartisan conservative coalition included nearly all Republicans and a fluctuating number of anti-New Deal Democrats. Besides opposing the increase in Presidential power, they urged slashing federal expenditures for New Deal programs. The conservative coalition favored terminating New Deal monetary, reciprocal trade, and work relief programs, disapproved of executive reorganization, and largely backed the Hatch Acts. The transportation issue, it should be noted, did not divide along New Deal-conservative lines. In addition, there are descriptions of the leaders directing the congressional battles for the New Dealers and the bipartisan conservative coalition on each particular measure. This book, through utilizing both published sources and manuscript correspondence, seeks to delineate the fundamental sources of contention between the New Dealers and the conservatives on each legislative question. The degree of leadership exhibited by President Roosevelt and the executive branch on each issue is explored to determine how much control they actually had over Congress. Through probing executive-legislative relations, this work shows whether the Senate and the House still followed the President's direction or had placed Roosevelt on the defensive. The relative impact of pressure groups is assessed in securing enactment of each economic and political measure.

Roll-call data supplied by the Inter-University Consortium for Political Research at the University of Michigan serves as the basis for making generalizations about party and sectional alignments which are scrutinized for economic and political issues. The Appendix Tables show these alignments on significant Senate and House roll calls.[13] They show the relative importance of party versus regional loyalties and how these loyalties shifted and to what degree in the Senate and the House. Eight major geographic regions were used to determine the impact of sectionalism.[14]

CONGRESS
and the WANING of the NEW DEAL

David L. Porter is an associate professor of history at William Penn College in Oskaloosa, Iowa. He received his Ph.D. in history from Pennsylvania State University. He is the author of articles in state and topical historical journals.

PART ONE

ECONOMIC REFORM ISSUES

1

EXTENSION
OF THE MONETARY PROGRAM

When the Seventy-sixth Congress convened in January, 1939, Democrats numerically dominated both the Senate and the House. Roosevelt's party held 70 percent of the Senate seats and 60 percent of the House positions, while Republicans filled most remaining places in Congress. Third parties blossomed only in the Middle West and played the most crucial role in the Great Plains Senate delegation. The South exhibited the least effective two-party systems, with the Democrats holding all Senate and House seats. One-party system, also prevailed in the Republican-controlled New England bloc and the Democratic-dominated border and mountain delegations. Those sections wielded a disproportionate amount of power in congressional committees because members had accumulated seniority more easily in one-party areas. Two-party systems flourished most readily among delegations from the Middle Atlantic and Great Lakes sections, which Republicans dominated in the House and Democrats controlled in the Senate.

Although Democrats maintained vast majorities in both chambers, President Franklin D. Roosevelt by early 1939 faced an increasingly rebellious Congress. In the Senate, Republicans had picked up eight seats in the 1938 elections, and twenty to thirty Democrats were disenchanted with New Deal programs. The situation looked even less promising for the Roosevelt administration in the House, where the Republicans had nearly doubled their strength by gaining eighty-one seats. Around one-third of the returning Democrats contemplated aligning with Republican representatives to oppose the extension of New Deal reforms.[1] Congressional conservatives not only began slicing appropriations for Roosevelt's relief agencies, but jeopardized the President's monetary policy.

Fiscal programs had changed drastically during the New Deal. Early twentieth-century presidents had vigorously supported gold as the exclusive national currency. Wrecked by the depression, western farmers had advocated increased currency circulation, and silverites had favored restoring a bimetallic standard. Congress in 1933 had authorized the President to enlarge the monetary supply by minting silver, printing greenbacks, or devaluing the dollar in terms of gold. The following year the legislative branch had established a $2 billion fund to stabilize the dollar in international exchanges. Roosevelt, recognizing that the depression had prompted acute deflation, had reluctantly pursued moderate inflationary policies. Besides taking the nation off the gold standard, he had subsequently devalued the dollar 40 percent in terms of gold. Congress in 1937 had extended both the Stabilization Fund and devaluation powers, but the chief executive's authority would expire in June, 1939.

In another inflationary action the Senate and the House in 1934 had sanctioned a controversial silver purchase program. The legislative branch had compelled the Treasury to purchase silver either until the metal comprised 25 percent of the monetary reserves or until the price of silver increased to $1.29 an ounce. Despite employing under five thousand, the silver industry had received larger federal subsidies under the program than the government had designated for farmers. These purchases, which endangered the currencies of China, Mexico, and Peru, had not ultimately accomplished their twin objectives—namely, the remonetization of silver and the promotion of inflation. Although an inflationist-minded Congress in 1937 had renewed the silver purchases, the program would terminate two years later unless extended.[2]

In early 1939 the Roosevelt administration seized the initiative and requested the increasingly hostile Congress to extend for two years the New Deal monetary program. Sending a message to Capitol Hill on January 19, Roosevelt urged continuation of presidential authority to devalue the dollar, to purchase foreign silver, and to utilize the $2 billion Stabilization Fund. Secretary of the Treasury Henry Morgenthau, Jr., vigorously defended the plan before the House Committee on Coinage, Weights, and Measures and in a letter to the Senate Banking and Currency Commitee chairman, Robert F. Wagner of New York. The administration insisted that continuation of the program would help to stabilize American economic conditions, which were endangered by high tariffs around the world. Roosevelt considered the extension a sound policy to help combat the worsening economic situation, while Morgenthau contended termination of the program would have "disastrous effects on our economy" and "impede the recovery of business." In the view of the executive branch, the program also would promote world trade. Roosevelt claimed his policy would "carry forward international monetary and economic cooperation," whereas Morgenthau considered the plan "a potent instrument for the protection of our stake in world trade." Besides insisting that continuation of the program would further stabilize the dollar, Morgenthau warned that termination would cause the dollar to "depreciate immensely."

The Roosevelt administration linked the monetary program with efforts to protect American security. They were apprehensive because of German expansion in Europe and Japanese movement in China. Roosevelt emphasized that the program would "safeguard the Nation's interests," while Morgenthau likened the policy to "a powerful navy in the field of defense against armed attack." At the same time the executive branch made clear that the program would not involve selling armaments to belligerent nations.[3] Since isolationists still dominated Congress and since the Roosevelt administration was seeking to repeal the arms embargo, they sought to alleviate congressional fears that the monetary plan would be linked to the sale of weapons.

The forty-three-year-old Andrew L. Somers of New York a week later introduced the administration measure in the House. The son of an educator, the Brooklyn Democrat had attended Manhattan College and Pratt Institute and had briefly headed a company manufacturing chemicals. He had entered politics as the protégé of John McCooey, a Brooklyn Democratic leader and personal friend of Andrew's father. Nicknamed the "Boy Congressman," he had been elected at age twenty-nine to the United States House of Representatives from a district filled with Jewish, Irish, Negro, and Italian constituents. A New Dealer, he chaired the House Committee on Coinage, Weights, and Measures and began guiding the administration measure through his committee.

Anti-administration forces did not fare well in the House Committee on Coinage, Weights, and Measures. Republican Chauncey Reed of Illinois directed committee resistance to the bill and was assisted by party colleagues Robert Luce of Massachusetts and August H. Andresen of Minnesota. Reed faced an almost insurmountable task from the outset, not only because Democrats outnumbered Republicans two to one in committee but also since Somers of New York chaired the committee. In the middle of April Somers easily steered the measure 9-5 through his committee. The Somers committee divided strictly along political lines, with the Democrats in favor and the Republicans opposed to the monetary policy. At the outset the House Committee treated the monetary issue as a political rather than an economic or sectional matter.

Political considerations had pervaded House attitudes from the beginning. Democrats eagerly espoused extension of the presidential program, but Republicans took the opposite view. Casting aside their anti–New Deal marriage with Republicans, southern and border Democrats led the battle for renewal of the monetary program. But the minority party vigorously opposed continuing the monetary authority of President Roosevelt.

Both parties relied upon influential representatives to lead their respective battles. Fresh from completing consideration of the Somers bill, the Coinage, Weights, and Measures Committee provided the bulk of the leadership. Chairman Somers of New York conducted strategy for the administration forces and benefited extensively from the help of non-members John E. Rankin of Mississippi and Wright Patman of Texas. Reed of Illinois, ranking Republican committee member, led the struggle for the monetary critics, with Jesse P. Wolcott of Michigan and Luce of Massachusetts lending valuable assistance.

The first major issue at stake concerned the proper role of the executive branch on economic questions. Stressing this aspect above all, Republicans hoped to increase the influence of the congressional branch because they did not occupy the White House. They opposed entrusting the executive branch in general and President Roosevelt in particular with unconstitutional monetary authority and endeavored to restore power to Congress on financial matters. Reed of Illinois urged Congress to rescind "this unwarranted, unlawful, and unconstitutional" measure, while Republican Coinage Committee members requested that "control of money should remain with Congress where it constitutionally belongs." On the other hand, Democrats denied the executive branch was wielding too much power because they controlled the White House. Patman of Texas and other Democrats claimed Roosevelt had not abused his devaluation authority.[4]

Congressmen from both parties argued strenuously whether the program would revive the American economy. Since the American people still suffered from unemployment, lagging production, and other vast internal economic problems, Republicans insisted charity should begin at home. Ralph O. Brewster of Maine complained that the United States was buying gold as "our people starve," while John M. Robsion of Kentucky denounced the United States for being a "Santa Claus." Republicans advocated a monetary program which would protect domestic industries and restore the gold standard. Democrats, however, stressed that the Roosevelt monetary program had helped the American economy. Southerners especially favored the bimetallic standard, which increased the availability of currency. Rankin of Mississippi warned that termination of the policy would "shut the door of hope in the face of the American people."[5]

The third issue concerned how the administration program would affect American foreign trade. Democrats concentrated primarily on this facet of the economic issue, stressing that the proposal would assist American foreign trade throughout the world. According to southerners, an extensive commercial policy would provide their farmers with markets. Democratic Coinage Committee members claimed the measure would afford "protection to our world trade," while Adolph J. Sabath of Illinois insisted the President's program had helped the United States "recapture and reestablish our foreign trade."[6]

The appropriateness of the Roosevelt monetary policy also was argued. Republicans insisted no economic emergency existed and considered the financial expenditure unwarranted. J. Will Taylor of Tennessee criticized the President for creating "more varieties of emergencies under the New Deal than Heinz had canned products," while W. Sterling Cole of New York protested Roosevelt's "raid on the Treasury." Rejecting this view, Democrats insisted that the measure would stabilize an unsteady world economy. Democratic Coinage Committee members boasted the administration program would "discourage other countries from further depreciating their currencies."[7]

The issue of American foreign involvement also arose. This aspect, which was raised more often by Republicans, attracted the least attention. Forming the core of the isolationists, Republicans feared the measure might cause the United States to drop neutrality policies and to intervene in foreign conflicts. Wolcott of Michigan, for example, warned that the extension of the monetary program might "destroy the neutral position." On the other hand, Democrats were confident that Roosevelt's monetary program would not lead to intervention in foreign wars.[8]

Wolcott and Reed shared the leadership for the opposition. Wolcott, who was ranking Republican on the Banking and Currency Committee, chaired a committee devising strategy to terminate the presidential authority on devaluation and to return to the gold standard. His committee on April 18 recommended the establishment of a joint congressional committee to propose monetary changes. Republicans almost unanimously endorsed the recommendations and attracted support from the Democrat Martin Dies, head of the House Committee on Un-American Activities and an ardent opponent of the Roosevelt administration.

The Republicans fought a losing battle on the House floor. They placed their principal hopes on amendments by Luce of Massachusetts to terminate the presidential power to purchase foreign silver and by Reed of Illinois to discontinue the executive authority to devalue the currency. Even though Republicans solidly supported both proposals, the numerically superior Democrats on April 21 were able to defeat the Luce and Reed amendments by 2 to 1 (152-84) and 3 to 2 (225-158) margins, respectively. Shortly afterwards the House, without taking a roll call, extended for two years the presidential monetary program.

Throughout the floor action the monetary issue remained a highly political question. The roll call on the Reed amendment differs strikingly from two hypotheses generally advanced by historians. Historians usually have considered monetary legislation as economic or sectional, but the outcome on the Reed amendment illustrates that political considerations pervaded on this question in the House.[9] Democrats solidly opposed and Republicans unanimously favored terminating the presidential devaluation authority. Since they did not control the White House, the minority party wanted to limit executive strength. Historians have also stressed the coalition of Republicans and conservative Democrats in disapproving New Deal programs, but the alliance did not exist on the Somers measure.[10] Southern and border Democrats did not ally with northern Republicans, coalescing instead with western Democrats. Wielding enormous numerical power, southern and border Democrats led the campaign against the Reed amendment and insured the ultimate approval of the President's monetary program. Northern Republicans, though, led the opposition to the Somers bill in the House.

Although political considerations played the most prominent role, economic factors also influenced the congressional outcome. Southern and border Democrats recognized the administration monetary program had helped to promote economic recovery for farmers. They also stressed that the measure had benefited their section by fostering world trade and by continuing a bimetallic standard, thus increasing the availability of currency. By contrast, northeastern Republicans traditionally advocated greater restrictions on world trade to protect their domestic industries and also favored returning to the gold standard. Western representatives surprised many by not insisting upon higher prices for silver. Wielding relatively few votes in the House, western members preferred to leave the bargaining for higher silver rates up to their more potent Senate counterparts.

The Roosevelt administration naturally welcomed the House outcome, but the measure now rested in the hands of the Senate Banking and Currency Committee. Roosevelt, who lauded the House action as "a model of excellent deliberative work," considered it "very vital" that the Senate committee act favorably on the measure. Wagner of New York, the sixty one-year-old committee chairman, held responsibility for guiding the monetary measure to passage. The son of a janitor, Wagner had migrated at age eight from Germany and had often arisen at 3 a.m. to sell newspapers in his slum neighborhood. "My boyhood was a pretty rough passage," he later admitted, "and impelled me to work for the passage of every measure that I thought would ameliorate the conditions I saw."[11] After graduating with honors from the College of the City of New York and from New York Law School, Wagner had befriended Tammany Hall and served from

1904 to 1918 in the state assembly and senate. Before being elected in 1926 to the United States Senate, he was a justice of the New York supreme court. Stocky, of medium height, the New Dealer had drafted the National Industrial Recovery Act, Social Security Act, National Labor Relations Act, and National Housing Act. Colleagues regarded him as persuasive in Senate cloakrooms, steadfast, persistent, probing, untiring, fearless, candid, courteous, and affable.

Wagner, as usual, performed his committee duty well. He played a major role in steering the administration proposal through the group without amendment, although it did not complete action until the end of spring. With Democrat Alva B. Adams of Colorado the lone dissenter, the committee on June 13 overwhelmingly approved the legislation. Political considerations did not figure nearly as prominently this time, because the five Republicans preferred instead to fight the bill on the floor. The delay in treating the measure, however, hurt the overall prospects for success because a powerful sectional coalition was threatening to defeat the bill.

The Senate approach differed significantly from that of the House. Although politics prevailed in the lower chamber, regionalism figured much more prominently in the Senate. Sectional motivations prompted western Democrats to oppose extension of Roosevelt's monetary program. Led by Key Pittman of Nevada and Adams, mountain Democrats advocated an increase in domestic silver prices. Agrarian western Democrats, directed by Elmer Thomas of Oklahoma, favored cheapening of the dollar and the issuance of some $2 billion in new currency. Pittman predicted that "unless the price of American-produced silver is restored to 77.57 cents an ounce mining conditions will be worse," while Thomas considered cheapening of the dollar as the principal method "to give the people greater buying power." Regional considerations also caused a few conservative Democrats, led by Carter Glass of Virginia, to seek removal of the presidential devaluation authority. Glass, for example, claimed, "No country in the world has ever benefited by cheapening its currency."[12]

Nevertheless, political considerations still played a prominent role in the Senate action. As in the House, support for the President's program came almost exclusively from Democrats. Southern Democrats led the struggle to extend the presidential purchasing powers, although Wagner of New York and Majority Leader Alben W. Barkley of Kentucky served at the helm. Continuing to oppose the monetary program, Republicans particularly preferred to eliminate the presidential power to purchase foreign silver. John G. Townsend, Jr., of Delaware considered the silver purchase program the "most careless scattering of our wealth abroad." Arthur H. Vandenberg of Michigan directed the Republican battle against the policy, receiving considerable help from Townsend and from Clyde M. Reed of Kansas. Lacking the numerical strength to block continuation of the money program, Republicans realized that forming an alliance with the disenchanted Democrats afforded the best opportunity of accomplishing their objectives. The minority party shunned their usual southern allies, coalescing instead with western Democrats.

In the Senate the principal issue centered upon how the administration program affected the American economy. Western Democrats considered this matter of paramount importance, while other senators gave somewhat less weight to this argument. Western Democrats contended the presidential monetary programs had hindered American mines and agriculture. Mountain senators complained that the domestic price of silver had dropped by 13 cents to 64 cents an ounce, thus causing silver production to decline 10 percent and unemployment to rise by 200,000 persons. On the other hand, agricultural senators protested that farm prices had declined precipitously. Republican William E. Borah of Idaho stressed "the frightful situation in the silver industry," whereas Democrat Thomas warned, "Money has been too scarce" and had caused "the lowest farm prices in history." Proponents emphasized less the domestic ramifications, insisting that the presidential program would promote internal economic recovery. The Banking and Currency Committee contended the extension of devaluation powers would bring "monetary stability to American producers."[13]

Executive power became another source of controversy. Republicans placed high premium upon this theme, but most Democrats did not follow suit. Republicans and a few non-devaluationist Democrats criticized vigorously this aspect of the Roosevelt economic program. As in the House, the minority party disliked the growth of presidential authority and hoped to give the legislative branch primary control over monetary matters. Vandenberg charged the Roosevelt administration with "whiplashing the Congress into a continuing rubber-stamp surrender of its own prerogatives." Conservative Democrats disapproved of the White House power to devalue the currency and hoped to restore legislative supremacy over the executive branch. Glass, a long-time personal foe of Roosevelt, deemed it "unsound for any Administration to have that power."[14] Like their House counterparts, proponents favored granting extensive monetary powers to the President. Wagner insisted the legislative branch would not administer the financial policy as effectively or deter foreign governments from depreciating their currencies.

The feasibility of the monetary program also aroused intense emotions. Critics stressed this particular point more than did proponents. Intensely disliking the purchase of foreign silver, Republicans did not want the President to issue additional paper currency backed by that metal. According to Reed of Kansas, the United States spent $1.2 billion for two billion ounces of silver "for which we have no earthly use." Proponents, though, stressed that the financial policy would stabilize the international situation and foster American foreign trade. Wagner, who considered international economic conditions unsettled, regarded the monetary program as "indispensable to the safeguarding of our export trade."[15]

The fate of the Administration measure depended largely upon the western Democrats. The mountain bloc had cooperated with the executive branch in the House, but possessed the numerical strength in the Senate to insist upon higher silver prices. Although representing only 3 percent of the nation's population, the mountain bloc wielded the balance of power on this issue because they held 18 votes. It vowed to oppose the measure unless Roosevelt agreed to raise the rate of domestic silver and to terminate the foreign purchases of the metal. Democrat Pittman led the powerful mountain bloc, assisted by Adams of Colorado. Pittman was the leading spokesman for western silver interests and for favorable monetary legislation, being convinced that his constituents considered economic prosperity paramount. As a delegate to the London Economic Conference of 1933, he shrewdly negotiated an international agreement compelling the United States to purchase nearly 25 million ounces of silver from domestic producers. Pittman in 1934 helped frame the Silver Purchase Act, whereby the federal government consented to buy existing stocks of the metal. Adams, chairman of a subcommittee of the Appropriations Committee, often helped lead efforts to slash government expenses. In an attempt to resolve the monetary deadlock, Adams proposed two amendments designed to remove the President's devaluation authority and to raise the silver price to 77.57 cents an ounce.

From the outset the silver bloc directed the fight in the Senate against the measure. Pittman on April 24 requested formation of a solid mountain bloc to oppose extension of the presidential devaluation powers unless the price of domestic silver was raised to 77.57 cents an ounce. The impetus for this move came largely from western governors, who at Reno, Nevada, on March 28 passed a resolution urging Congress to increase the internal rates immediately from 64.64 cents an ounce to a higher, fixed level. Most mountain senators, including Democrat Carl Hayden of Arizona and Borah, eagerly supported Pittman's proposal. "I have always followed your leadership on silver matters," Hayden wrote Pittman, "and I am glad to join with you in any representation which you may care to make looking toward the reasonably permanent establishment of a higher price for domestically mined silver." Borah likewise agreed to participate in the bloc, but opposed making an increase in internal rates "a condition" for supporting extension of the President's devaluation powers. At the same time Pittman and Hayden planned to visit the White House to seek presidential endorsement for establishing through June, 1941, a definite domestic silver rate of 77.57 cents. In late April Hayden remarked, "Senator Pittman and I plan to call upon the President before very long and discuss with him the possibility of increasing the prices paid for this metal." [16]

By the middle of June the mountain bloc broadened its base of support to include agricultural members. Democrat Pat McCarran of Nevada on June 15 made an arrangement of mutual interest with party colleague Thomas of Oklahoma. Thomas promised that the farm delegations would join the battle to fix silver prices at $1.04 an ounce, while McCarran pledged that the mountain bloc would advocate the issuance of $2 billion to help tillers of the soil. "The Thomas-McCarran substitute proposal," Hayden vowed, "will be supported by western Senators interested in stabilizing the price of silver." [17]

At this juncture, however, these senators disagreed sharply over strategy. Thomas and McCarran both favored filibustering against the administration proposal as the best means of accomplishing their twin objectives, and on June 20–21 thwarted several attempts by Majority Leader Barkley of Kentucky to obtain a vote on the bill. McCarran argued in cloakrooms that the struggle was "much broader than the question of the price of silver alone," while Thomas occupied the floor for several hours to prevent any roll calls. Pittman, Borah, and several other mountain senators, though, strongly disapproved of the dilatory tactics. Pittman assured Roosevelt, "I have nothing to do with a filibuster," while Borah warned that the western delegation "might debate the silver question here with no practical result whatever." [18] Instead they both favored an alliance with the non-devaluationists and Republicans to terminate the purchase of foreign silver and to fix the price of domestic silver.

Broadening their coalition a second time, the silverites reached an understanding with the non-devaluationists. A few conservative Democrats already had opposed extending the presidential authority to devalue currency. Upon learning that non-devaluationists would support increasing the domestic silver rate to 77 cents an ounce, Borah proceeded quickly to arrange a compromise with Glass. Borah and Glass used the two amendments by Adams of Colorado, a non-devaluationist and a silverite, as the basis for reaching a settlement. Adams earlier had proposed amendments to remove the President's devaluation authority and to raise the silver price to 77.57 cents an ounce. Borah pledged the silver bloc would support the Adams non-devaluationist amendment, while Glass promised the non-devaluationists would favor the Adams silver proposal.

Joining the silverites and non-devaluationists in this arrangement were the Republicans. Reed of Kansas negotiated for the minority party, which particularly opposed the foreign silver purchase program. An amendment by Townsend to terminate all such acquisitions from abroad enabled Reed to work out a compromise with disenchanted Democrats. Glass and Borah both agreed their forces would support the Townsend measure, while Reed pledged Republican backing for both Adams proposals. Reed subsequently admitted that the Republicans had engaged in a deal and claimed, "I was the most active man in making the arrangements." Higher domestic rates, he argued, were a small price to pay for removal of the foreign silver purchase program. Reed explained acquisitions from overseas cost $135 billion annually, twenty-seven times the amount of the raising of the internal price.[19]

The silver–agricultural–non-devaluationist–Republican alliance jeopardized several Roosevelt administration programs. Besides threatening to delay action on the monetary question, the Senate postponed consideration of crucial tax, relief, and neutrality measures. The White House wanted Senate approval before the fiscal year ended June 30 of a revenue proposal designed to extend nuisance taxes to raise $1.8 million daily. In addition, the President hoped the upper chamber would designate immediately appropriations for the relief programs because the Works Progress Administration already was operating with deficient funds. The executive branch urged Senate removal of the arms embargo against belligerent nations, but Foreign Relations Committee members were deadlocked on the question. According to an April 7 survey made by *Congressional Intelligence* Magazine, only 11 of the 23 committee members either definitely supported or leaned in favor of repeal. Although conducting hearings on neutrality revision from April 5 to May 8, Committee Chairman Pittman then postponed action indefinitely because of the logjam. In order to secure senatorial performance on these vital measures, President Roosevelt needed to make concessions to the silver bloc. Pittman already had warned the President, "We have 18 votes," and inquired, "What are you going to do about it?"[20]

Roosevelt declined at first to reach any type of settlement with the silver bloc. Since the American price was 23 cents above the world market rate, he insisted the federal government already was subsidizing domestic miners. The President claimed the assistance proportionately exceeded that given to wheat and cotton farmers and noted "the world does not seem to want our silver." Buying foreign metals, the State Department contended, helped American relations with Mexico, China, and other nations.[21] But Roosevelt's refusal to bargain with the mountain members soon backfired on him because the silverites insisted upon substantial increases in the domestic price.

By late June the silver–non-devaluationist–Republican coalition clearly prevailed over the White House. The alliance had grown from a small mountain bloc to a large group encompassing non-devaluationists and Republicans. Besides easily pushing through both the Adams devaluation and silver rate proposals by 47–31 and 48–30 margins, the alliance on June 26 also secured approval by voice vote of the Townsend silver purchase amendment. To the dismay of the Roosevelt administration, the coalition had terminated the President's authority to devalue the currency and to purchase foreign silver. At the same time the coalition had raised the price of domestic silver from 64 cents an ounce to a permanent 77 cents an ounce. Keeping their previous pledges, the vastly outnumbered Republicans supported termination of the presidential devaluation rights and an increase in silver rates. The Democrats disagreed sharply on both amendments, signifying that political party played a less prominent role in the Senate than in the House. Mountain members fulfilled earlier promises to support discontinuation of presidential devaluation powers, while some conservatives supported the proposal to raise silver prices.

Regional patterns figured prominently on both Adams amendments, although shifting more than political patterns. In order to improve silver production and increase employment opportunities in mining states, the western bloc led the fight for the two amendments. Sectional considerations, though, prompted other delegations to switch votes. Southern and border Democrats led the opposition to efforts to remove the presidential devaluation power, but furnished less resistance to the silver price increase. They insisted previous executive actions had helped stabilize the currency for world trade, upon which their farmers depended heavily. On the other hand, the Middle Atlantic delegation directed the opposition to the silver price increase. They considered the rate augmentation as a subsidy to greedy silver producers and claimed the amendment would not benefit the gold-oriented Northeast. New England and Great Plains senators also were more inclined towards discarding the presidential devaluation powers than towards increasing the silver price. The federal government, they complained, was subsidizing mining products to a much greater extent than New England dairy and Great Plains wheat products.

Two unusual voting trends occurred. Although the large, experienced southern delegation normally exerted the most power in the upper chamber, the mountain bloc in this instance determined the outcome. The diligence of the silver bloc had already paid dividends on the Adams amendments, indicating that historians may have underemphasized the influence of western Democrats on economic issues. A few non-devaluationist southerners aligned with northern Republicans, but most conservative Democrats did not coalesce this time with their anti–New Deal partners. Sharply disagreeing with the southern Democrats on the Adams devaluation amendment, Republicans allied instead with western

Democrats. The same pattern also emerged on the Adams silver purchase proposal, signifying that a Republican–western Democrat coalition flourished on economic issues.[22]

Statistics, though, do not tell the full story. Besides the silver–non-devaluationist–Republican combination, two other factors hurt the administration. Since Senate Republican Leader Charles L. McNary of Oregon was bedridden at this time, Reed assumed leadership on this issue. McNary traditionally had acted much more cautiously than Reed in strategy matters and, according to Majority Whip Sherman Minton of Indiana, would not have allowed the Republicans to "get out on that limb" and make an arrangement with the silver bloc.[23] The President also shared major responsibility for the outcome by refusing to compromise with the western bloc. If Roosevelt had agreed to a slight increase in silver rates, the western Democrats probably would have abandoned the non-devaluationists and Republicans and voted to maintain the presidential monetary powers. Now the fate of the measure rested in the hands of the conference committee.

Administration leaders, who naturally protested the outcome vigorously, resolved to take a more flexible attitude in the future. Roosevelt strongly opposed the Senate action on all three amendments, centering his criticism on the Adams proposal terminating the presidential devaluation powers. Besides warning that foreign trade and exchange would be hindered, he argued the Adams amendment would permit Wall Street interests to regain control of the national currency. Since monetary powers were to expire on June 30, Roosevelt needed to act quickly. He concluded that making concessions to the silver bloc was the best method to induce the conference committee to restore presidential devaluation and silver purchase powers. Reaching a classic understanding with Pittman, Roosevelt promised to accept an increase in the price of silver to 71.11 cents an ounce. In return Pittman promised that several silver bloc members would support the conference report and restoration of the presidential devaluation authority. McCarran, Adams, and three other mountain Democrats, however, refused to participate in the arrangement because they advocated much higher silver prices and also opposed unconditionally the executive monetary powers.

The outlook for the Roosevelt administration quickly improved. After the President expressed a willingness to compromise on domestic rates, the silver bloc conferees no longer resisted the measure. Pittman claimed Roosevelt's flexibility relieved the silver industry of "the uncertainty of bureaucratic domination."[24] Conferees quickly accepted the basic House version, continuing for two years the presidential prerogatives to devalue the dollar and to purchase foreign silver. In addition, they set the price for domestically mined silver at 70.95 cents an ounce. Although House members on June 30 promptly approved the conference report, the President's battle was not yet finished. Unless the Senate acted by midnight, Roosevelt's monetary authority would terminate.

Strongly rejecting the conference report, a powerful coalition of Republicans and non-devaluationist Democrats obstructed final action. Upset over the desertion by some silver bloc members, they vowed to let the presidential monetary powers expire. Republicans Vandenberg and Townsend, along with Democrats Adams and McCarran, led the filibuster against the measure. "I have never known of a single instance," Townsend complained, "when the will of the Senate was so completely ignored and cast aside by a conference committee." Echoing similar views, Vandenberg denounced the committee restoration of devaluation and silver purchase power as "humiliating and wholly indefensible." [25] Republicans and non-devaluationist Democrats monopolized the Senate debate until after midnight, thus ostensibly terminating the presidential monetary powers. As Hayden noted, "Its enactment by midnight June 30 was prevented by filibuster supervised by Eastern Republican Senators opposed to extension of dollar devaluation power." [26]

Around midnight the conference report critics made a tactical mistake by not insisting upon an immediate roll call. Since the conference report had reached the Senate only four hours before midnight, Republicans and non-devaluationist Democrats appeared to have enough votes to defeat the conference report. Urging the filibuster leaders to request a roll call, Republicans Reed of Kansas and Robert A. Taft of Ohio noted that 38 of 73 senators present disapproved of the conference report and argued that critics had gained "all the advantage that prolonged debate could give them." But Vandenberg, Townsend, Warren R. Austin of Vermont, and other minority party members considered the vote margin too close to risk a roll call defeat. "If the darned fools had listened to Bob Taft and myself and taken a vote on the monetary legislation," Reed subsequently claimed, "I think we would have won." In Reed's view, the delay "would only give the administration a chance to strengthen their lines." [27]

Consternation rocked the Roosevelt administration camp. Besides conversing continually with Senate leaders throughout the evening, the President remained at the White House ready to sign the measure. Roosevelt wanted to risk an immediate roll call vote, but Senate leaders preferred to postpone such action because of the formidable resistance by the dissatisfied Republicans and Democrats. Many opponents, detesting the growth of Roosevelt's executive authority, favored letting the monetary powers expire. "The suspicion with which he is regarded," charged Republican Hiram Johnson, of California "now makes the Congress distrustful of what he desired, and this was confirmed by his bitterness when the Senate refused to extend the time."[28]

As the midnight hour approached, Roosevelt increasingly realized no action would occur that evening. Attorney General Frank Murphy, at the President's request, conveniently issued an opinion stating that Roosevelt's monetary powers would continue in operation if the Senate failed to act before midnight. Because of the stalemate, Majority Leader Barkley persuaded his weary colleagues to adjourn at 1:53 a.m. and to delay any vote until July 5.

Opponents naturally resented the last-minute intervention by the Roosevelt administration. They claimed that the executive branch unfairly employed the attorney general's ruling to avert an almost certain defeat. "When it was obvious the President was beaten," Johnson maintained, "they rushed to us the opinion of the Attorney General." Foes, though, could do little beyond question the legality of Murphy's opinion. In their view, Roosevelt would utilize the Independence Day recess to rally support for the existing monetary authority. "I think the conference report on the devaluation bill," Johnson predicted, "will be approved by the Senate." In addition, Johnson feared "the President will claim his powers are not affected by the time limitation, and he may soon proceed to further devalue our dollar." They also doubted that the Roosevelt-controlled Supreme Court would make any effort to overturn Murphy's decision. "The opinion of the Attorney General," objected Johnson, "is a shot-gun opinion, and the trick is obvious. I presume, however, with the Supreme Court constituted as it is now, he will be able to have his will."[29]

During the Independence Day recess the Roosevelt administration seized the initiative from the disenchanted Republicans and Democrats. Although Pittman urged Roosevelt to issue a proclamation instituting the silver rate increase, the President wanted to work behind the scenes on individual senators.[30] Secretary of the Treasury Morgenthau persuaded the American Farm Bureau Federation to approach some wavering midwestern members, while administration leaders Barkley and Minton induced Carl A. Hatch of New Mexico, Burton K. Wheeler of Montana, and other mountain Democrats to support the conference report because of the proposed increase in silver prices. The administration strategy paid dividends as the Senate on July 5 narrowly adopted (43–39) the conference report restoring the presidential monetary powers.

Ironically, senators had approved a measure almost identical to the one rejected earlier. Ten Democrats, including eight westerners, swung the pendulum in favor of the conference report by joining border, southern, and Middle Atlantic party colleagues. Welcoming the increase in silver rates, western senators abandoned their alliance with Republican critics of

Roosevelt's foreign policy. If the measure was sent back to committee, several senators feared that the domestic silver price increases would be removed.

Still posing formidable resistance, the Republican-Democratic coalition nearly prevented approval of the conference report. Republicans almost unanimously opposed the conference report, criticizing the section continuing foreign silver purchases. On the other hand, some Democrats, including five silver bloc members, protested the presidential devaluation policy. New England and Great Plains Republicans directed the foes of Roosevelt's monetary program, signifying once more that the presidential alliance with conservative Democrats did not apply.

The Roosevelt administration, along with southern and border Democrats, deserve credit for passage of the measure. Besides clearly presenting its objectives at the outset, the executive branch testified before congressional committees and intervened at a critical time in the Senate struggle. At the same time the White House should have made concessions earlier to the silver bloc on domestic prices. The executive branch had far more at stake in continuing the devaluation and purchase programs than in permitting a small increase in internal silver rates. Conservative border and southern Democrats, exerting more influence in the House, led the campaign in Congress for extension of the presidential monetary policy because they favored the bimetallic standard.

Above all, the silver bloc made possible the extension of the President's monetary policies. Pittman and most other mountain senators helped insure congressional approval of the conference report, after the President consented to raise slightly the domestic silver price. Although preferring substantially higher rates, Pittman explained that the westerners "got the best price that could be gotten at this time." Hayden added, "It was a genuine pleasure for me to be helpful in the establishment of a permanent price for domestically mined silver." [31] Without the willingness of most silverites to compromise, the President's measure would not have survived in the Senate. To the chagrin of fellow Republicans, Borah joined the other westerners in endorsing the compromise. Johnson groaned, "We lost again because of the action of Borah, who voted with the President, and succeeded in having his young colleague Clark of Idaho follow him." [32]

Opponents, still disturbed over administration tactics, nevertheless had waged a very spirited battle. They still insisted the Senate lacked authority to act on the conference report because the President's monetary powers already had expired on June 30 at midnight. As Johnson argued, "You cannot breathe life into a dead Act." Although participating in a losing cause, critics had forced the White House to rescue the floundering monetary program. "It was a good fight," Johnson remarked, "and required all of the power of the Administration to win it, and even with a Senate which is three-fourths Democratic, they won by a majority of but four."

In the final analysis, Congress had wielded considerable authority on the monetary question. An intense struggle occurred before the legislative branch consented to restoring the President's devaluation and foreign silver purchase powers. Congress, instead of functioning as a rubberstamp for the executive branch, had acted quite independently on this economic measure. At the same time the legislative branch reflected this autonomous attitude on the very complex issue of transportation reform.

2

BROADENING TRANSPORTATION
REGULATION

About the same time railroad companies appealed to the federal government for immediate assistance. Trains handled approximately two-thirds of the nation's traffic and hauled the most freight, but suffered from inadequate earnings and extensive bankruptcies. They protested that the Interstate Commerce Commission strictly regulated them by requiring standard minimum rates for carrying goods. Severe competition came from inland water carriers, which charged much lower prices for transporting agricultural and industrial products. According to the railroads, the federal government provided large subsidies to develop internal waterways and yet did not compel them to adopt minimum rate levels. The United States Maritime Commission had regulated intercoastal carriers before 1940, but the executive branch never had exercised control over inland river, lake, or canal operators. In an endeavor to establish uniform national transportation policies, the train companies urged Congress to place the interior water carriers under the jurisdiction of the ICC.

Railroads had faced serious problems for at least two decades. Automobiles, trucks, buses, inland waterways, and coastal shippers had increasingly competed with trains, causing declines of 10 percent in freight traffic and 35 percent in passenger service. Oil pipelines had diverted enormous traffic, while large shippers had frequently prevented the consolidation of railroad companies. Since numerous lines had collapsed by 1932, the Reconstruction Finance Corporation sought to rescue them with loans.[1]

New Deal programs had afforded some relief to the trains. Congress had permitted lines to retain all excess profits and had loosened rate-making restrictions, but railroads still complained that other modes of transportation were competing unfairly and advocated uniform federal control. The eleven-member ICC had begun to reorganize train finances, combine lines wherever possible, and regulate competitors. In another move to assist the railroads, Congress in 1935 had permitted the ICC to establish guidelines for rates and finances of buses and trucks competing in interstate commerce. The legislative branch, though, had not authorized the ICC to manage inland water carriers, who were charging lower rates to transport goods.

From the outset internal water operators resisted any federal controls. Since they could compete with the railroads only by assessing lower prices for carrying products, water carriers did not advocate any change in existing national policy. Labeling the ICC as a railroad-minded body, they feared executive agencies would compel them to raise minimum rates to a standard level. Such a step, they warned, would give the railroads a monopoly of traffic and eventually would drive the water shippers out of business.

Two presidential committees laid the initial foundation for solving the transportation problem. President Roosevelt in 1938 ordered two separate committees, consisting of three ICC members and six railroad people, respectively, to investigate the entire travel network. He hoped to utilize the recommendations of both committees as a basis for ameliorative legislation. In April, 1938, the three ICC members urged immediate financial assistance to the railroads and insisted that a single unspecified government agency regulate water operators and all forms of transportation. Eight months later the other committee wholeheartedly endorsed the ICC's recommendations, giving the President a more comprehensive program to rescue train companies. They urged the ICC to establish guidelines and uniform rates for all types of transit and requested the establishment of a board to examine the financial and physical conditions of all carriers. Both committees ignored the attitudes of inland water carriers, who were not represented in either group. By not inviting inland water carriers to participate in committee activities, Roosevelt had made a serious mistake which later haunted him.[2]

Finding a Senate sponsor for the potentially controversial issue proved rather difficult. George Harrison and Carl Gray of the railroad committee in early January asked Democrat Wheeler, chairman of the Interstate and Foreign Commerce Committee, to introduce transportation legislation encompassing their earlier recommendations. Wheeler was regarded as one of the Senate's foremost friends of the railroads and headed a committee sympathetic to trains. Although hoping to prevent the railroads from becoming bankrupt, Wheeler initially declined to introduce the bill. His relations with Roosevelt had soured considerably ever since he had opposed the President's Supreme Court reorganization proposal. Wheeler instead suggested that one of the loyal New Deal Democrats Harry S. Truman of Missouri, Minton, or Lewis P. Schwellenbach of Washington sponsor a transportation measure. After Harrison and Gray failed to change Wheeler's mind, the President in early 1939 summoned the Montana senator to the White House. Giving assurance that the court issue was "water over the dam," Roosevelt urged Wheeler to direct the Senate battle. Wheeler eventually agreed to introduce transit legislation after the President promised to cooperate fully with the Montana Senator.

From the outset Chairman Wheeler influenced the committee to align with the railroads. Fifty-seven-year-old Wheeler, the son of an impoverished Hudson, Massachusetts, shoemaker, had studied law at the University of Michigan. After journeying further westward, Wheeler had settled in Butte, Montana, with just $50 in his pocket and had begun practicing law there. Before joining the U.S. Senate in 1922 the outspoken liberal Democrat had belonged to the state House of Representatives and was U.S. district attorney for Montana. In 1924 the Progressive Party presidential candidate Robert LaFollette had selected the Montana Democrat as his running mate. Wheeler was described as "a lanky, rumpled man who walks with a rapid shamble, smiling quizzically, his glance a friendly, direct glare through octagonal spectacles, smoking a cigar with the superb nonchalance of Groucho Marx." Although supporting early New Deal programs, he had aligned frequently with conservatives after the court reorganization controversy. Wheeler particularly advocated federal assistance to railroads because the train brotherhoods had provided him enormous backing in previous campaigns.[3]

Wheeler, along with Interstate Commerce Committee members Truman and Clyde M. Reed, favored legislation to rescue the trains from bankruptcy. Residing in rural regions heavily dependent upon railroads for transporting products, they complained that the federal government had developed and yet had not regulated water carriers. Truman had already sponsored a bill requiring federal licensing of commercial motor vehicles in interstate traffic and had chaired an Interstate Commerce subcommittee investigation on the financial status of railroads. Wheeler, Truman, and Reed, a Kansas Republican, performed most of the tasks confronting the committee. Wheeler and Truman drafted an omnibus measure assisting the train lines, while Reed arbitrated on several controversial questions.

Although sympathetic towards the railroads, the committee still wrestled for several months with the transportation problem. Wheeler's committee drafted a measure very slowly because of the enormous scope of the transit question and unexpected opposition from certain federal agencies. Besides seeking to establish an equitable relationship among the various operators, the committee hoped to recodify the entire Interstate

Commerce Act of 1887. Reed of Kansas stressed that Wheeler's committee faced "hard work" and performed "a tough job" because they handled "a multitude of technical subjects" and wrote "the largest bill yet presented to this session!" In addition, the ICC and the U.S. Maritime Commission openly opposed the committee's intentions. Although favoring transportation reform, the ICC resisted any attempt to recodify the original act. They disliked subjecting inland water carriers to the same regulations as railroads and protested establishing uniform rates for all operators. The U.S. Maritime Commission objected to surrendering its authority over the interior water companies to the ICC. According to Maritime Chairman Emory Land, "Users of water transportation would be footing the bill for the sole benefit of the railroads."[4]

Dismayed over the resistance from federal agencies, Chairman Wheeler urged President Roosevelt to intervene on behalf of the Senate committee. Wheeler speculated that White House pressure could induce the ICC and the U.S. Maritime Commission to support his group's efforts. Besides stressing that the two presidential committees solidly favored the transportation reform, Wheeler warned Roosevelt, "We are going to have enough trouble as it is."[5] The President, ignoring an earlier pledge to assist the Montana Democrat, remained silent. Since he already had split with Congress over New Deal measures, Roosevelt did not want to alienate any executive agencies too. He also hoped to obtain the complete cooperation of the federal bureaucracy for executive reorganization, which Congress had begun considering.

By the middle of May Wheeler's committee had drafted a measure resembling the recommendations of the earlier presidential committees. Besides recodifying the entire Interstate Commerce Act, they requested placing inland water carriers under federal jurisdiction and urged creation of a temporary transportation board to investigate the relative fitness of each type of carrier. Most committee members endorsed the final version, but left room open for additional changes. Wheeler lauded the measure as "a sound, realistic and carefully considered approach" to "one of the most grave problems," while Truman remarked, "The bill has been considerably changed since it was first introduced, and I think, much for the better."[6] On the Republican side, Reed claimed the committee "made the railroad bill much better than was proposed in the beginning." At the same time Wheeler and Reed both conceded that the committee might have overlooked other possible improvements for the transportation system. Reed admitted the committee proposal "isn't what I would write."[7] Nevertheless, Farmer-Laborite Henrik Shipstead of Minnesota alone opposed the railroad-oriented committee measure.

Irate over these developments, waterway pressure groups began lobbying extensively against the Wheeler bill. Iron, steel, coal, and other companies, which often utilized internal water routes, feared the ICC would raise water rates to protect rail traffic. The Mississippi Valley Association and other water carrier organizations had previously transported commodities at relatively low prices without federal regulation. Water pressure groups began flooding Congress with mail and, according to Wheeler, "lined up most of the senators along the Mississippi River against my proposals."[8]

Senate leadership on the transportation issue differed considerably from that on the monetary question. In the upper chamber conservatives supplied the strategists for both the railroads and the water carriers. Advocates relied principally upon pro-railroad Interstate Commerce Committee members, with Wheeler directing and Truman and Reed providing considerable assistance. The Commerce Committee, which traditionally favored the waterways, furnished the leadership for the opposing forces. Committee chairman Josiah W. Bailey of North Carolina, the state having the most highly developed inland waterway system in the United States, devised the tactics for the disenchanted Senators seeking to prevent federal regulation of inland water carriers.[9] Bailey cooperated closely with Democrats Bennett Champ Clark of Missouri and Morris Sheppard of Texas.

The principal issue for both sides, of course, concerned whether the ICC should regulate inland waterways. According to railroad-minded senators, all forms of transportation including inland water vessels should be governed uniformly by the federal government. Wheeler insisted, "If you are going to regulate one form of transportation, regulate them all," and vowed the measure would "not put out of business any water carriers." Inland waterway operators, Truman argued, "are bitterly opposed to repeal of the laws regulating other methods of transportation, but are not willing to come in on an equal basis themselves. Either the whole system of regulation ought to be done away with or everybody ought to be treated alike." Other transportation lines initially had resisted any federal regulation, but subsequently found control by the ICC beneficial. "We had exactly the same arguments from the bus and truck people," Truman noted, "when we were passing the bus and truck regulatory law, and now the buses and trucks are asking for more regulation." If the committee bill were enacted, Truman prognosticated, "nothing in the world could persuade the water carriers to have it repealed."[10] On the other hand, critics claimed the ICC would compel inland shippers to raise rates and restrict profits. Democrat A. Victor Donahey of Ohio warned that "shipping industries will be irreparably damaged" by federal control, while Shipstead predicted the measure would "stifle, retard, and possibly prevent" coastal waterway improvements.[11]

Senators also argued over how the measure would affect the railroads. Trains, opponents charged, would enjoy a monopoly over the other forms of transportation and would be favored by the ICC. Clark complained railroads would utilize enormous capital to "put the water competition out of business," while Sheppard feared the ICC would protect "the profitable operation of the railroads." Accenting the plight of trains, advocates of the committee version protested water shippers were reducing rates unfairly. As Reed of Kansas remarked, "our railroad situation is not only critical but desperate." Democrat Clyde L. Herring of Iowa considered the railroads a "great and distressed industry" in "grave need of rehabilitation and restoration to prime fitness." [12]

Sectionalism again figured prominently, with the opposing factions disagreeing over the impact of the measure upon the American economy. Critics especially seized this issue, citing adverse affects upon agriculture and railroad labor. Farmers favored continuation of the lower rates afforded by water shippers, while train unions feared the bill might lead to train consolidations threatening numerous jobs. In the view of Shipstead of Minnesota, the measure would not "help railroad labor in any manner." By contrast, advocates claimed the transportation measure would be advantageous to both farmers and train workers. Midwestern wheat growers, Reed complained, had not received "a particle of benefit from inland water transportation." [13]

The feasibility of the measure likewise provided considerable debate. Opponents especially warned that federal regulation would have an adverse impact upon the consumer and stressed that inland water shippers transported only a small percentage of national traffic. Republican Borah cautioned that the "effects of this bill upon water rates will not be helpful to the people of the United States," while Bailey indicated that railroads carried twenty-two times the freight hauled by river and canal operators. On the other side, advocates insisted the Wheeler-Truman bill would provide a more economical national transportation system. The measure, Reed pointed out, was designated "so each form of transportation may be efficiently and economically utilized." [14]

Striking differences appeared between the transportation and earlier monetary questions. Besides producing different leadership and widespread party division, the Wheeler-Truman measure did not provoke a contest over executive and legislative power. Senators seldom raised interventionist or foreign trade issues on the Wheeler-Truman bill, which mainly concerned the domestic economy.

In the Senate debate critics adopted a twofold strategy to modify the Wheeler-Truman measure. Since they lacked numerical strength to defeat the transportation bill outright, opponents concentrated on attaching a Bailey amendment preventing federal regulation of inland water carriers. Bailey argued that neither the interior shippers nor the American public had clamored for federal agencies to extend jurisdiction over transportation. If the Senate rejected the Bailey amendment, opponents then would attempt to secure approval of a more moderate proposal by Democrat John E. Miller of Arkansas. The Miller amendment would authorize any carriers to reduce prices "so long as such rates maintain a compensatory return to the carrier." Under the Miller plan shippers could lower rates to remain competitive with railroads and to enable the public "to enjoy the benefit and economy afforded by each type of transportation."[15]

The game plan backfired. On May 25 senators easily (57-22) buried the Bailey proposal, thus subjecting the inland water carriers to ICC regulation. The railroad bloc received overwhelming support from both Democrats and Republicans, signifying that the Senate considered transportation as a sectional rather than a political issue. Regionally, railroad-minded Middle Atlantic and Great Lakes delegations led the opposition to the Bailey amendment. Mountain and Great Plains members, also representing regions carrying enormous train traffic, joined the railroad bloc to insure the defeat of the Bailey proposal. Besides capturing relatively little backing from either political party, the opposition garnered majority support only in the shipping-oriented border and Pacific regions. Other water sympathizers came from southern and New England states, both of which transacted widespread inland water operations.

Party and regional alignments shifted considerably from the monetary patterns. Republicans and Democrats alike favored the transportation measure much more vigorously than the earlier bill. The transit problem produced greater internal division among Republicans, while the monetary legislation split the Democrats more openly. The southern and border delegations were more enthusiastic about the monetary bill, but Great Lakes and mountain members found greater sympathies for transportation reform. In marked contrast, two delegations were consistent on both issues. The Middle Atlantic senators favored the transportation and monetary bills, while Pacific legislators helped direct the resistance to both proposals.

Although thwarted in their principal objective, the water bloc enjoyed wider success on the milder Miller amendment. After Miller consented to delete a provision making it unlawful to establish non-compensatory rates for any purpose whatever, Wheeler temporarily agreed to accept the Arkansas Democrat's proposals. Wheeler, though, fully intended to drop the Miller amendment in conference committee. His temporary compromise with the water bloc upset Reed, who complained the Montana Democrat did not give "proper consideration" to the "unworkable" amendment.[16]

At this juncture the water bloc divided into two factions. Most shipping sympathizers, led by Bailey, realized they lacked numerical strength and did not attempt to prevent further Senate action on the Wheeler-Truman bill. According to Borah, "As the set-up was, perhaps nothing could have been accomplished." [17] This wing preferred to leave principal resistance to the House, where they anticipated greater success. On the other hand, a small determined faction, led by Clark and Sheppard, favored continuing the resistance. With the water bloc split asunder, the Senate on May 25 overwhelmingly approved (70-6) the omnibus transportation measure. Clark and Sheppard attracted support only from die-hard water advocates, including Democrats Tom Connally of Texas and John H. Overton of Louisiana, Republican Lynn J. Frazier of North Dakota, and Farmer-Laborite Shipstead.

The railroad bloc received overwhelmingly strong backing from both political parties and all regional delegations. Because of the change of strategy by the water forces, the Republicans, Democrats, and most sections clearly sided with the rail lines. Democrats and Republicans differed little, signifying politics did not figure prominently. Sectionally, deviations appeared much less than before, largely because the Bailey faction of border, Pacific, and New England members did not support the water bloc.

Senators were less enthusiastic about the railroad measure than the decisive roll call indicates. In several cases members either did not understand the full implications of the Wheeler-Truman bill or did not have the time to read the long, technical proposal before the floor debate. At the same time they faced agricultural, housing, and other significant New Deal measures. Two senators who voted affirmatively on the final roll call later denounced the transportation bill. Democrat Theodore G. Bilbo of Mississippi admitted having "grave and serious doubts about the wisdom of this legislation," while Borah claimed, "If I had to do it over again, I would more earnestly oppose it." [18]

Wheeler, Truman, and Reed had insured Senate passage of the transportation bill. Above all, Wheeler had guided the measure ably through both the Interstate Commerce Committee and the Senate chamber. Wheeler confessed, "I worked on the railroad bill to the exclusion of almost everything else," while Truman gave him "the principal credit" for the outcome. A cosponsor of the measure, Truman had performed yeoman service for Wheeler in committee and on the floor. Truman conceded, "I have spent nearly three years with Senator Wheeler trying to get the bill to the point of passage," while the Montana Democrat commended him for being "conscientious and loyal." [19] On the Republican side Reed contributed substantially to the success of the railroad forces. Wheeler allegedly considered Reed "the only man that knows what is in the bill" and claimed that without the Kansas Republican the Interstate Commerce Committee "would not have. . .gotten the job done." Reed, though, exaggerated his role and downgraded the influence of Chairman Wheeler, who belonged to the opposing party, besides boasting that "with the traffic and transportation experts my voice carries further than that of any man in public life." Reed asserted, "None of the real experts among traffic and transportation regard Wheeler as an authority on the subject." The Montana senator, Reed contended, "gets the publicity because of his seniority as a Senator and as Chairman of the Interstate Commerce Committee."[20]

The transportation measure, however, faced a more formidable hurdle in the House. Republican James W. Wadsworth, Jr., of New York warned, "There is very little chance that a bill of such length and involving such implications can pass at this session of Congress," while his political colleague Clifford R. Hope of Kansas expected "a very bitter fight on the waterways provision." [21] Since the water bloc was more effectively organized and pressure group activity intensified, the prospects for the railroad bill looked less certain in the lower chamber. The water bloc, especially consisting primarily of members of the Rivers and Harbors and Merchant Marine and Fisheries committees, posed a serious challenge to the railroad forces. Under the direction of Democrat Lindsay C. Warren of North Carolina with assistance from Democrat J. J. Mansfield of Texas, the shipping forces vigorously resisted federal regulation of inland shippers. Forty-nine-year-old Warren, the son of a distinguished lawyer, was born in Washington, North Carolina, studied at the University of North Carolina, and began practicing law in his home town. After serving as attorney for Beaufort County and as a state senator and assemblyman, he in 1925 joined the U.S. House of Representatives. A New Dealer, he became an authority on government organization and eventually won plaudits from the Washington press corps as one of the ten ablest congressmen. Various reporters lauded the dynamic, eloquent Warren as an exceptionally able legislator, an effective organizer, and a persuasive operator in cloakrooms. Representing a coastal region, he had advocated the development of an inland waterway system to improve North Carolina's transportation facilities. He had witnessed the completion of waterways traversing the entire eastern portion of North Carolina, giving that state the greatest expanse of inland waterways in the United States.

Pressure groups, meanwhile, played a much more crucial role than on the monetary bill. By late spring, more federal agencies and private pressure groups began lobbying congressmen to defeat the transportation proposal. The War and Agriculture departments, along with the ICC and the U.S. Maritime Commission, protested the railroad bill. Besides considering inland waterway development vital to national defense, the War Department feared the shippers would be "regulated and taxed out of existence." The Agriculture Department warned that compelling water carriers to raise rates for transporting foodstuffs would hurt the farmer, whose income had declined nearly one-half since World War 1. In the view of Secretary Henry A. Wallace, the railroad bill would "make this vicious attack on the farm standard of living worse." Private agricultural and railway groups and inland waterway companies also opposed the transportation measure. The American Farm Bureau Federation, the National Grange, and other agricultural organizations echoed the sentiments of Secretary Wallace, while train unions feared consolidations would cause widespread unemployment. A. F. Whitney, president of the Brotherhood of Railroad Trainmen, implored unions to "Act Now" in "asserting and exercising their democratic rights." With interior waterway companies at the forefront, these sundry groups began flooding congressional offices with mail and testifying before House committees. Interstate Commerce Committee Chairman Clarence F. Lea of California, who was sympathetic to the railroads, complained that these lobbyists were "making a strenuous effort . . . to create fear of agriculture that its rates will be raised injuriously." [22] On the other hand, pressure groups representing companies already regulated by the ICC lobbied strenuously in favor of the bill. The American Association of Railroads, the American Trucking Association, and several other transit organizations supported congressional efforts to broaden the scope of federal control. In addition, congressional offices were deluged with letters and telegrams. "I am very conservative," Truman of Missouri remarked, "when I say that we have had at least five thousand letters from individuals on this bill." [23]

Lea's Interstate Commerce Committee favored the railroads. Lea, medium-sized and sixty-four years old, had grown up on a farm near Highland Springs, California, attended Stanford University, and then studied law at Denver University. After practicing law in Santa Rosa, California, and being district attorney of Samona County, he in 1916 had joined the U.S. House of Representatives. The California Democrat, who eventually represented his district in Congress longer than any Pacific Coast member ever, had faced Republican opposition only twice. Besides chairing the House Democratic caucus in 1933, he had supported most New Deal programs and had favored abolition of the electoral college system. An opponent of further regulation of railroads, he had urged more federal government control over inland water carriers and airlines.

Sympathetic with the basic provisions of the Senate measure, Lea's group espoused federal regulation of shippers and all other forms of transportation. Lea, as well as most other committee members, represented sections relying largely upon railroads for service. Besides hoping to deny water carriers the privilege of charging lower rates, they wished to restore more equitable competition among transit companies. Refusing to make this issue political, the committee almost unanimously supported the railroad measure. Elated with the committee cooperation, Lea praised his group for showing "great fidelity" without the "slightest partisanship."[24]

Lea's committee changed considerably the Senate version. They merely revised the existing provisions and created a section covering water carriers rather than try to codify the entire Interstate Commerce Act. Besides rejecting plans to create a transportation board, Lea's committee permitted the Reconstruction Finance Corporation to provide railroads with loans and authorized the ICC to prescribe maximum and minimum rates for both railroads and water shippers.

On the House floor the leadership differed considerably from that on the monetary issue. With Lea serving at the helm, the chief strategists for the railroad measure came from the Interstate Commerce Committee. Under the direction of Warren of North Carolina, the water bloc devised opposition strategy. Republicans Wadsworth and Francis D. Culkin of New York, along with Democrats Mansfield and Vincent F. Harrington, afforded invaluable assistance to Warren.

Following the Senate pattern, the regulation of inland shippers remained the most controversial issue. Railroad forces, who particularly stressed this aspect, urged elimination of special treatment for water carriers. Republican John M. Vorys of Ohio favored uniform federal control of all forms of transportation to create "an equitable balance between rates, taxes, and subsidies," while Democrat John H. Kerr of North Carolina insisted upon national jurisdiction over water transport so as "to be fair to all types of shipments."[25] On the other hand, the water bloc argued the ICC would force inland shippers to raise rates and consequently lose business to the railroads. Mansfield warned that the transportation measure would "increase the freight bill of the shippers," whereas Democrat Vincent F. Harrington of Iowa predicted, "the incarceration of the waterways in the straight jacket of Interstate Commerce Commission regulation will only serve to saddle an additional burden on the farmers and shippers, the consumers, and the general public of this country, and further tend to stagnate the sources from which our domestic commerce springs."[26]

The relative status of the railroads also caused sharp disagreement. Relying most heavily upon this point, the opposition again insisted the ICC usually sided with the train companies. Warren denounced the measure as a "railroad bill" instigated to "destroy all water competition." According to Mansfield, transportation legislation gave the ICC "dangerous powers over industry."[27] The plight of the rail lines, advocates countered, warranted uniform regulation of all forms of transportation. Republican Clifford R. Hope of Kansas maintained, "We ought to do everything we can to build up our railroads," whereas Vorys denounced federal discrimination in favor of shippers both as "foolish" and as "a racket." Republican George H. Bender of Ohio warned, "The destruction of our railroad transportation has far too many implications to be lightly ignored" and contended that "it is cowardice to throw in the sponge and turn the railroads over to the mercy of fate."[28]

The water bloc stressed how the measure would affect the American economy. Fearing the transportation bill would damage agriculture, Warren protested that federal regulation would "endanger the economical water services for which the farmer has waited so long." If railroad companies merged, route service would be reduced and thousands of workers would lose their jobs. Harrington warned that "a million railway workers would suffer from a devastating program of railroad consolidation."[29] In the railroad camp these contentions were rejected. Hope argued agriculturalists were "absolutely dependent" upon shippers "for transportation," while Vorys alleged the proposal guaranteed "forever the present status of any railway labor involved in a merger."[30]

Representatives, especially the water bloc, likewise debated vigorously the feasibility of the measure. According to the opposition bloc, public consumers feared the measure inevitably would elevate transportation rates. Mansfield saw "no public demand for this legislation," while Wadsworth interjected "public sentiment simply will not stand for the regulation of rates."[31] On the other hand, railway sympathizers argued the federal government had utilized tax revenues unwisely on waterway development. Vorys vowed "the interests of the public will be better served by preventing cut-throat competition between the various types of transportation," while Hope denounced national funding of unregulated shippers as "a ridiculous and an inexcusable waste of Government money."[32]

Two original issues arose in the House. One dispute, particularly raised by the railroad bloc, concerned whether federal agencies or private sources should be utilized to assist trains. Railroad defenders advocated extensive federal action to help railroads, but opponents countered that train companies should ameliorate their own situation. Wadsworth claimed, "The only thing that will help the railroads is more traffic," while Republican John Taber of New York predicted the "very dangerous" proposal would hasten "the demoralization of our transportation system." Harrington stressed, "Simply because one member of a family has squandered his resources and, partly perhaps through no fault of his own, has landed in the poorhouse, is no reason every other member of the family should be placed in the poorhouse to share the pauperism of the first unfortunate."[33]

During debates the sectional implications at stake received more attention. Viewpoints of representatives depended largely on whether they came from a region primarily utilizing rail or water transportation. The emphasis placed by representatives upon sectional considerations differed strikingly from that on the more highly political monetary issue. Opponents insisted that their states benefited principally from water shippers, while advocates represented sections depending upon railroads. In defense of the water carriers, Warren considered it "inconceivable" that any southern member would surrender "the last club we have in our hope to obtain lower freight rates." On the other side Hope vowed railroads should have a "fair deal" because they were "the principal source of transportation" in Kansas.[34]

The water bloc organized much more effectively in the House. On June 7 Mansfield invited several members of the Rivers and Harbors and Merchant Marine and Fisheries committees to his office to plot strategy. At the meeting they pledged to oppose any federal regulation of inland shippers because such action would raise shipping costs and hurt American consumers. Two weeks later the same bloc urged Congress to postpone further action indefinitely so as to give more time to examine the effects of the measure upon agriculture, industry, and commerce. Unable to augment their ranks initially, the water forces needed the time to solidify membership. In order to keep House members "fully informed" about the adverse affects of the measure, Warren urged the formation of a "nation-wide protest."[35]

During July the water bloc intensified its activity. Since Congress was hurrying towards adjournment, they feared representatives would seek "to jam this bill through. . .without adequate debate or consideration." On July 17 Mansfield, Warren, and Culkin agreed to expand their campaign against the measure. Five days later they sent letters to all House members urging them to reject the omnibus transportation measure. Besides criticizing the Lea bill for providing "no comfort to the shipper or to the public," the water bloc rallied behind an amendment by Wadsworth to restore the earlier Miller proposal. Wadsworth represented a district situated on the Genesee River near the old Erie Canal route. He therefore had encouraged the development of inland waterways and had opposed strenuously any federal regulation of that form of transportation.[36]

In order to secure adoption of the Wadsworth amendment, though, the water bloc needed to increase its numerical strength. In a move reminiscent of the earlier silverite–non-devaluationist–Republican alliance, they arranged a bipartisan coalition with the agricultural and train union forces. The farm bloc, directed by Democrat Marvin Jones of Texas, feared the Lea measure would raise transit costs over inland waterways. To secure agricultural backing for the Wadsworth amendment, the water forces consented to support a Jones proposal preventing industrial shippers from taking freight rate advantages over agricultural carriers. Under the direction of Harrington of Iowa, train union supporters warned that railroad consolidation would cause widespread joblessness. The water bloc pledged to vote for a Harrington amendment preventing any railroad mergers from displacing workers and received promises from the union bloc of backing for the Wadsworth plan.[37]

The alliance operated as adeptly as the Senate coalition on the monetary issue. Shipping, farming, and railway labor factions united to hamstring the transportation bill. On July 24 the House easily adopted both the Jones and Harrington amendments by 72-32 and 96-78 margins. Representatives the following day approved (149-119) the Wadsworth proposal, which Warren lauded as "the first thing that has been offered in behalf of the American public."[38]

Lea's railroad sympathizers stood virtually powerless against the formidable tripartite coalition. Despite determined resistance by Democrats Lea, Sam Rayburn of Texas, and Alfred L. Bulwinkle of North Carolina, the advocates of the transportation bill could not prevent House adoption of the three amendments. Lea vociferously denounced the three plans on the House floor, while Bulwinkle and Rayburn sought to prevent teller votes on the various proposals. Since the alliance held the numerical advantage, Lea and Rayburn were forced to secure postponement until the next day. Lea considered intervention by the executive branch as the best means of salvaging the transit legislation and in late July urged Roosevelt to issue a public statement supporting the measure.[39]

Throughout this congressional battle the President had remained unusually silent. Although endorsing the original recommendations of the two transportation committees, he had not defended the Wheeler-Lea bill for several months. ICC member Walter Splawn had informed Roosevelt of legislative developments, but the President had not studied this issue very carefully and did not desire to alienate those federal agencies already opposing the Wheeler-Lea measure. Roosevelt also was preoccupied with neutrality preparedness, work relief, lend-spend, housing, and other critical matters. In late July the President pleased Lea by releasing a statement wholeheartedly backing the railroad bill. Besides the pressure from Lea, two transportation committee members persuaded Roosevelt to intervene more directly. In late July Lea's subcommittee visited the White House and warned the chief executive that the coalition of water, agricultural, and railway labor forces threatened the entire transit proposal. Harrison and B. M. Jewell of the Presidential Commission also urged Roosevelt to advocate publicly federal regulation of inter-coastal shippers.[40]

The President's timely intervention revitalized the Lea side and rescued the transportation measure. After the President issued his public state-ment, the water bloc on July 26 suffered several major setbacks. Represen-tatives rejected an amendment by Democrat Charles L. South of Texas to exempt inland water carriers from national control and overwhelmingly repudiated (273–99) Wadsworth's proposal to recommit the bill without instruction. The lower chamber then approved the Lea measure, which Senator Reed of Kansas had considered "the biggest piece of major legisla-tion brought up in this Congress." Roosevelt's intervention may have persuaded many agricultural and railroad labor members to desert the water bloc on these votes and, according to ICC Commissioner Splawn, had "saved" the transit bill.[41]

The Wadsworth recommittal motion attracted relatively little following from either party, although it appealed more to Democrats. As in the Senate, transportation was not a political issue. The Warren water bloc did not secure majority support in any section, faring best in the Pacific section dependent upon shipping. Some southern and Middle Atlantic representatives also belonged to the water bloc, but the remaining sections supported the Lea measure.

The water bloc in the House differed considerably from its counter-part in the Senate. Democratic representatives exhibited more enthusiasm for shipping concerns, while the opposite pattern occurred among Republi-cans. Sectionally, the water bloc varied extensively in the two chambers. Middle Atlantic representatives, along with border and New England senators, sympathized with shippers much more than their respective counterparts in the opposite chamber. Pacific members consistently pro-vided the water forces with the largest following, but backed this group less enthusiastically in the House. Great Lakes legislators, especially those in the Senate, gave the shippers the least support.

Under the circumstances, the water bloc had fared well. Beginning with minimal support, it had formed a powerful coalition and had modified the measure substantially. The faction, according to Warren, had scored "a 90% victory" in the House and had prevented Lea's original strategy "to rush" the legislation through "with practically little debate." On the negative side, the Warren forces had not succeeded in exempting inland water carriers from federal regulation. They also feared that the con-ference committee, dominated by railroad advocates, would delete the Wadsworth, Jones, and Harrington amendments.[42]

Several months elapsed before the conference committee met. Although Lea urged the conferees to arrange a compromise quickly, Wheeler and Reed realized considerable time would be required to resolve the substantial differences in form and content between the Senate and House bills. The outbreak of World War 2 in September, 1939, forced the committee to procrastinate on settling the transportation question. Providing immediate military assistance to Great Britain and France dominated congressional attention.

During early 1940 the railroad-dominated conference committee began trying to reconcile differences between the Senate and House versions. Most members, including Senators Wheeler, Truman, and Reed, and Representative Lea, sympathized with the railroads from the outset and advocated federal regulation of intercoastal waterways. Since the two versions differed considerably in both substance and form, the committee faced a very difficult task. The Senate had recodified and clarified the entire Interstate Commerce Act, while the House had retained the existing law and had written a completely new section governing water carriers. In addition, representatives had inserted the controversial Wadsworth waterway, Harrington railway labor, and the Jones agricultural amendments. Senate conferees, deploring these changes, preferred instead to restore the original version. As committee member Truman remarked, "The House amended it and, of course, wrecked it."[43]

Interest groups continued playing a prominent role. Throughout early 1940 waterway, labor, and agricultural organizations bombarded conferees with telegrams, letters, and petitions defending the House version. Shippers urged the committee to retain the Wadsworth compensatory rates amendment and to exempt intercoastal operators from federal control. The Mississippi Valley Association considered national regulation of inland water carriers "harmful and vicious," while the New York State Waterways Association denounced the Wheeler-Lea measure as "fraught with danger for the water carriers and shippers."[44] Since railroad consolidations might promote widespread joblessness, train unions urged the committee to maintain the Harrington proposal. The Brotherhood of Railroad Trainmen and the Brotherhood of Locomotive Firemen claimed mergers already had doubled the unemployment rate. Led by the American Farm Bureau Federation, agrarian lobbyists opposed elimination of competition in rates and thus solicited the conferees to keep both the Jones and Wadsworth amendments.[45]

Government agencies likewise pressured the conference committee. The ICC rejected Senate recodification as "a forced and hurried job" performed under "great difficulty" and urged adoption of the non-codified House version containing "matters of principal importance." In a joint letter to Senator Bailey, the directors of the War and Agriculture departments and the U.S. Maritime Commission unequivocally supported continued federal exemption of intercoastal shippers.[46]

The vocal hostility of the executive agencies shook the confidence of the railroad-minded conferees. "I hope that when we get through," Truman remarked, "we will have something worthwhile. Sometimes I am not sure that we will even get a bill." Upon learning about the joint letter to Bailey, Wheeler speculated that the President no longer supported the transportation measure. On March 7 Roosevelt summoned Wheeler to the White House and assured the Montana Democrat he had not changed his attitude. At a press conference the next day, the President vigorously endorsed the Wheeler-Lea bill and desired "very much" that Congress approve the measure at this session. Roosevelt, speaking out publicly on this issue for the first time in over seven months, particularly advocated federal regulation of all forms of transit.[47] The rejuvenated conferees redoubled efforts to secure a satisfactory settlement.

In addition, Harrington and Jones urged the committee to keep their proposals. Harrington submitted a petition signed by 275 representatives requesting the conferees to retain the railroad labor amendment. Around 100,000 Americans, including railroad workers, businessmen, professionals, and civic groups also had sent petitions urging Congress to reject the transportation measure if the conferees removed the Harrington amendment. At the same time Jones pleaded with Senate conferees not to remove his amendment so as to prevent industrial producers from enjoying "advantageous freight rates" over agricultural producers.[48]

These lobbying activities, however, largely failed. In late April, 1940, the railroad-minded committee regained the momentum from the water bloc by writing the bill to conform with the Senate version. Undeterred by the vocal pressure groups, the conferees dropped both the Wadsworth and Jones amendments. Senate members also advocated deleting the Harrington proposal, which Wheeler denounced as both "imperfect" and "very drastic." In order to secure House approval of the committee version, the conferees made concessions to the railway labor unions. They agreed to eliminate the consolidation provisions, causing the railway labor unions to drop further opposition to the transportation measure. According to Lea, the conferees "struck the consolidation provision" with "the understanding" that railroad brotherhoods would "support the bill."[49]

The conferees expected their version would confront limited resistance. According to Reed, the committee solution would be both "reasonably acceptable to all interests" and "the beginning of a Sound Transportation Policy." Besides considering the compromise "as fair as could be made by twelve men," Reed claimed the conferees "leaned backwards to protect the waterways." On the Democratic side, Truman denied the conference report "would be injurious to the waterways." Truman wrote one disenchanted inland shipper, "You will be a lot better off under the proposed legislation than you are at this time."[50] Although placating the railway labor forces, they had done nothing to alleviate the fears of waterway or agricultural groups.

Shipping and farm organizations immediately protested the committee solution. Coastal maritime and longshoremen's unions strenuously disapproved of the deletion of the Wadsworth amendment and were determined to protect water carriers from federal regulation. Agricultural organizations denounced the committee removal of the Wadsworth and Jones proposals, warning that the transportation measure would continue to give railroads a monopoly. In a telegram to President Roosevelt, twenty farm groups complained that the committee action would "retard the national economic recovery" and "stifle competition."[51]

The committee version merely revitalized the formidable alliance of waterway, agricultural, and railway labor factions. The conferees, the coalition charged, had exceeded their authority by removing the Wadsworth, Jones, and Harrington amendments. On May 1 Warren's water bloc determined strategy for restoring the Wadsworth proposal and for reviving the earlier alliance. Shipping advocates again lured the support of both the farm and train union forces by promising to back restoration of the Jones and Harrington amendments. The agrarian wing had contended the removal of the Jones proposal would increase the cost of distributing their products and would decrease their purchasing activity, while the train unions had warned that deletion of the Harrington amendment would leave laborers unprotected in consolidation cases. In return the farm and railway labor factions pledged to battle for reinserting the Wadsworth amendment. The coalition concentrated on enacting a Wadsworth recommittal motion, which would instruct the conference committee to reinstate all three amendments. Warren, who predicted the House would approve the Wadsworth motion by at least 75 votes, confessed, "I have never known more vicious legislation since I have been in Congress." Kerr of North Carolina remarked that the transportation measure was "about as controversial as any that has been put in Congress."[52]

Railroad backers, again placed on the defensive, turned to the White House. Since the President had helped them on other occasions, they hoped Roosevelt would once more intervene to counter the powerful House alliance. Wheeler and Lea, fearing the opposition might "become an important menace to the bill," urged the President to endorse the committee solution publicly "as soon as possible." With the 1940 presidential election approaching, Roosevelt refused to align with the railroad forces this time. Since he contemplated running for an unprecedented third term because of worsening European conditions, the chief executive did not want to alienate the increasingly hostile Middle West. Secretary of Commerce Harry L. Hopkins, along with Agriculture Secretary Wallace, warned Roosevelt of "serious political" opposition throughout the midwestern regions.[53] The President also was preoccupied with foreign policy and preparedness questions because Germany had just expanded into the Scandinavian countries.

On May 9 the House temporarily killed the transportation bill by approving (209–182) the Wadsworth recommittal motion. With the powerful waterways-agriculture-labor coalition taking charge, representatives agreed that the conferees either should have rewritten the entire bill or not eliminated the three major amendments. Pennsylvania Democrat Herman P. Eberharter complained that the committee proposal was "designed solely for the benefit of a special interest"—namely, the railroads —and that it denied "the time-honored principle of fair competition in industry." Mansfield, Wadsworth, and especially Warren had caused the demise of the committee proposal. According to Eberharter, Warren deserved "by far the major credit for the victory" because he was "responsible for the strategy employed" and "led the fight" in an "intelligent and vigorous manner." In addition, shipping, farming, and railway union organizations helped swing the tide against the committee version. A railroad sympathizer, Vorys of Ohio complained representatives were "subjected to more high-pressure lobbying on this than on any other bill since I have been down here."[54] Roosevelt's refusal to intervene also contributed to the outcome.

Political party alignments on the Wadsworth motion may explain the President's silence. Roosevelt's Democratic Party furnished the nucleus of the Warren coalition forces, while Republicans supplied a substantial majority of the railway bloc. Although personally sympathetic to the train companies, Roosevelt did not desire to alienate such a large segment of Democratic representatives in an election year. Political party differences surfaced much more this time, resembling Democratic and Republican disagreements on the monetary question.

The House response bitterly disappointed backers of the committee version. The willingness of railroad labor to continue aligning with the water bloc rather than following general union sentiments particularly perplexed the Lea forces. Hope insisted "the railroads and railroad employees would both be the losers," while Taber of New York protested the railroad brotherhoods "made a deal with their own enemies and got nothing for it except a kick."[55] In hopes of reviving the transportation issue, Lea in early June attempted to persuade several congressmen from the coalition to oppose the amendments. Besides denouncing the Harrington amendment for compelling employees "to be continued on a full salary basis without work to perform," he criticized the Wadsworth proposal for seeking to establish "an arbitrary minimum rate rule." Lea's overtures seemingly fizzled, though, because Congress was increasingly disturbed over German moves into the Low Countries and France and preoccupied with foreign policy and preparedness efforts. Vorys pronounced the measure "dead for the rest of this session," while Senator Truman dejectedly commented, "I feel as if my four and a half years hard work has been practically wasted." [56]

On the other hand, jubilation filled the opposition camp. Eberharter of Pennsylvania viewed the outcome as "delightfully surprising to all of us who joined together in the bloc" recommitting the transportation bill. If the conferees "again attempt to circumvent the will of the House," he remarked, "I hope we can again throw them for a loss." Warren, confident the transportation issue was buried for the remainder of 1940, vacationed in rural Beaufort, North Carolina, completely unaware that the conferees were planning another offensive. [57]

ICC devised a strategy to entice away the agrarian and labor wings from their coalition with the water bloc. Commissioner Splawn urged the conferees to strengthen the Jones amendment by giving exported farm products the same preferences accorded to manufactured products. In the commissioner's view, uplifting the Jones proposal would appeal to agricultural organizations and would provide a face-saving solution for train unions. Solid labor support for the Jones amendment, Splawn argued, would help unions take a united stand for the rest of the transportation measure. [58]

The railroad-minded conferees eagerly pursued the ICC strategy of isolating the water forces. Catching the shipping bloc off guard, the conferees drafted a considerably modified bill. Following the ICC recommendations, they sought to lure the farm bloc to their side by strengthening the Jones amendment. In an effort to woo the labor forces, the conferees went beyond Splawn's original recommendations and altered the Harrington amendment. They now advocated requiring railroads either to pay a dismissal wage or to maintain veteran employees for at least four years. Conferees of course still refused to make any concessions to the water bloc and repudiated the twice-approved Miller-Wadsworth amendment. "The Miller-Wadsworth Amendment," Truman warned, "would raise freight rates in every section of the country and would prevent the railroads from reducing passenger fares—in fact the passenger rates would all be more than double." In reviving a virtually dead measure, the committee had accomplished an incredible task in a diligent manner. "No legislation, in my seventeen years in the United States Senate," Wheeler remarked, "has received the careful, detailed, and thorough consideration that has been accorded this bill." Truman likewise lauded the measure as "the most excellent piece of transportation legislation that has ever been offered to the country."[59]

The latest turn of events angered the water bloc. They complained the conferees had exceeded their authority by inserting material not included in either bill. Besides protesting that different language had been substituted for the Jones amendment, they charged the committee had substantially altered the Harrington proposal. To counter the conferees' move, Warren's water bloc concentrated on securing congressional approval of a Wadsworth motion recommitting the bill with instruction to restore the New Yorker's amendment. The shipping faction also denounced the conferees for having "utterly ignored instructions to restore the Miller-Wadsworth amendment, which had been approved by both chambers." Wadsworth deplored the committee action as "without precedent in legislative history," while Culkin attacked it as "parliamentary Hitlerism."[60]

The absence of Warren and the defection of the agricultural and labor forces destroyed the effectiveness of the water bloc. Warren had ably directed the opposing coalition in May, while agricultural and labor representatives had provided the margin of victory for the water bloc. The vacationing Warren, who did not know the conference committee had revived the transportation measure, subsequently admitted being "caught by surprise" and claimed "it was simply impossible for me to get back."[61] Wadsworth, who attempted to assume Warren's leadership role, did not capture the same degree of legislative support. With an election impending, several Democrats refused to follow the ardent anti-New Deal Republican Wadsworth. Conference committee concessions on the Jones and Harrington amendments also had induced several agricultural and labor representatives to desert the once formidable coalition. On August 10 the water bloc urged representatives either to "recommit this report or reject it entirely."[62] Two days later, however, the House buried (212–112) the Wadsworth recommittal motion and easily adopted (247–75) the conference report. The shipping faction attracted less support from both political parties, particularly the majority Democrats. Most agrarian and many pro-labor representatives from Roosevelt's party aligned against the water bloc, thus helping cause rejection of the Wadsworth amendment. Railroad-minded Republicans also joined these Democrats in defeating the Wadsworth recommittal motion.

Transportation remained largely a sectional question. Pacific and southern members, representing regions with large shipping interests, continued to comprise the foundation of the water bloc. Shipping forces still attracted substantial following in the water-oriented New England and border sections. Mountain, Great Lakes, and Middle Atlantic delegations, representing constituents dependent on large railroad traffic, insured the demise of the Wadsworth recommittal motion.

Attempting to rebound from this enormous setback, the water bloc concentrated on the Senate. Clark and Sheppard, coleaders of the shipping forces, faced a formidable task because the railway faction had easily prevailed there before. Employing the House strategy, opponents stressed that the conferees had disregarded the will of Congress by removing the Miller-Wadsworth amendment. Independent George W. Norris of Nebraska insisted the conference committee had "no right to take it out."[63] In order to prevent any Senate action on the transportation measure, the water bloc supported Clark's motion that the conferees had exceeded their authority.

The executive branch refused to align with the railroad forces this time. At the White House in early September, Roosevelt told Wheeler, "I do not think you can get the bill through the Senate."[64] Roosevelt opposed taking a public stand on the measure allegedly because he had not studied the legislation. The President also wanted wholehearted congressional support for the destroyer-base deal, selective service, and excess profits tax legislation and thus did not want to alienate party members belonging to the water bloc. Since the presidential election was rapidly approaching, Roosevelt did not desire to lose potential electoral support of water carrier, agricultural, and other organizations. In addition, the President's decision may have been influenced by Assistant Attorney General Thurman Arnold and other executive officials opposing the measure. Arnold complained the conferees had changed the bill drastically by granting "the greatest extension of railroad monopoly power attempted since 1912."[65]

Despite the President's response, railroad forces overcame the water bloc's resistance. They remained unalterably opposed to the Miller-Wadsworth proposal, which Reed claimed "would have destroyed the whole system of regulation of rates."[66] On September 9 the Senate decisively (51-23) overrode Clark's point of order, ruling the conferees had not exceeded their authority. The Wheeler forces established a significant precedent on the Clark motion, permitting future conferees the widest possible latitude when either chamber had rewritten a bill. At this point, however, enactment of a transportation measure far outweighed any technical deviation from previous procedural rules.

The Senate sounded the death knell for the water bloc by overwhelmingly approving (59-15) the transportation measure. Although having furnished formidable resistance in the House, the shipping forces could not overcome the railroad faction in the upper chamber. In addition, the water bloc did not capture majority backing among either major political party or any geographic region. Most Republicans and Democrats approved the conference report, signifying again the subordinate role of politics on this issue. Only three sections—namely the coastal southern, New England, and inland Great Plains regions—gave any support to the water bloc this time.

Although solidly defeated, the shipping forces had fared better than in April, 1939, in the Senate. The water bloc, benefiting from capable leaders, had enticed more senators from both major political parties and from the southern, Great Plains, and especially New England sections. Clark utilized his expertise in parliamentary procedure to considerable advantage, while Bailey, Sheppard, Shipstead, and Vandenberg argued effectively on the floor that the measure might create a railroad monopoly. Wheeler, who readily admitted the water bloc had posed formidable resistance, considered the transportation issue "one of the most exasperating and wearying victories of my career."[67]

Congress had approved one of the most significant transportation measures in American history. The act, Truman predicted, would "do more for transportation than any bill which has been passed since the Interstate Commerce Commission was set up" and would "do more for waterways than any piece of legislation that has ever been before Congress."[68] Although Truman exaggerated the importance of the legislative action, the Senate and House had promulgated a national transportation policy to bring rail, motor, and water carriers under uniform, centralized control and had placed inland shippers under federal jurisdiction for the first time. In an effort to create an equitable standard, Congress had authorized the ICC to establish maximum and minimum rates for rail, motor, and water carriers. A board would examine the fitness and economic status of transportation systems and would recommend railroad consolidations whenever necessary. The board, though, never became an effective body because its reports were delayed and obscured by American entry into World War 2.

In the final analysis, the railroad bloc had triumphed over the shipping forces. To help alleviate the economic plight of railroads, intercoastal water operators had been subjected to the same essential regulations as the rail and motor companies. The persistent shipping forces, by contrast, ultimately had failed in their quest to exempt inland water carriers from federal control. Since the water bloc had posed formidable resistance, however, the railroad-minded conferees had made substantial concessions to the agricultural and labor factions. Congress, meanwhile, had to decide whether to extend or discontinue the President's reciprocal trade program.

3

CONTINUATION
OF RECIPROCAL TRADE

American commercial policies were reevaluated when the transportation measure was buried in conference committee. President Franklin D. Roosevelt's reciprocal trade program, which had lowered tariff duties considerably, was scheduled to expire in June, 1940, unless extended for three years by Congress. During early 1940 the legislative branch had to decide whether to continue the reciprocity arrangement or to raise duties on imports.

In the 1920s American tariff rates had reached unprecedented levels. Congress in 1922 had established high imposts and had applied them to new products. Republican administrations not only had wished to protect domestic industries but had hoped to stimulate internal demand for farm goods. The Hawley-Smoot Tariff of 1930 had restricted American trade further by raising duties on foreign agricultural and textile products. Foreign nations had retaliated with high rates, causing American trade abroad to decline drastically.[1]

Democrats, who regained control of the presidency in 1933, had initiated a reciprocal trade program. Reflecting their traditional party stance, they complained that high tariffs had hurt international relations, restricted foreign trade, raised prices for both consumer and farmer, and encouraged monopolies. In order to expand American foreign markets and to enlarge domestic productivity, the Roosevelt administration had championed freer trade and tariff reductions. Congress in 1934 had authorized the President to lower rates by 50 percent and to negotiate international commerce agreements for a three-year period without Senate ratification. Although Republicans had despised the reciprocal trade program, the Democratic-controlled Congress in 1937 had secured extension of the Roosevelt policy for another three-year period.

Foreign trade had helped the American economy recover from the depression. The State Department by 1939 had negotiated arrangements with seventeen Latin American countries, Canada, Sweden, France, and Great Britain, covering over 60 percent of American commerce. These areas, especially those in Latin America, could not compete on an even basis economically with businessmen and farmers from the United States. Domestic exports to reciprocity nations had jumped 63 percent from 1934 to 1939, twice as much commerce as with other nations. American imports from trade agreements countries had risen only 22 percent, or around one-third of the export figures. Domestic producers thus had profited considerably because exports from the United States had increased at a much faster pace than imports. In addition, the tariff rates on some American products had remained highly protectionist. Many duties from the Hawley-Smoot Tariff of 1930, in fact, had continued at such prohibitive levels that a 50 percent reduction was insufficient to allow certain competitive products to enter the United States. Before any rate could be reduced, lobbyists from interested American domestic industries were allowed to make appeals to the Tariff Commission. If conclusive evidence was presented that any contemplated agreement would harm domestic industries or agriculture, the Tariff Commission then canceled the proposed revision. Domestic producers, for example, prevented the lowering of taxes on copper, oil, fruit, beef, and other key Latin American exports. The most favored nation requirement also had kept tariff reductions limited in scope because any advantages granted or received by the United States could be secured by any other nation consenting to make similar concessions. The Roosevelt administration had not lowered the duty on Brazilian meat because domestic cattlemen opposed the extension of reduced rates to Argentine meat.[2]

The Roosevelt administration acted much more decisively on the trade issue than on the transportation question. In his annual message in January, 1940, Roosevelt urged Congress to renew the trade policy for three additional years. Secretary of State Cordell Hull and Secretary of Agriculture Henry A. Wallace, ardently battled for the program before the House Ways and Means Committee and the Senate Finance Committee. High tariff policies of previous Republican presidents, the administration argued, had fostered widespread unemployment and had destroyed international economic stability. Hull blamed the high Hawley-Smoot Tariff of 1930 for "the unprecedented economic collapse," whereas Wallace denounced the protectionist rates for encouraging a "world wide economic disaster of cataclysmic proportions." The executive branch also stressed that Roosevelt's commercial policy had opened up foreign markets for American goods and had encouraged non-discriminatory trade practices among nations. Besides lowering trade barriers, Wallace boasted that the agricultural exports to agreement countries had increased 15 percent over a four-year period.[3] With the European situation worsening, the White House connected reciprocity with attempts to defend American security. Roosevelt considered low tariff arrangements "indispensable" to "any stable and durable peace" among nations.[4]

In its quest to secure continuation of the reciprocal trade program, however, the executive branch faced worsening European developments and an increasingly hostile Congress. The outbreak of World War 2 threatened to destroy low tariff arrangements. Germany in September, 1939, had launched a devastating attack on Poland, while Russia three months later had attacked Finland. Adolf Hitler was planning a full-scale invasion of the Scandinavian and western European countries, thus endangering American commercial agreements with England and Sweden. On the domestic front the anti–New Deal coalition had continued to resist Roosevelt's economic and social programs.

As on the monetary question, representatives stressed political considerations. Democrats favored continuation of the commercial policy, while Republicans were determined to restore higher tariffs. Southern and border Democrats, temporarily setting aside their differences with Roosevelt, directed the administration battle to extend reciprocal trade. On the Republican side, representatives solidly disapproved of delegating such extensive economic power to the executive branch. Both political parties, cognizant that commercial policy could become a major issue in the upcoming presidential election, hoped to seize the initiative in Congress. Secretary Hull, who had arranged most of the agreements, loomed as a possible Democratic presidential candidate.

Party leadership this time came principally from House Ways and Means Committee members. Chairman Robert L. Doughton, a seventy-four-year-old North Carolina Democrat, directed the administration struggle in the House. The Laurel Springs, North Carolina, native had grown up on a farm and had graduated from high school there. Besides farming 5,000 acres and raising a prize herd of Hereford cattle, he also had headed a savings bank in North Wilkesboro. After a brief apprenticeship in the state senate, he was elected easily in 1910 to the U.S. House of Representatives. Doughton worked hard for his constituents, arriving at the Capitol by 6 a.m. and personally opening all mail. The big-boned, wiry, 6-foot Doughton always dressed somberly and walked with a "yard-long gait that forces his companions to trot to keep up." During his first two decades in the House, he had seldom delivered a speech. Upon becoming chairman in 1933 of the Ways and Means Committee, the avid New Dealer held responsibility for originating all congressional revenue measures. His committee had shaped the Social Security Act of 1935 and drafted numerous tax bills to finance public works programs, relieve unemployment, and stimulate business.[5] A vigorous advocate of low tariffs, in early January, 1940 he introduced a measure to continue the reciprocal trade program for three years. Democrats Jere Cooper of Tennessee and Carl Vinson of Georgia gave Doughton considerable assistance in waging the battle in 1940 for renewal of the low tariff policy. On the other hand, Republicans Allen T. Treadway of Massachusetts and Roy A. Woodruff of Michigan directed strategy for the high tariff advocates urging immediate termination of the reciprocal trade program.

The political parties disagreed sharply over what role the executive branch should play on economic questions. Since the Republicans did not occupy the presidency, they placed very high priority on reasserting congressional supremacy over the executive branch. Republican Karl M. Le Compte of Iowa insisted that "we should maintain that constitutional safeguard." The minority party certainly opposed allocating further authority to Roosevelt, who they feared might seek an unprecedented third term in office. The anti-New Dealer Hamilton Fish, Jr., of New York denounced reciprocal trade as "the worst delegation of power in our history" and warned that the Hull program would "destroy the very essence of representative and constitutional government." In control of the White House, Democrats contended the measure did not surrender legislative power unduly to the executive branch. Opponents, Cooper claimed, had made no "successful challenge" to the constitutionality of the trade policy.[6]

Representatives argued whether or not low tariff policies would revive the American economy. Republicans, who historically had favored protectionism, contended the Hull trade program adversely affected American agriculture and industry. Treadway complained foreign companies were "flooding" the domestic markets with products "which we do not need," while Daniel A. Reed of New York charged reciprocity brought "ruin to agriculture." On the other side, Democrats insisted the Republican protectionist programs had helped to cause the economic depression in the United States. The Hawley-Smoot Act of 1930, Doughton asserted, was "an old fashioned, log-rolling tariff" leading industry and agriculture into "utter ruin."[7]

The feasibility of extending a massive foreign trade program likewise provoked political controversy. Giving top priority to this theme, Democrats praised the accomplishments of the numerous economic agreements with European and Latin American countries. Between 1935 and 1939 American exports to participant nations had increased 23 percent more than shipments to other countries. Republicans, however, claimed the United States derived few benefits from Roosevelt's policy and urged higher tariffs promoting greater reliance upon domestic agricultural and industrial producers. "American producers," Hope of Kansas warned, "are being sacrificed on the altar of good will and diplomacy." Republican Benton F. Jensen of Iowa argued that American farmers were being "sold down the river with respect to the reciprocal trade treaties" and protested that "foreign agricultural products grown by what virtually amounts to slave labor can come into this country and undersell those same products raised here."[8]

Interventionism also was connected with reciprocal trade. Democrats, who favored assisting the Allies against possible German aggression, predicted the Hull program would bolster England, France, and other European nations economically and would keep the United States out of World War 2. According to Doughton, the administration economic policy had enabled foreign governments to lower their trade barriers without involving the United States "in a European conflict."[9] Republican isolationists, though, predicted that reciprocal trade extension would lead to greater involvement in European affairs and more direct American assistance to Great Britain and France. The United States, August H. Andresen of Minnesota contended, had become "the prize sucker of the world" and "the champion Santa Claus for the rest of humanity." Since some reciprocal trade critics were not isolationists, the extension technically was not an interventionist issue. Wadsworth of New York, who ardently supported American economic and military help to western European nations and had considered the arms embargo "unwise," refused to endorse the Hull trade policy.[10]

Reciprocal trade issues resembled the monetary question much more than transportation. The devaluation bill had focused upon the relationship between the executive and legislative branches, the probable effect upon the American economy, the feasibility of foreign trade, and the role of interventionism in the European war. In both instances representatives had responded to an essentially economic measure in a highly political fashion. By comparison, the transportation problem did not concern intervention in a European war or the impact of foreign economic policy upon the United States.

During late 1939 Republican representatives commenced their battle against reciprocal trade. Ways and Means Committee members Treadway and Woodruff recommended the formation of a Republican trade committee "as soon as possible" to draft an alternative commercial program.[11] In late January, 1940, Woodruff challenged Secretary Hull to explain why he had opposed lower tariffs as a Tennessee senator eleven years earlier. Hull, annoyed over Woodruff's query, claimed he now supported low tariff policies because President Hoover's protectionist approach had caused "awful conditions" in the United States. Republicans concentrated on attaching two amendments to the Doughton bill, one of which would limit presidential power by requiring Senate ratification of all executive agreements. In an endeavor to assist American farmers, they proposed preventing price reductions on agricultural imports when commensurate domestic rates were below parity.[12]

Pressure groups, although less vocal than on the transportation legislation, posed additional resistance. At Ways and Means Committee hearings business, mining, and agricultural organizations charged reciprocal trade encouraged foreign competitors to deluge domestic markets with cheaper goods. The National Association of Manufacturers and the mining lobbyists contended that tariff reductions discriminated against their products, while agricultural groups opposed dropping rates on farm commodities selling below parity. Besides condemning the most favored nation clause, these organizations labeled the executive agreements as "unconstitutional."[13]

The House Ways and Means Committee treated the Doughton bill as a political issue. Although waging determined resistance, Republicans did not succeed in amending the measure because Democrats controlled 60 percent of the committee seats. Doughton, who had sponsored the measure, chaired the committee and steered the proposal (14-10) through his committee. Committee members voted almost exclusively along party lines, with majority Democrats insuring favorable action. A member of Congress since 1911, Doughton observed that the Republicans posed "the most stubborn and determined fight that I have experienced."[14]

The undaunted Republicans furnished formidable resistance on the House floor. Since Democrats easily controlled the lower chamber numerically, the minority party did not expect to defeat the Doughton bill. "Democratic knees," Woodruff charged, "grow weak and the spines grow boneless in an election year." Before the House began floor debates, Hope of Kansas conceded his party "did not have any chance to defeat" the measure.[15] Nevertheless, the Republicans rallied behind a Treadway recommittal motion designed to kill the trade program. Treadway wanted the Ways and Means Committee to secure additional protection for domestic producers against foreign competition and to require congressional approval of all new agreements. In another setback for the Republicans, the Democratic-controlled House on February 23 rejected the Treadway motion and approved a three-year extension of the trade program by 221-163 and 218-168 margins.

Reciprocal trade, like the monetary issue, produced unusual voting patterns. Both major parties achieved over 90 percent loyalty on an issue normally decided along economic or sectional lines. Democrats solidly favored Roosevelt's commercial program, while the Republicans almost unanimously opposed the economic policy. As on the devaluation question, the anti–New Deal coalition of Republicans and southern Democrats took opposite viewpoints this time. Southern and border Democrats wielded enormous power in guaranteeing approval of the program, setting aside political differences with the President. Northern Republicans, on the other hand, spearheaded resistance to the Doughton measure.

Despite high political party allegiance, economic considerations also affected voting behavior. Southern Democrats urged continuation of reciprocal trade because their section exported to Latin America enormous amounts of cotton, tobacco, and rice. New England, midwestern, and mountain representatives opposed extension partly because foreign producers had flooded domestic markets and competed unfairly with American industrialists and farmers.

Besides Doughton, several individuals or groups had insured the survival of reciprocal trade. Southern and border Democrats, led by Doughton, had enabled the continuation of a commercial policy that most other sections considered unpopular. In addition, the executive branch had continued to intervene more directly than on the transportation question. State Department officials, especially Secretary Hull and Assistant Secretary Breckinridge Long, had provided invaluable assistance behind-the-scenes. Hull had persuaded about one dozen wavering representatives to support reciprocal trade, while Long had consulted privately with administration leaders in the House and had made certain that practically all Democrats were in Washington on the roll call date.[16]

Roosevelt, though, did not play a direct role in the trade struggle. Although ardently favoring continuation of the low tariff policy, the President wisely let State Department officials handle the administrative strategy. Roosevelt, intensely cognizant that Congress had opposed numerous presidential policies since 1937, feared that forthright leadership on his part might further antagonize legislators. With the European situation becoming more ominous daily, he needed the full cooperation of Congress for his preparedness and foreign policy measures. Republican representatives also suspected Roosevelt might seek an unprecedented third presidential term.

Senators, meanwhile, responded to reciprocal trade in the same manner as on the monetary issue. Western Democrats, again led by Pittman of Nevada and assisted by Edwin C. Johnson of Colorado, furnished the principal resistance to low tariff policies. A few conservative Democrats directed by Carter Glass, still allied with the westerners because too much power already was vested in the executive branch. The third segment of the monetary alliance, namely the agrarian southwesterners, did not join the opposition forces on this issue because their section had profited from lower rates.

Senators still placed much premium upon political factors. Republicans, who again gave top priority to this theme, objected to executive control of the trade agreements policy because their party did not occupy the White House. Under the direction of Vandenberg of Michigan, the minority Republicans hoped to make reciprocal trade a major issue in the impending 1940 presidential campaign. Vandenberg's party especially wanted the issue "sharply defined for campaign purposes" and vowed the matter should be settled conclusively in November, 1940, at the polls.[17]

Republicans still lacked the numerical power to defeat the administration proposal in the House. Casting aside their customary alliance with anti-New Deal southern Democrats, they renewed their partnership with the western Democrats on this economic issue. Rejoicing over the division within Roosevelt's party, Republicans anticipated much greater success than in the House. Hope of Kansas noted that "the agricultural States are numerically much better represented" in the Senate, while Vandenberg detected "a general unanimity of opinion" among midwestern and western members from both parties against "many phases" of the Hull program.[18]

Democrats, as on the monetary question, provided almost sole support for the low tariff program. Southern Democrats again directed the administration struggle; northeastern members played a less active role than on the devaluation measure. Democrat Pat Harrison of Mississippi, fifty-seven-year-old chairman of the Finance Committee handling reciprocal trade matters, led the battle for continuing foreign trade. His father was an impoverished Crystal Springs, Mississippi, storekeeper, who died of a crippling disease in the late 1800s and left four children. In order to support the family, young Pat had sold newspapers and driven a two-mule hack. After attending Louisiana State University the tall, lanky, beak-nosed Harrison had returned to Mississippi to teach public school and to play semi-professional baseball. He had practiced law for several years and served from 1911 to 1919 in the U.S. House of Representatives. An intelligent, shrewd, and witty campaigner, Harrison in the 1918 Democratic primary had ousted veteran James K. Vardaman from the U.S. Senate. The Mississippi Democrat, who was an exceptional leader and debater, had guided the National Recovery Act and other New Deal legislation through the Senate. When Roosevelt selected the more liberal Barkley of Kentucky over Harrison for Majority Leader in 1937, he began aligning with the anti-New Dealers. In 1939 the Washington press corps lauded the Finance Committee chairman as the most influential and persuasive member of the entire chamber. Blaming the Hawley-Smoot Tariff of 1930 for hindering American export trade, he had sponsored in 1934 the initial Senate measure on reciprocal trade and had utilized his considerable authority three years later to insure continuation of low rates.

Senators debated heatedly how reciprocal trade would affect the American economy. Western Democrats, along with Republicans, protested the Hull program had impeded domestic economic growth. The renewal of Roosevelt's policy, Democrat James E. Murray of Montana warned, would promote "a serious condition of unemployment and business stagnation." In addition, the opposing coalition stressed how low tariffs adversely affected both miners and farmers. Pittman denounced the administration program for encouraging the "flooding" of the domestic market with foreign copper, silver, and other mining products, while Republican Arthur Capper of Kansas feared "swelling imports of competitive farm products" were "displacing American goods."[19] Democrat Joseph C. O'Mahoney of Wyoming warned that "tariffs protecting agricultural items may be reduced in order to secure concessions from foreign countries for manufactured goods." On the other hand, proponents deplored the high tariff policies of previous Republican administrations and argued that reduced rates stimulated the American economy. Democrat Guy M. Gillette of Iowa protested that, during the Harding, Coolidge, and Hoover presidencies, "the great export markets for the raw materials of America were, to all effective purposes, totally destroyed." Harrison contended reciprocity created "economic stability," while Truman insisted that "domestic agriculture has been substantially aided by the trade agreements program."[20]

The role of executive power likewise caused considerable controversy. Republicans and western Democrats particularly despised the growth of the President's economic power and hoped to reassert congressional supremacy over Roosevelt. Commercial agreements, Pittman insisted, "must be ratified by the Senate" since they were treaties affecting federal revenue and industrial prosperity. In a similar vein, O'Mahoney argued "We cannot preserve democracy and popular government by abandoning the processes of that government."[21] On the Republican side Vandenberg denounced the Hull program as "a grossly unconstitutional delegation of legislative power to the executive branch." "There is no doubt," Hiram Johnson asserted, "but what these tariff agreements are treaties. The Administration has got over the Constitution by simply disregarding it."[22] Reciprocal trade supporters did not object to executive control of both the negotiation and ratification stages of agreements. Truman of Missouri claimed the Roosevelt administration "placed the adjustment of tariff duties in the hands of the most competent men available for the purpose, men beyond the reach of political logrolling and tariff lobbying at the expense of national welfare." In addition, reciprocity backers argued that the federal courts had sanctioned the principle of executive control over commercial arrangements. "The Supreme Court," Hayden of Arizona stressed, "has many times upheld the power of the Congress to delegate authority to negotiate reciprocal trade agreements without requiring their confirmation by a two-thirds vote of the Senate."[23]

Another volatile issue concerned the appropriateness of an extensive foreign trade program. Republicans and western Democrats preferred restoration of protectionist rates so as to increase profits of domestic businessmen and farmers. The Hull program, McNary of Oregon charged, had made American industries "practically prostrate." On the other hand, low tariff defenders contended that the administration policy had promoted considerable economic growth and had increased employment opportunities in the United States. As Hayden noted, "improved foreign trade resulting from the trade agreement program has meant domestic employment to millions of Americans."[24]

Senators occasionally linked reciprocal trade with the European war. Some isolationists opposed the Hull program because they disapproved of economic or military assistance to Great Britain and France. Capper insisted the United States should be "determined to keep out of war," while McNary contended the European conflict had created "additional hardships" for Americans.[25] In the internationalist camp, senators stressed that lower tariffs would bolster western Europe economically against future German expansion. The Hull program, Democrat Theodore F. Green of Rhode Island claimed, already had facilitated the "path to international peace."[26]

Reciprocal trade, as in the House, should not be considered as an interventionist-isolationist issue. Some internationalists, such as Pittman and Glass, had urged American economic and military assistance to Great Britain but disliked the reciprocal trade program. Pittman had played an instrumental role in late 1939 in securing Senate repeal of the arms embargo, which he complained "helps Germany while injuring Great Britain and France." A rabid interventionist, Glass had remarked that "Germany should be wiped off the map" and demanded that the "disgraceful" limitations of the Neutrality Act of 1939 be "expunged." Pittman fought reciprocal trade largely for sectional considerations, while Glass favored increased Senate control over presidential power in foreign affairs.[27]

The bipartisan coalition nearly prevented the Finance Committee from reporting the bill. Although controlling around three-fourths of the committee seats, Democrats were so split that Chairman Harrison had to exert adept leadership to salvage the administration measure. Although the committee in early March approved the measure (12-9), five Republicans, three western Democrats, and Progressive Robert M. LaFollette, Jr., of Wisconsin posed very formidable resistance. Despite the narrow margin, the Senate was expected to approve without amendment the administration's economic policy. A February poll indicated low tariff advocates held the initial advantage, with 45 of 85 senators favoring reciprocal trade extension and 11 being undecided.

Western Democrats led the Senate battle to defeat the measure, while Republicans pursued a divide-and-conquer strategy. Although stressing sectional considerations during the currency struggle, western Democrats utilized different tactics this time because fewer opponents came from mining states. In an effort to broaden the opposition coalition, the Pittman forces sought to lure any senators deploring the unfavorable economic impact of lower tariffs or denouncing the growth of executive power. Pittman, who claimed the agreements were treaties necessitating Senate approval, concentrated on testing the legality of the Hull agreements and proposed an amendment requiring Senate ratification of all such accords. Seeking to capitalize on the dissension within Roosevelt's party, Republicans were content to remain silent and let the western Democrats conduct the floor debate. As Vandenberg observed, "So many Democrats want to present amendments" to the measure, the Republicans would "let them do the fighting." [28]

The Roosevelt administration, visibly alarmed by coalition tactics, intensified its campaign to preserve the trade program. In his first public statement on the issue since January, Roosevelt warned senators that the Pittman amendment would retard foreign trade. Assistant Secretary of State Long, working feverishly behind the scenes, sought to dissuade both Pittman and Democrat Clark from opposing continuation of the low tariff approach. [29] At the insistence of the executive branch, Harrison and Majority Whip Minton agreed to intensify their activities on the Senate floor against the Pittman amendment. Harrison, who ably conducted the administration floor fight, cautioned his colleagues that the Pittman proposal would stymie future trade arrangements and urged wavering senators to oppose the western Democrat's plan. After polling colleagues in late March Harrison favored an immediate vote because 48 of 94 committed members disapproved of the Pittman amendment. Minton advised all Democrats supporting reciprocal trade extension "under no circumstances" to leave Washington because the tally would be "so close" they could not "risk any absentees." [30]

The administration had seized the offensive. Dismayed over the poll results, the western Democrats sought postponement of a roll call on the Pittman amendment for a few days so as to convert a few wavering senators to their side. Undermanned opposition forces, however, faced an unenviable task because Pittman could not always find speakers available to filibuster against the measure. Before the roll call Johnson of Colorado even conceded the Pittman amendment would lose by at least two votes and refused to "bet a lead nickel" against supporters of the Hull program.[31] After Harrison forced the question to a vote, the Senate on March 29 narrowly (44–41) rejected the Pittman amendment.

Several considerations had doomed the Pittman amendment. A substantial majority of Roosevelt's party favored low tariff policies, thus preventing the bipartisan coalition of Republicans and western Democrats from modifying the bill. As on the monetary question, political allegiance figured less prominently than in the House because of the Democratic split. President Roosevelt's strong commitment to existing reciprocal trade programs may have induced some senators to oppose the Pittman proposal, but regional factors were paramount. Southern and border members, opponents of protectionist rates, led the battle to defeat the Pittman amendment. Middle Atlantic and Great Lakes delegations, likewise disapproving of high tariffs, also tipped the scales against the Pittman forces. Harrison played a more decisive role than any other senator, winning his initial confrontation with the bipartisan coalition.

The reciprocal trade program had survived a very close call. Opponents of the increasing economic powers of Roosevelt almost succeeded in limiting executive authority. Senators from farming and mining states had nearly installed a procedure for checking foreign trade and restoring high tariff rates. Although losing their initial struggle the undaunted Republicans and western Democrats still vowed to resist the Hull program.

Dissenters quickly sought to broaden their coalition. Repeating strategy utilized on the currency question, the Pittman forces attempted to reach an understanding with the southerners. In an effort to attract southern support, the coalition drafted two amendments. Democrat Pat McCarran of Nevada, cognizant that some southern cottonseed oil and petroleum producers disliked foreign competition, proposed exempting those goods from reciprocal trade negotiations. Shipstead drafted a comprehensive plan excluding all agricultural items from tariff agreements. In return the coalition hoped to secure pledges from southerners to battle against extension of the Hull program. Southern senators, however, refused to cooperate, because their section had benefited from foreign trade, and helped defeat both amendments.

As on the monetary question, dissension developed within the administration camp. In early April the Majority Whip Minton disclosed to newspapers that Vice President Garner was working behind the scenes to limit the extension of the Hull program. Garner, who had opposed numerous New Deal measures, was competing with Secretary Hull and Postmaster General James A. Farley in 1940 for the Democratic presidential nomination. According to Minton, Garner was seeking "to line up votes in the Senate" for an amendment by isolationist David I. Walsh of Massachusetts to limit to only one year continuation of the trade agreements. Since Garner declined to comment on the story, rumors circulated around the Capitol that Minton's accusations were correct. Roosevelt, who was furious with the Vice President, allegedly "really let go his temper" at the next cabinet meeting. Garner abruptly ceased his clandestine maneuvering and did not even preside over the Senate when the final roll call was taken. Several of the Vice President's closest friends opposed the Walsh plan, which was easily rejected.[32]

The upper chamber on April 5 narrowly approved (42-37) extension of the Hull program. Despite behind-the-scenes activity by the Republicans and western Democrats, political party and regional voting patterns had changed relatively little. Sectional considerations overshadowed political motivations, with low tariff Democrats preserving the life of the commercial program. Since three Republicans converted to the administration viewpoint, the opposing coalition dropped slightly in numerical strength.

Several elements had contributed to the outcome. As earlier, southern and border Democrats led the battle to renew the trade program and received considerable assistance from Great Lakes members. Minton and especially Harrison provided adept leadership to insure senatorial approval of the reciprocity policy. Roosevelt lauded Harrison for "piloting through" the measure, while Secretary Hull praised the Mississippi Democrat for "fine leadership" and claimed that no senator "could have rendered more splendid service."[33] In addition, Minton had assisted immeasurably in rounding up votes. The executive branch, especially Secretary Hull and Assistant Secretary Long, played dynamic roles. Long, according to Pittman, converted two western Democrats to the reciprocal trade camp only hours before the final roll call. Pittman claimed his coalition had held a three-vote majority the previous night, but "were fighting a losing battle" after the State Department's decisive intervention.[34]

The spirited bipartisan coalition thus had failed in its quest to terminate the reciprocal trade agreements program. "The battle over the trade pacts was about as vigorous as could be," O'Mahoney concluded, "but we apparently just did not have the votes." A realist, he added, "close as the contest was, we were unable to muster more than 41 [votes] at any time."[35] Opponents, who blamed the outcome on intense pressure applied by the Roosevelt administration, found limited consolation in making the battle very close. "The White House," Johnson of California remarked, "had to break its neck to put them over this time, and did it then by a very scant majority. Old Hull is a 'nut' and he had gathered about him some superannuated free traders, and some young men who have adopted that as a philosophy of government. Each time we have been getting closer to whipping him, so I don't feel particularly badly about the present extension."[36]

The Roosevelt administration had succeeded in extending reciprocal trade for three years. On April 12 an ecstatic Roosevelt praised the "splendid" congressional action as a step for "strengthening the foundations of world peace."[37] The Hull policy had survived an intense legislative struggle without being altered. President Roosevelt and the State Department had retained the right to negotiate trade treaties without Senate ratification. Since Hitler was planning a massive spring offensive, the renewal of the commercial program helped to bolster economically Great Britain and the other western European countries.

In the final analysis, Congress still remained quite autonomous from the White House. The House and Senate once again had posed formidable resistance to an executive program. Although less successful this time, opposition forces almost altered drastically the Hull trade policy.

PART TWO

POLITICAL REFORM ISSUES

4

MAINTAINING WORK
RELIEF PROGRAMS

Political issues likewise aroused considerable controversy on Capitol Hill. By early 1939 dissension pervaded in Congress more than at any time in the New Deal period. President Franklin D. Roosevelt already had antagonized many senators and representatives with his actions on the Supreme Court and purge questions. He also had not ruled out seeking an unprecedented third term in office, which encouraged opponents to center on the dangers of excessive presidential power. A formidable coalition of conservative Democrats and Republicans, fresh from triumphs in the 1938 congressional elections, planned a major assault on the Works Progress Administration.

Work relief programs had become a trademark of the New Deal. The stock market crash of 1929 and subsequent economic depression had triggered the development of federal assistance for the unemployed. By 1932 nearly 13 million Americans, or 26 percent of the adult population, had lost their jobs. During the "first hundred days" in 1933 Roosevelt had established the Civilian Conservation Corps, the Federal Emergency Relief Administration, and the Public Works Administration to help alleviate the plight of the unemployed citizens. These New Deal agencies had provided substantial direct relief to numerous persons or families, but soon were overshadowed by the WPA.[1]

The WPA, headed by Harry L. Hopkins, by 1939 had become the most comprehensive, ambitious, and controversial government program. Congress in April, 1935, had authorized the agency nearly $5 billion for hiring unemployed persons to participate in construction and conservation projects. A vast cadre had built public parks, schools, post offices, highways, roads, streets, bridges, flood control levees, and fish hatcheries. In addition, the agency had recruited numerous jobless artists, musicians, and actors to participate in sundry community projects. Remuneration had varied according to the skill required and the region involved, but pay scales in 1936 averaged slightly above $52 a month. Anti-New Dealers, though, had attacked the WPA program, charging administrators had used discriminatory rate scales, padded relief rolls, permitted ultra-liberals to participate, and intervened in political campaigns.[2]

The Senate Campaign Expenditures Committee, headed by Democrat Morris Sheppard, had damaged further the reputation of the WPA. Conservatives already had accused local Democratic politicians of misusing staff and funds for political purposes, charging that agency relief rolls had ballooned to 3.3 million workers shortly before the 1938 congressional elections and then mysteriously dropped by 250,000 persons within sixty days. The Sheppard committee, consisting of four Democrats and Republican Austin, investigated the use of WPA funds in states holding senatorial races and failed to sustain most accusations. On the other hand, the committee found agency officials had diverted some funds to support New Deal Democrats in Kentucky, Tennessee, and Pennsylvania.

On the first day of the Seventy-sixth Congress, the Sheppard committee issued a report describing each instance of political manipulation. In the Kentucky senatorial primary Democratic officials had canvassed WPA workers for political affiliations and had solicited $24,000 from agency employees to help Majority Leader Barkley triumph over Governor Albert B. "Happy" Chandler. Senator Thomas Stewart, who defeated George L. Berry in Tennessee, had received substantial donations from federal civil service and relief workers supposedly under "intimidation and coercion." Pennsylvania Democrats also had raised funds illegally from WPA employees to assist Governor George H. Earle in an unsuccessful Senate campaign against incumbent Republican James J. Davis. Besides selling tickets at political gatherings to agency personnel, WPA officials there had ordered Republican workers to join the Democratic Party or risk loss of their jobs. Sheppard's committee cleared political candidates in those states of direct responsibility, but demanded legislation preventing relief administrators from coercing employees.[3]

Vice President Garner also insisted upon sharp reductions in WPA programs. A liaison between congressmen and government agency officials, and a presidential contender, Garner had often infuriated Roosevelt by cooperating with conservative Democrats. Garner and Representative Clifton A. Woodrum of Virginia, a major figure on the Appropriations Committee, dropped a bombshell on New Year's eve by insisting that a $500 million ceiling be placed on additional funds for the agency. In addition, they urged the removal of considerable personnel from relief rolls and the disbanding of unwarranted projects. Fearing the rapid growth of presidential power, they requested that states and local communities play a larger role in administering and financing these programs.[4]

The Roosevelt administration, meanwhile, urged continuation of the WPA. Citing widespread unemployment, it claimed millions of persons would have lived in abject poverty without agency assistance ranging from $19 to $94 monthly. WPA officials had carried an average of 2.5 million Americans on rolls before 1939, affording relief to nearly one-fourth of the entire adult working force. On January 5 President Roosevelt warned that agency funds would evaporate within one month and requested Congress quickly to approve an $875 million deficiency appropriation to keep the WPA in operation for the remainder of the 1939 fiscal year. Although expecting relief rolls to drop, he urged "speedy action" so as "to prevent disruption of the program and consequent suffering and want on the part of the unemployed." Concerned over reaction to the Senate scandals, he ordered the agency to stay "completely free from political manipulation" and demanded "the imposition of rigid statutory regulations and penalties by the Congress."[5] In testimony before the House Appropriations Committee the next day, WPA Administrator Fred Harrington adamantly defended agency programs and stressed that at least 750,000 other eligible Americans were being denied relief because of financial limitations.[6]

House members split into two basic camps, both being led by Appropriations Committee personnel. The economy bloc and New Dealers formed the two factions, with the fiscal conservatives enjoying numerical control. Moderate and conservative Democrats, under the direction of subcommittee Chairman Woodrum of Virginia, dominated the economy forces and favored reducing the President's request from $875 million to $725 million. Fifty-two-year-old Woodrum, the son of a Roanoke, Virginia, lawyer, had studied medicine and run a pharmacy in his home town. Following his father's footsteps, he had pursued law at Washington and Lee University and in 1908 had commenced practice in Roanoke. Before joining the U.S. House of Representatives in 1923, Woodrum was commonwealth attorney in his home town and judge for the Hastings courts. Washington correspondents lauded the vigorous, gregarious Appropriations Committee member as one of the five ablest representatives. A gifted orator and frequent lecturer, the Virginia Democrat impressed colleagues as an industrious, persistent, highly principled, and very influential legislator. Although supporting early New Deal programs, he eventually had insisted upon slashing federal domestic expenditures. At the 1937 and 1938 sessions Woodrum had successfully inserted amendments requiring relief to be allocated on a monthly basis and to make ineligible any workers who had declined higher paying private jobs. Rabid fiscal conservatives, including Republicans and anti-New Deal Democrats, also belonged to the economy bloc. Appropriations Committee members Taber of New York and Edward Eugene Cox of Georgia headed this contingent, which insisted upon slicing the WPA amount far below the $725 million figure.

On the other hand, New Deal Democrats favored allotting the WPA the entire $875 million. Although prevailing in the House on most issues until the 1937-38 session, they had begun losing ground to the economy bloc. Appropriations Committee Chairman Edward T. Taylor of Colorado, the oldest member of Congress at age eighty, helped conduct the battle this time for the liberal forces. Fifty-nine-year-old Clarence Cannon, Jr. of Missouri, a prominent member of the Appropriations Committee, provided much more vigorous leadership for the New Dealers supporting the original amount requested by the President for the WPA. A small group of flamboyant urban liberals, headed by American-Laborite Vito Marcantonio of New York and Democrat John M. Coffee of Washington, also aligned with New Dealers. Marcantonio and Coffee argued that Roosevelt had understated the crisis facing the WPA and clamored for increasing agency funds above the $875 million figure.

Representatives treated WPA mainly as a political question, with alliances fitting traditional stereotypes. Liberal Democrats rallied behind the proposal by Taylor of Colorado authorizing the entire $875 million requested by President Roosevelt. Conservative party members rebelled against the President this time and allied with Republicans in seeking to reduce agency appropriations. If the bipartisan coalition succeeded in slicing WPA funds, they could set the tone for the new Congress and strike a penetrating blow at presidential prestige.

The two factions clashed boldly concerning the seriousness of the unemployment situation. New Dealers, who attached highest importance to this theme, stressed that joblessness had spiraled markedly in the 1938 recession and warned that families denied relief might face starvation. "What would you do," Democrat John J. Cochran of Missouri queried, "if after tramping the streets all day looking for work and you come home and find your wife and children crying for food?" Democrat Martin L. Sweeney of Ohio argued, "it is the Government's obligation to feed and clothe and give shelter to those of our brothers who, because of no fault of their own, find themselves empty-handed." WPA finances, they cautioned, would become exhausted within a few weeks, threatening one-third of agency employees with loss of jobs. As Democrat Arthur D. Healey of Massachusetts remarked, reduction in WPA funds would cost 97,000 agency positions in Ohio and Pennsylvania, 90,000 in Illinois, and 66,700 in New York City.[7] On the opposition side, representatives argued that no deficiency appropriation was needed because conditions were improving steadily and employment was increasing nationally. Taber protested, "We are building up our roll in the WPA contrary to the trend of unemployment" and charged that one-half did not need relief.[8]

Politicization of the WPA split the two sides. Citing the numerous agency scandals, critics complained the WPA was exploiting the misery of Americans by padding rolls just before elections. "The administration of relief under the present set-up," Republican Treadway argued, "has been nothing short of a national scandal. Money appropriated for human needs has been used to build up a political machine and entrench the present administration in office." "The whole rotten mess," remarked party colleague Fish, "stinks to high heaven," while Republican Vorys of Ohio charged that it was "perfectly rotten to use needy women and hungry children for political purposes."[9] Maladministration and abuse of the WPA, they asserted, would infringe upon individual liberties and damage democratic institutions. "If corruption, political manipulation, favoritism, and partisanship are permitted to continue in relief," Republican J. William Ditter of Pennsylvania predicted, "the results will be an undermining of free government and an abridgement of personal liberties that can eventuate only in the collapse of our Constitutional Government." New Dealers countered by accusing opponents of playing petty politics at the expense of the unemployed and of exposing trivial abuses in the WPA program. Sweeney stressed, "we have in our midst want and misery and poverty, with members of Congress who have to talk to a hundred souls a day and watch strong men shed tears because they can't get employment." "I have seen scores of them," he added, "jump at the opportunity to take up a pick and shovel and go down into the ditch that they may earn their daily bread."[10]

Centralization of relief programs also provoked controversy. Fiscal conservatives lamented that the spendthrift federal government already wielded too much power and urged states to take primary responsibility for providing unemployment assistance. "I am not going to vote," Republican Dewey Short of Missouri vowed, "to give any man in the White House, be he Republican, Democrat, or new dealer, blank checks" over "sums which he can spend at any time and in any manner." According to anti-New Dealers, the WPA served as a symbol of an erratic, inefficient bureaucracy. Anti-New Dealers also argued that private enterprise should be encouraged to hire more workers, thus decreasing reliance upon federal relief programs. "The National Government," Bender insisted, "must alter its policies, so that we can look forward to the return of thousands of our working people to private employment. We must take steps to liquidate unemployment through stimulating private work."[11] Since state and local communities lacked financial resources to handle the recession, WPA supporters countered that the broad scope of unemployment compelled massive financial commitments at the federal level. "There are those who deserve work and who are not able to find it," remarked Democrat Doughton, who argued, "If local authorities cannot take care of this class of people, it is up to the Federal Government to look after them." In addition, New Dealers claimed the executive branch had access to more direct information than Congress on the national economic situation. President Roosevelt, Democrat John W. McCormack of Massachusetts stressed, "is in the best position to know the conditions existing throughout the country . . . from a national angle and not from a sectional or local angle."[12]

The two factions likewise disagreed over the contributions made by the WPA. Agency defenders lauded the enormous number of projects built or refurbished in the latter portion of 1938, including 30,000 miles of roads and streets, 4,000 bridges, and 1,500 miles of sidewalks. Fiscal conservatives countered that the WPA had wasted much money of taxpayers and insisted that the $40 billion national debt militated against continuing spendthrift programs. Republican Richard B. Wigglesworth of Massachusetts condemned relief administrators for "waste and extravagance, with the scandalous use of money appropriated." "The days of our national Santa Claus," Robsion of Kentucky pointed out, "are numbered. The pocket is empty." Bender protested, "We are plunging this country into debt, and the Government of the United States is not only the laughing stock of citizens generally but is the laughing stock of those engaged in that work and on the jobs." According to Bender, "that kind of morale is not in keeping with the thing that has made America great."[13]

Anti–New Dealers also denounced the wage discrimination among various regions and insisted that leftist organizations had infiltrated WPA rolls. According to rural Democrat Malcolm C. Tarver of Georgia, agency employees in industrial states often received wages at least 25 percent above pay scales for those holding similar jobs in less populated states. Salaries for laborers ranged from 18 cents an hour in Tennessee to $1.02 an hour in Illinois, while remuneration for skilled workers varied from 31 cents an hour in several southern states to $2.25 an hour in New Jersey.[14] Some WPA writers and actors, opponents argued, belonged to the socialist Workers Alliance seeking to overthrow the federal government. Republican J. Parnell Thomas of New Jersey charged, "These Federal writers projects and the Federal theater projects in certain of our large cities, notably New York, are honeycombed with communism." Echoing a similar theme, Republican Frank Horton of Wyoming demanded that "all those belonging to un-American organizations should be purged from WPA rolls" so as to "make millions of dollars available for the actual needy which is now reaching the hands of those who have no business receiving them." [15]

The first major test came in the House Appropriations Committee, where economy advocates prevailed. Chairman Taylor of Colorado could not utilize his authority to preserve intact his $875 million appropriation measure. Although Democrats controlled a majority of committee seats, Woodrum and other conservatives revolted, shattering any hopes Taylor had of securing unified party backing for his proposal. Anti–New Deal Democrats, along with Republicans, instead pushed through a Woodrum amendment slashing the President's supplementary relief request from $875 million to $725 million. Woodrum's proposal, which triggered the first revolt by the newly convened Congress against domestic spending programs, compelled the WPA to spread funds over the remainder of the 1939 fiscal year and stripped the executive branch of any authority to request additional money.

At the other end the committee action did not satisfy the most persistent fiscal conservatives. Taber insisted his colleagues slice agency funds even further to $350 million, but committee Democrats united temporarily to squelch that proposal. Speculating that a drastic reduction would not survive in the House at large, anti–New Deal Democrats did not join minority party members endorsing the Taber amendment. Four Republicans, including Taber, also requested a comprehensive investigation of WPA political activities. Besides contending improved business conditions militated against increasing agency employment, they argued additional funding would bankrupt the public treasury. "Each relief bill," Taber protested, "has been designated to promote useless, wasteful, and extravagant programs of expenditures of public money which has (sic) brought Americans to the brink of ruin." [16]

Roosevelt administration officials, New Deal congressmen, and liberal pressure groups all denounced the slicing by the committee of agency appropriations. At the insistence of the President, White House Assistant Stephen Early sent to all representatives a letter warning that the $150 million reduction in WPA funds would require the discharge of 500,000 persons from relief rolls and would jeopardize the future of the program. [17] Defending the New Deal position, Cannon charged that his committee colleagues had "met with the preconceived determination to cut the amount recommended in the Budget. No matter what amount had been recommended, the committee would have cut it." The Congress of Industrial Organizations and the socialist Workers Alliance urged increasing agency funds above $1 billion. "We want to give solemn warning,"

Workers Alliance head David Lasser wrote Chairman Taylor, "that these unemployed cannot and will not accept this edict for their starvation; nor can the liberal forces of this nation stand idly by while the recovery movement is smashed."[18]

As debate opened on January 13, tension filled the air in the House. Woodrum, who commenced floor debate for forces championing the $725 million committee version, claimed the WPA could remove 400,000 to 500,000 workers from relief rolls "without causing any deserving person to actually suffer." A moderate Democrat, he charged the agency had retained 10 percent of its employees on relief rolls for nearly four years and urged private business and industry to create 1,500,000 jobs. If the House allocated the entire $875 million presidential request, Woodrum warned additional burdens would be placed on the taxpayer. On the other hand, he ruled out as dangerous any proposals to reduce the figure below the $725 million amount because unemployed persons "have to be taken care of."[19]

Cannon countered with a vigorous plea for allocating the entire $875 million requested by the administration. The Woodrum proposal, he warned, would force the WPA to dismiss over 1 million workers and would deprive at least 4 million dependents of primary financial support. In addition, the Missouri Democrat stressed that the agency had certified over 500,000 additional persons for whom jobs could not be found because of budgetary cutbacks. Laborers, veterans, clergymen, economists, businessmen, municipal government officials, and other groups, he cited, favored restoring the original $875 million figure. "The proposal to reduce the amount," Cannon protested, "is so unwarranted, so at variance with the evidence, so unjustified by the statistics submitted to the hearings."[20]

The keynote for forces seeking drastic reductions in WPA allocations was sounded by Taber. Besides urging that the agency be funded with only $350 million through April 7, he implored relief administrators to eliminate wasteful projects and dismiss 500,000 excess workers. "The WPA rolls," he argued, "can be reduced by getting off a large number of people that do not belong there." In addition, he complained that members of leftist organizations had infiltrated WPA literary and acting groups in attempts to overthrow the federal government. Agency employees, Taber charged, included people "who are writing articles and guidebooks for sale by the WPA subversive of the Government of the United States and designed to stir up class hatred."[21]

Marcantonio, along with Coffee, presented the case for those members urging substantial increases in agency funding. Primarily representing labor and municipal government interests, they stressed that the serious unemployment situation compelled the continuation of massive federal assistance. If Congress retained the committee amount, Marcantonio asserted, "private industry will be hurt, recovery set back, and business will be dealt a staggering blow." "As long as private industry fails to give the unemployed of the country an opportunity to work," he implored "it is the solemn duty of the Government of the United States to give work to unemployed Americans." WPA employees, he and Coffee contended, were working at subsistence wages and might resort to violence if relief rolls were curbed drastically. Coffee remarked, "The wages paid them are so inadequate, for even a minimum standard of living, that WPA workers are enduring great suffering and privation. Congress," he warned, "will have upon its head the responsibility for the riots, the bloodshed, the social disorder that may occur."[22]

New Dealers enjoyed a few bright moments. Liberal and moderate Democrats defeated by a 214–154 teller vote Taber's motion to reduce WPA appropriations to $350 million for the next two months and to investigate the entire agency operation in the meantime. After an impassioned plea by McCormack, the House reduced restrictions upon persons over 65 and mothers with dependent children. Urban representatives also rejected a proposal by rural members to secure uniform wage scales nationally regardless of living costs. "The boys from the South and West," Democrat Lex Green of Florida pointed out, "voted . . . for the same scale of wages . . . but the members of Congress from the populated areas of the East were in the majority."[23]

On the crucial votes, however, fiscal conservatives overrode the liberals. Republicans and anti-New Deal Democrats survived several major challenges, shouting down an amendment by Coffee to raise agency funds over $1 billion and decisively rejecting a Marcantonio proposal in a 199-21 teller vote to increase WPA authorizations to $915 million. By a much closer 171-138 teller vote, the conservative coalition inserted a motion by Tarver to prohibit relief administrators from exceeding 25 percent in wage differentials between states. Rural representatives complained that WPA workers from urban, industrial states had received salaries far outdistancing those granted to agency employees in their home districts.

Liberals suffered their most disappointing setback when the conservative coalition easily defeated an amendment by Cannon. In a decisive 226-137 teller vote the House rejected Cannon's proposal to restore the original $875 million appropriation. Representatives disregarded an appeal by Cannon, who disapproved of dropping 1.5 million from relief rolls "arbitrarily, unscientifically, without supporting evidence either in the hearings or on the floor." Nearly one-half (107) of 226 Democrats opposed the White House this time, while Minority Leader Joseph W.

Martin lined up 119 of the 123 Republicans against the Cannon plan. Since the onset of the New Deal in 1933, Republican members had rarely displayed such unity on a major piece of legislation. Anti-New Dealer Wadsworth, who had served in the House for the entire period, boasted "the Republicans, to all intents and purposes, were solid."[24]

Liberals dropped further resistance, hoping the Senate would restore the $875 million amount. Representatives then resoundingly (397-16) adopted the Woodrum motion appropriating the $725 million amount through June 30. Both parties overwhelmingly backed the $725 million figure, as only 10 Republicans and 6 Democrats dissented. Bender lauded the House for "smashing all party lines to cut down the President's excessively large WPA proposal. That measure was checked by a line-up of Democrats and Republicans, which could never have been assembled 2 years ago." Southern and western delegations, controlled by Democrats, unanimously endorsed the Woodrum plan, but a sprinkling of opposition came from New England and Great Plains congressmen.

The burgeoning conservative mood, coupled with dynamic roles by key individuals, produced the dramatic House outcome. Fresh from a mandate in the 1938 elections to balance the budget, anti-New Dealers followed the public demand for reduced expenditures. Rebelling against the President, conservative Democrats had aligned with a solid Republican phalanx to slash a major appropriation bill for the first time in the New Deal period. Woodrum had ably directed the Democratic revolt, while Minority Leader Martin had organized the most effective Republican opposition in several years. Roosevelt, who did not intervene actively in the House battle, watched congressmen slash the program regarded as the cornerstone of domestic relief. Besides signaling to Roosevelt that future spending proposals emanating from the White House would be scrutinized closely, representatives had diminished presidential influence on Capitol Hill. "The real test," Wadsworth later admitted, "was on whether the House would follow the President or follow its own judgment."[25]

Roosevelt administration officials, not wanting to suffer two consecutive setbacks, intervened more actively in the Senate battle. At a press conference on January 17, the President urged senators to restore the $875 million request or to risk the discharge of 400,000 workers in six weeks. Before the Appropriations Committee the same day, WPA Administrator Harrington warned that his agency otherwise would be compelled to drop a million persons from relief rolls by the end of June. On January 18 Roosevelt invited Democrat Adams and Republican Borah to the White House to discuss the employment situation. Adams, who conducted the economy bloc in the Appropriations Committee, still opposed increasing the $725 million figure and predicted the reduced amount would compel dropping only 600,000 workers in the first half of 1939 from relief rolls. A former backer of New Deal programs, Borah likewise disappointed the President by conceding that the committee probably would retain the $150 million reduction.[26]

Liberal pressure groups, likewise infuriated with the House outcome, intensified lobbying efforts on Capitol Hill. The American Federation of Labor, the Congress of Industrial Organizations, and the U.S. Conference of Mayors recommended the Senate restore the original $875 million, while the Workers Alliance campaigned for even additional funding. "Any reduction in this amount," AFL President William Green protested, "will mean a lowering of relief standards and a decrease in the amount supplied those who have suffered very greatly because of unemployment." In a similar vein CIO Secretary James Carey challenged the Senate to "show its independence of reactionary interests" by supporting the President's initial request.[27]

Although less partisan than representatives, senators still viewed relief as a political issue. A majority of Democrats favored authorizing the $875 million presidential request, but southern and Great Plains anti-New Dealers opposed increasing the House figure. Hostile sentiments towards both Roosevelt and organized labor, coupled with a desire to balance the budget, influenced Republicans to reject almost unanimously restoration of the $875 million amount. Content to pursue a divide-and-conquer strategy, the minority party elected again to watch Democrats engage in one of the most spirited confrontations of the entire Seventy-sixth Congress.

As in the House, members were divided into two basic camps conducted by Appropriations Committee personnel. The economy bloc and New Dealers again vied for control, with the two sides approximately equal numerically.The economy bloc had not been very powerful until 1937, when President Roosevelt tried to enlarge the Supreme Court. Southern Democrats and a nearly solid phalanx of Republicans now formed the nucleus of the fiscal conservatives, who favored either maintaining the $725 million amount or slicing WPA funds even further. Adams commanded strategy for the anti-Administration forces. A native of Del Norte, Colorado, he was the son of a prosperous storekeeper and banker and had earned degrees from Yale University and Columbia Law School. Upon returning to Colorado, Adams began practicing law in Pueblo and held the posts of Pueblo County attorney and city attorney. He became a member of the U.S. Senate in 1923, briefly filling a vacancy caused by the death of the Democrat Samuel Nicholson, and then resumed law practice in Pueblo. In 1933 the diligent, conscientious Adams rejoined the U.S. Senate and held moderate-conservative views on New Deal issues.

He denounced the President's Supreme Court reorganization bill of 1937 and especially resented Roosevelt's attempt to purge him in the 1938 Democratic primaries. Adams, a major figure on the Appropriations Committee, often had advocated slashing federal government expenses and particularly opposed granting full amounts for Roosevelt's work relief programs.[28] Veteran Southern Democrats Harrison and James F. Byrnes of South Carolina assisted Adams for the economy bloc. Although supporting early New Deal legislation, Harrison and Byrnes subsequently urged balancing the federal budget and reducing the scope of work relief programs.

New Deal Democrats, on the other hand, favored restoring the $875 million figure for the WPA. Although no longer dominating the Senate numerically, they were prepared to plunge into a vigorous battle to defend the relief agency. Seventy-year-old Democrat Kenneth D. McKellar of Tennessee conducted the campaign for those favoring restoration of the original amount. The son of a prosperous Richmond, Alabama, attorney and farmer, he had earned undergraduate, master's, and law degrees from the University of Alabama and had begun a lucrative law practice in Memphis, Tennessee. McKellar, who never married, befriended Memphis political boss Edward H. Crump. After serving three terms in the U.S. House of Representatives, he had defeated the Prohibitionist Governor Ben Hooper in 1916 in the first popular election ever held for the United States Senate. The very courteous, industrious McKellar had performed innumerable favors for Tennessee constituents and had frequently obtained federal appropriations for state dams, bridges, post offices, and public works. As chairman of the Post Office Committee, he had become an expert on parliamentary maneuver and had sought to remove postal employees from civil service. McKellar, who read prodigiously, had written a massive volume chronicling the history of Tennessee senators and had vigorously defended the Tennessee Valley Authority. A New Dealer, he enlisted the help of Majority Leader Barkley and Wagner of New York in defending the WPA.

Economy advocates clashed with New Dealers in the Appropriations Committee. Adams and Byrnes vied with McKellar in an intense race to sway the votes of several committee members undecided between the $725 million and $875 million figures. Some moderates were lured to the economy camp, when Adams agreed that WPA Administrator Harrington should not dismiss more than 5 percent of workers before April 1 and that Roosevelt could request additional funds should an emergency arise. The Committee rejected 17-7 an attempt by McKellar to restore the $875 million presidential figure and then promptly approved the $725 million figure. Following the vote, jubilant Adams forces argued that "some steps toward reduction in governmental expenses must be taken in order to avoid possible impairment of government credit." Dejected McKellar supporters denounced the final action as "an arbitrary reduction without regard to questions of actual need."[29]

As in the House, the bipartisan conservative coalition haunted New Dealers in the Appropriations Committee. Although Democrats controlled 18 of the 25 committee seats, 10 members of Roosevelt's party joined 7 Republicans in rejecting the $875 million amount. Four southern Democrats, including Byrnes, Glass, John H. Bankhead of Alabama, and Richard B. Russell of Georgia, ignored McKellar's pleas by opposing an increase in WPA appropriations. New Dealers Chavez of New Mexico and Truman also cast lots with the Adams forces, smoothing the way for fiscal conservatives. On the losing side, WPA advocates belonged to the Democratic Party and typically resided either in the mountain or New England states.

Before floor debate began, the bipartisan coalition worked actively behind the scenes to sustain the cut. At Vice President Garner's office Byrnes, Harrison, Adams, and other economy senators quickly planned strategy for upholding the $725 million amount. "We've got to economize," the Vice President stressed, "and we've got to start now." In an effort to rally additional support for the $725 million figure, Adams, Byrnes, Harrison, and others circulated in Senate cloakrooms and invited moderates to their offices. On the Republican side Minority Leader McNary secured pledges in advance from all twenty-three members except Borah, Davis of Pennsylvania, and Frazier of North Dakota to support the committee amount.[30]

On January 24 Adams and McKellar commenced floor debate in spirited fashion. In a vigorous defense of the $725 million amount, Adams deplored the $40 billion national debt and pointed out that relief programs had absorbed more than one-half the total federal government income. Seeking to balance the budget, the Colorado Democrat warned, "Unless the tendency to extreme appropriations is turned we will break down the greatest humanitarian movement in the history of the world." Adams denied conservatives were slashing WPA funds, arguing instead that funds for the agency were being increased only 17 percent less than the President wished.[31] Unless the Senate restored the original $875 million amount, McKellar countered, relief officials would be forced to drop 75 percent of their workers and to deny jobs to other unemployed persons eligible for assistance. "That," McKellar protested, "is a long step to take in six months." Besides noting that every committee witness and practically all mayors favored raising the appropriations to at least $875 million, he argued that the President could view the WPA situation from a much broader perspective than Congress. Roosevelt, McKellar contended, "declared the emergency, he has fixed the amount after the most careful preparations, after the most careful examination by those in charge."[32]

Senators debated the same basic issues as representatives. Senate acceptance of the $725 million, New Dealers argued, would compel relief administrators to slice 2 million persons from rolls and refuse positions to 750,000 qualified individuals. "Hundreds of thousands, and even millions, of these people," Borah emphasized, "are actually in want." Unless Congress appropriated the entire $875 million, Democrat James E. Murray of Montana feared massive layoffs "creating another psychological condition, ending possibly in another downward spiral of depression."[33] Rejecting these contentions, the economy bloc claimed the agency still could pay relief workers for several months. Glass accused the administration of exaggerating the unemployment situation "so that they can get all of the money possible out of the Treasury."[34]

National spending and centralization of power again sparked additional disagreement. Fiscal conservatives insisted the federal government already had wasted too much of the taxpayers' money on New Deal programs and were alarmed over the rapid growth of executive agencies. During the next five months, Byrnes predicted, "we will spend more money than has been spent by the Government in time of peace in the history of this nation." Shipstead denied that "that form of spending is any more effective in bringing about recovery than for a man to think he can drink himself sober."[35] In response, New Dealers stressed that saving American lives far outweighed any desire to slice federal expenditures and asserted state and local governments lacked financial resources to fund WPA operations. A drastic reduction, Wagner of New York cautioned, would "bring misery and privation to millions of American citizens" and would "seriously threaten our entire recovery movement" with "national suicide." Liberal Claude Pepper of Florida warned, "If we think that private industry . . . is going to absorb these unemployed men and women, we are just cherishing a pipe dream."[36] The federal government, WPA defenders insisted, should continue providing public service jobs until private industry could offer more employment opportunities. "I regard relief appropriations as necessary," O'Mahoney of Wyoming argued, "until we find the way to stimulate private industry." On the other hand, O'Mahoney stressed, "It is essential that without delay we must get private business running" because relief jobs "afford no future for the unemployed" and constitute "an increasing danger to the national credit."[37]

Citing the 1938 congressional elections, anti–New Dealers capitalized on the politicization of the WPA. If political officials had not diverted relief funds, conservatives maintained the WPA would not need even the $725 million amount. They also accused elected officials of placing personal financial gain above relief and demanded the removal of all wealthy Americans from work rolls. "If the President had thought about these hungry workers when he was using relief funds to purge members of Congress," Democrat Rush Dew Holt of West Virginia charged, "we would have more cash in the treasury to feed the hungry." Although embarrassed by exposures of agency scandals, New Dealers contended that the Sheppard committee found relatively few incidents of corruption and stressed the volume of WPA activities. According to Democrat Miller, the WPA had engaged in 37,031 projects involving construction or repair of highways, roads, and public buildings.[38]

Administration forces initially prevented the economy bloc from seizing the initiative. On the day before floor debate was scheduled to begin, Roosevelt held a strategy session with Majority Leader Barkley. If the Senate approved only $725 million, the President warned, "nearly 2,000,000 people will be dropped from the relief rolls" between March and July. Roosevelt and Barkley decided to concentrate on securing adoption of the McKellar amendment designed to restore the full $875 million amount, but refused to press for an immediate vote. In the meantime they hoped city officials, local chambers of commerce, retailers, and labor pressure groups would avalanche Senate offices with telegrams urging restoration of full appropriations. On January 24 and 25 Barkley shrewdly recessed the Senate to prevent any WPA votes and spent the time canvassing moderate members. Democrat Elmer Thomas of Oklahoma gave administration forces time to round up additional votes by delivering a 16-page dissertation on the American dollar. Barkley, who expected the McKellar amendment to win by three to five tallies, carefully arranged the time and circumstances of the roll call. Administration forces appeared to control the floor situation so firmly that, two hours before the actual vote on January 27, one economy bloc member conceded defeat.[39]

But bipartisan conservatives surprised New Deal officials. By a razor-thin 47–46 margin the Senate rejected the McKellar amendment, terminating liberal hopes of restoring WPA funds to $875 million. A majority of Democrats favored authorizing the entire presidential request, but 38 percent revolted against Roosevelt to prevent adoption of the Tennessee senator's motion. The action by rebellious Democrats, including eight senators on the President's 1938 purge list, delighted Republicans. The outcome, Johnson of California stressed, "taught a lot of weak-kneed Senators that they can stand up and vote as their consciences dictate without falling dead."[40] Twenty of 21 Republicans, along with third-party member Shipstead, joined defecting Democrats to swing the momentum against the McKellar forces. Since the WPA issue was so crucial, only Democrats Chavez and Elbert D. Thomas of Utah and Republican Styles Bridges of New Hampshire missed the roll call.

Before the vote three key senators defected from the McKellar camp. Barkley had counted on support from New Dealers Shipstead, Davis, and Scott W. Lucas of Illinois, but they switched sides at the last minute because Roosevelt later could ask for additional WPA funds. New Dealers charged Republican representatives had converted Davis, prompting an instant denial by the former secretary of labor. "No Republican Congressman," Davis countered, "spoke to me or urged me to vote against it." In addition, he predicted that "no WPA workers will be forced off the rolls" because of the vote change and promised to support agency appropriations "as long as they are necessary."[41]

Sectional alignments contrasted markedly with those on economic issues. Mountain senators, who had cooperated with Republicans in opposing presidential monetary and trade programs, joined border members this time in seeking restoration of the entire $875 million. In both these sections the WPA had employed numerous jobless persons and had constructed and improved numerous facilities. Southerners, firm backers of New Deal economic legislation, insisted upon slicing expenditures in retaliation against Roosevelt for seeking to purge several conservative members in the 1938 primaries. Although switching leadership roles, Great Plains and New England senators rejected both the President's economic and WPA programs. Great Plains members, alarmed over spending and purge trends, directed the battle against WPA appropriations, whereas the New England bloc had led the assaults on Roosevelt's economic policies.

Population density also influenced voting patterns. With the exception of Lucas of Illinois and purge target Frederick Van Nuys of Indiana, all urban-based Democrats favored restoration of the full $875 million amount. Democrats A. Victor Donahey of Ohio, Francis Maloney of Connecticut, and Walsh of Massachusetts set aside their conservative philosophy this time because they represented numerous municipalities benefiting from agency relief funds. On the opposing side rural Democrats and practically all Republicans accused the WPA of discriminating against less populated areas. Although usually backing the administration, Democrats Bankhead and Truman repudiated the McKellar amendment because they represented predominantly agricultural constituents. The precise impact of population density upon voting, however, is difficult to determine because political party loyalty influenced the behavior of urban Republicans and rural Democrats.

WPA opponents encountered mixed success thereafter. McKellar forces the same day attached amendments guaranteeing that no more than 5 percent could be removed from relief rolls before April 1 and permitting Roosevelt to request more funds at any time. In addition, liberals shouted down a proposal by Russell preventing WPA wage differentials between states from exceeding 25 percent. On the other hand, fiscal conservatives approved a Barkley amendment prohibiting government employees from offering any benefits to or soliciting any political contributions from WPA workers. Anti–New Dealers triumphed ultimately, as the Senate on January 28 adopted the limited $725 million appropriation.

Economy moods prevailed to a lesser extent in the Senate than in the House. Senators came within one vote of restoring the entire $875 million, although representatives had rejected an identical motion by a much wider margin. Republicans solidly favored slashing funds in both houses, but more of the Democratic congressmen had rebelled against the President's wishes. The Senate would have insisted upon the larger $875 million figure if fiscal conservatives had demanded removing over 5 percent from WPA relief rolls before April 1. The economy bloc also had permitted Roosevelt to request further deficiency funds at any time before June 30.

Several forces had kept the momentum on the side of the anti–New Dealers. Bipartisan conservatives, consisting of the solid Republican phalanx and 38 percent of the Democrats, had resisted efforts by the McKellar camp to restore the President's request. Roosevelt's direct intervention hardened resistance by the economy bloc against fully funding the WPA. Johnson of California claimed, "There was not very much to fight about, but the President made it a great question by insisting that everybody should toe the mark, and go down the line, and some of us took up the challenge." Roosevelt, the California Republican remarked, "met certain individuals who were just as obstinate as he, and just as determined on the result—so it made a pretty fight about nothing in which his presence suffered greatly." Several conservatives, most notably Adams of Colorado, deserve credit for the outcome. Steering a course reminiscent of Woodrum, Adams ably directed anti–New Deal committee members and senators in sustaining the House cuts. As shown by the 1938 elections, numerous Americans had urged reductions in federal spending and closer congressional scrutiny of presidential power. Nevertheless, the determined, well-organized McKellar forces had made the Senate battle extremely dramatic. "It was," Johnson concluded, "an amazingly close fight."[42]

Senate rejection of the McKellar amendment and endorsement of the House course infuriated President Roosevelt. Upon first learning of the Senate outcome at a cabinet meeting, he supposedly stared at the wall and orally remarked, "Well, that is that. Now we will go on to chapter 2." After cabinet members left the room, Roosevelt analyzed the vote of each senator and was especially angry over defections within his party. The President initially planned to veto the bill "on the grounds of its inadequacy to meet human need," but did not follow through with the threat because the conference committee accepted the Senate amendments. Besides agreeing that no more than 5 percent could be removed from relief rolls before April 1, conferees had permitted the chief executive to request additional funds at any time. After receiving these assurances the President reluctantly signed the measure granting the WPA $725 million.[43] The chief executive's reaction, meanwhile, hardly surprised the conservative bloc. "Roosevelt," Johnson charged, "is such a singular man, that he is perfectly insane over a defeat such as this, and vindictively waits for an opportunity to pay back the recalcitrant ones."[44]

In retrospect, the executive branch had overreacted to the legislative outcome. Congress had authorized over four-fifths of the amount requested by the President, although the national debt had risen sharply in the New Deal period. Senators also had given Roosevelt a loophole through which to seek further monies. "There will be no man on WPA," Johnson stressed, "that will go hungry, or to whom relief will be denied. The only thing we did was to cut $150,000,000, and then, if emergency should arise, the President should at once make it plain to us, and the money would be forthcoming."[45] On the other hand, Congress had inflicted another penetrating blow to Roosevelt's prestige and influence by limiting the scope of the most publicized New Deal program. The legislative branch also had taken a major step towards seeking short-term solutions to unemployment problems and had restricted the power to spend government money.

President Roosevelt quickly took advantage of the loophole. In a message to Congress on February 7, he insisted that the $150 million be restored to cover projected WPA deficits through June. Roosevelt complained that the WPA had removed 350,000 persons from its rolls in four months, causing "undue suffering" among the numerous able-bodied unemployed. If the $150 million increase was rejected, the President feared relief programs would face "a very drastic reduction . . . far beyond those that can be absorbed by industry."[46]

Economy-minded congressmen moved very slowly on the President's latest request. Denying that any new emergency had arisen, Woodrum and Adams prevented their respective appropriations subcommittees from considering Roosevelt's proposal. "The situation has not changed within a week," remarked Woodrum, who was convinced the recent $725 million amount would cover WPA expenses for the remainder of

1939. An unidentified Republican tabulated that Roosevelt had proclaimed emergencies once every eight weeks and quipped, "Is it any wonder that the people are emotionally exhausted?"[47] During late February Marcantonio discussed the WPA issue daily on the House floor and urged colleagues to force the Appropriations Committee to give the President's proposal immediate attention. Failing to break the impasse, New Dealers began requesting Roosevelt to drop demands for $150 million and to compromise instead at $100 million figure. "Because of my deep interest in you and in the Democratic Party," Representative William L. Nelson of Missouri in early March wrote Roosevelt, "I suggest that . . . the amount be placed at not exceeding $100,000,000. This can be put through without a serious fight. The larger amount means a battle, and I fear defeat."[48]

Undeterred by congressional resistance, the White House stubbornly refused to compromise. On March 9 WPA Administrator Harrington warned reporters that one-third of the 3 million WPA workers would be removed from the rolls by June 30 if Congress failed to grant the entire $150 million amount. In a letter to Congressman Nelson, Roosevelt made clear he would not surrender to the conservative coalition. "The appropriation of a lesser amount," the President argued, "would entail hardship, privation and additional harm or suffering among people who have already suffered acutely." He also declined to "take responsibility for asking for less money than Colonel Harrington says will relieve the situation."[49] On March 10 Roosevelt summoned Democratic members of the Appropriations Committee, including Woodrum and Taylor, to the White House and urged enactment of his original $150 million request. Most other committee members, including Woodrum, doubted any new emergency had occurred. Unless a congressional investigation revealed that the WPA required the full amount to survive, the committee members intended to reject the President's move. "I have not seen or heard anything," Woodrum told reporters, "that makes me feel I made a mistake."[50]

Administration officials still continued their battle. In a message to Congress on March 14, Roosevelt appealed again for the full $150 million amount and argued that diminished funds would force WPA Administrator Harrington to discharge before June 30 over 1.2 million workers. Since "needy persons, out of work, should not be allowed to starve," the President affirmed, "it was an obligation of the Federal Government to give work to those able to work." At the insistence of the White House, Appropriations Committee Chairman Taylor introduced a bill requesting the complete $150 million and on March 15 commenced hearings. Fiscal conservatives were infuriated. Taylor bypassed Woodrum's subcommittee and vowed to resist any rush tactics.[51]

In retaliation the economy bloc sponsored a drive to investigate the

WPA. On March 15 the anti–New Dealer Cox of Georgia introduced a resolution funding the Appropriations Committee with $30,000 to probe agency operations and to curb funds not being used directly for relief purposes. In a radio chat that evening Woodrum wholeheartedly supported the inquiry and accused WPA officials of diverting hundreds of millions of dollars for political activities. The conservative-dominated Rules Committee on March 22 approved the investigation by a 7–4 margin and speedily sent the resolution to the House floor. Five days later representatives overwhelmingly (352-27) supported the investigation. Majority Leader Rayburn predicted the probe "will reflect credit on the administration of WPA," while Cannon defended the Cox measure "not because there's anything to investigate, but because there's nothing to conceal."[52] A sprinkling of opposition came from urban Democrats representing Middle Atlantic, Great Lakes, and Pacific constituents. Woodrum directed the WPA investigation, which disclosed malpractices and abuses within the New Deal agency.

Tensions flared between urban and rural congressmen. Metropolitan representatives threatened to battle against farm programs unless the economy bloc promised to support President Roosevelt's WPA request. During late March urbanites infuriated agrarian members by opposing a farm appropriation bill. "If men from the farm states want our help on parity payments," Rules Committee Chairman Sabath insisted, "they should help us get the $150 million for relief." "We would like to go along with the farmers," another metropolitan Democrat explained, "but we would like to have some assurance that if we do we will get real consideration from the Appropriations Committee on the Relief Bill."[53]

Conservatives, meanwhile, dominated Appropriations Committee proceedings. WPA Administrator Harrington, who testified before the subcommittee for the entire $150 million, encountered another stormy reception from Woodrum and Taber. Woodrum accused Harrington of attempting to create a crisis and charged that the WPA employed 150,000 persons not needing relief. In addition, conservatives asserted that the agency could operate through June without additional funds and protested that some employees in New York City were paid $250 monthly. Inflicting another setback upon the White House, Woodrum steered through the committee an amendment slicing $50 million from Roosevelt's request. Although some fiscal conservatives demanded further reductions, Woodrum persuaded most members to accept the compromise $100 million allocation and to postpone any floor fight until completion of the WPA inquiry. Four Republicans, including Taber, however, issued a mimeographed statement recommending the House slice the amount to $55 million.[54]

Appropriations Committee members again led the opposing camps. Woodrum still directed the economy bloc seeking to sustain the $100 million amount and was assisted by Republicans Taber and J. Will Taylor. Taylor, who served in a state delegation controlled by Democrats, ardently defended fiscal conservatism in floor debates. On the administration side, Cannon conducted the WPA forces and was aided by American-Laborite Marcantonio and Democrat James Fitzpatrick of New York. Serving a metropolitan district with one of the worst unemployment rates in the nation, Fitzpatrick urged restoration of the original $150 million request.

On March 30 spectators crowded the galleries to witness Woodrum and Cannon commence floor debate. Defending the committee $100 million version, Woodrum claimed New Dealers exaggerated national unemployment figures and accused agency officials of padding relief rolls. "There is no emergency in WPA today," he asserted, "save the emergency that it has created itself." Congress, Woodrum insisted, already had ordered the WPA "to restrict its operations, to purge its rolls, and to reduce its administrative expense." In an effort to counter these contentions, Cannon boasted the agency had constructed thousands of schools, hospitals, bridges, and other public buildings. Through the WPA, he assured colleagues, "we have saved untold thousands of American families from suffering and privation." Cannon also maintained the relief agency had outstanding leadership and had employed only around one-half of those eligible for relief. "No calumny," he stated, "can detract from the glory of achievement, from the record of honesty and efficiency and integrity, which is bridging over one of the greatest economic crises in American history."[55]

During the two-day debate members clashed over the basic issues. Woodrum forces, who controlled the opening session, argued that the national budget deficit had skyrocketed and urged fiscal conservatism in all relief programs. "Let us restore confidence," Taber remarked, "by stopping foolish expenditures." On the other hand, the Cannon camp insisted that the plight of jobless Americans should not be subordinated to economy drives. "But let us not in the name of economy," Democrat Jed Johnson of Oklahoma cautioned, "wreak our vengeance on the unfortunate unemployed citizens of America who today become innocent victims of our folly."[56]

Other familiar economic and political themes filled the House chambers. Cannon forces concentrated on describing a grim national unemployment situation and lauding relief administrators. Besides urging colleagues "to prevent another business recession and economic chaos," Marcantonio protested that slicing agency appropriations "to the tempo of oratorical swing and by means of a rhetorical Susie Q. is twentieth century

Bourbonism." "I believe," Pennsylvania Democrat Michael Bradley boasted, "the record of the WPA under the previous administrator, Mr. Hopkins, and under Colonel Harrington, presents a picture with regard to efficiency and honesty that is unsurpassed in the history of the country."[57] In the conservative camp Woodrum forces claimed WPA officials had spent allocations recklessly and had engaged in political corruption. "If the money was not wasted," Republican George A. Dondero of Michigan charged, "there would be no need for appropriating further sums," while Taylor of Tennessee accused the WPA of "reeking with partisan politics, favoritism, nepotism, and . . . communism."[58]

Liberals wholeheartedly endorsed a Fitzpatrick amendment to restore the original $150 million amount. If Congress sliced $50 million, Fitzpatrick warned that WPA officials would be forced to remove over 10 percent of the 3 million unemployed on relief rolls. Since principal resistance to WPA came from rural areas, he highlighted the benefits farmers would receive from the relief program. "I appeal to those from the agricultural sections today," Fitzpatrick remarked, "to support the $150,000,000 so that the people in the cities can have purchasing power to buy the produce from the farmers throughout the country."[59] Despite Fitzpatrick's plea, the budget-conscious representatives on March 31 rejected 205-156 the proposal to restore the President's full request.

Moderates prevailed on other major amendments. In an alliance with rabid conservatives, they defeated 207-160 a proposal by Democrat Joseph E. Casey of Massachusetts to raise WPA funds to $125 million. On the other hand, they joined New Dealers in repudiating Taber's motion to kill the bill altogether (277-130) and Cox's amendment to slice agency appropriations to $50 million (161-111). By an even wider 259-75 margin the moderate and liberal wings disapproved a proposal by Republican Dudley White of Ohio to reduce the amount to $75 million.

The House resoundingly adopted (292-110) the Woodrum motion appropriating the WPA $100 million through June. With the bipartisan coalition in firm control, 91 percent of the Democrats and 43 percent of the Republicans supported the $100 million figure. To the dismay of President Roosevelt, New Dealers deserted the administration side this time because they realized the $100 million allocation was the highest sum acceptable to the Woodrum forces. A majority of Republicans, along with nearly two dozen southern Democrats, preferred a more drastic cutback in WPA funding. Since a larger proportion of Democrats and considerably fewer Republicans backed the Woodrum motion this time, the composition of the bipartisan conservative coalition had shifted markedly since the January WPA vote.

Woodrum's solution attracted majority backing in every section, dividing less along urban-rural lines. Southern Democrats furnished largest numerical support for the $100 million, with border and western members lending almost unanimous support. New England Republicans directed the WPA opposition and aligned with Great Lakes and Middle Atlantic colleagues in urging further monetary reductions. Population density played a less dynamic role this time because opponents represented a broader cross section of industrial and rural regions. Rural northeastern and midwestern Republicans and southern Democrats replaced urban liberals from those same sections as the principal foes of the Woodrum motion this time.

For the second time in less than three months, representatives had slashed a major presidential request for WPA funds. Conservative Democrats had bolted from the administration camp and aligned with minority Republicans to destroy White House hopes of receiving the entire $150 million. Southerners had played the most important role, preventing liberals from restoring the original amount and resisting demands by anti-New Deal Republicans for more drastic reductions. Woodrum again had assumed the leadership cudgels, influencing the committee to slash the original request to $100 million and managing floor operations from the economy bloc side. Rising national debt, which had triggered the House drive for balancing the budget, had left the massive WPA program as one of the principal targets.

Alignments on the Woodrum motion differed considerably from voting patterns on previous issues. Economic legislation provoked a deeper split between major political parties. Democrats still remained quite united, while Republicans were far more divided on the Woodrum proposal than on either monetary or trade questions. Sectional delegations clustered closer together on work relief than on either devaluation or tariff issues. In contrast to economic measures, border and western state representatives opposed Roosevelt's WPA program more than did southerners. New England members still led the resistance to the White House, but Great Lakes rather than Great Plains colleagues were their strongest allies this time.

Representatives again had defied the wishes of the Roosevelt administration. Several urbanites, who previously had defended New Deal programs, swelled the ranks of the conservative coalition. If senators restored the original amount, economy-minded representatives were determined to block any $150 million appropriation in conference committee. White House hopes now hinged on whether New Dealers would battle for the entire presidential request or accept the $50 million reduction.

Majority Leader Barkley, who personally favored authorizing the entire $150 million, reluctantly defected from the Roosevelt camp this time.

After consulting with McKellar, Chavez and Hatch of New Mexico, and around a dozen other New Dealers, Barkley opted for the figure already approved by the House. "It was (sic) almost unanimous judgment of these Senators," he noted, that the $100 million appropriation was "the wisest course to pursue." Besides hoping to prevent further dissension within his party, Barkley feared economy forces would control the conference committee and block any amount exceeding $100 million. "I am not going to kid the Senate, or kid the people of the United States," he said, "by holding out hope that they can get something they cannot get."[60] On April 5 Barkley pledged that New Dealers would not attempt to restore the original $150 million figure, prompting Adams and Byrnes to drop plans to slash WPA funds further. The Senate Appropriations Committee unanimously backed the House $100 million version, enabling floor debate to begin.

Democrats, though, ignored Barkley's pleas for party unity. Barkley summoned party members to urge their support of the $50 million cut, but encountered resistance from both conservatives and liberals. Boycotting the session, Byrnes, Harrison, and the other fiscal conservatives refused to believe the majority leader would defy the wishes of the President on such an important issue. Pepper, a 38-year-old New Dealer and one of the most articulate, energetic members, replaced McKellar as commander of the Administration forces seeking restoration of the entire $150 million. Ignoring Barkley's pleas for party harmony, Pepper led over one dozen disenchanted Democrats refusing to reduce the President's original request. Barkley, who was chagrined over Pepper's defection, exhibited mediocre leadership in the ensuing floor debate. As La Follette summed up, the Majority Leader could not "crack the whip" or "keep the votes lined up."[61]

Floor leadership this time also had a sprinkling of other new faces. Mead of New York and Farmer-Laborite Ernest Lundeen of Minnesota assisted Pepper in floor debate for restoring the $150 million amount. Adams again assumed the helm and Byrnes was a valuable subordinate for the economy bloc. Barkley, who nearly always had supported Roosevelt, concentrated this time on securing approval of the $100 million authorization.

Pepper and Adams served as principal spokesmen for the respective sides. Beginning the floor debate on April 6, Pepper stressed that over 10 million Americans still were unemployed and complained that WPA officials already had been forced to dismiss 200,000 agency workers. Chastising the Appropriations Committee, he argued, "It has definitely sabotaged the effort of the Government of the United States to solve the existing chaotic situation." "Eight hundred thousand American men, women, and children," Pepper lamented, "have this month, on one day, lost their whole income."[62] Presenting the economy bloc's case five days later, Adams charged that Director Harrington had padded relief rolls and sponsored extravagant projects. Adams claimed that reducing relief expenditures would encourage private industry to hire more personnel and warned that the rising national budget deficit would bankrupt the federal government. "We will have spent," he remonstrated, "more than one-half of the total income of the United States Government for the WPA."[63]

Familiar themes dominated the Senate debate. WPA forces, who played a more vocal role than in the House, argued that unemployment remained so severe as to warrant restoration of the $150 million. Democrat Allen J. Ellender of Louisiana cautioned, "Unless we do take care of the hungry and the poorly clad, there will lurk ahead a force that will know no bounds and that may cause our cherished institutions to crumble."[64] Local government, they contended, lacked resources to fill any vacuum left by the economically productive WPA. According to Mead, it was "unfair, unwise, and unsportsmanlike, at this time, for the Federal Government to shift a great degree of the burden on already overloaded and overburdened local relief agencies." Defending WPA accomplishments, Independent Norris boasted, "Even centuries after they are gone those who are to follow will benefit from their toil."[65] In the Adams camp fiscal conservatives deplored both the spending for agency projects and increasing bureaucracy in government. Democrat Millard E. Tydings of Maryland protested, "We are going into our fifth or sixth year of recurring deficits" amounting to nearly $3 billion, while Republican Alexander Wiley of Wisconsin counseled Americans that they "sooner or later must cease to depend on Washington for continued subsidies."[66]

Around fifteen liberals filibustered the measure from the outset, evoking angry reactions from the economy bloc. New Dealers controlled floor debate for several days, seeking to rally majority support for a Pepper amendment reviving the President's entire $150 million request. On April 7 Pepper lectured colleagues for several hours about the dangers of cutting WPA funds and was followed by Ellender, Mead, and Norris. Irate over the impasse, Barkley the next day sought unsuccessfully to terminate floor debate and begin voting before adjournment. Pepper, who refused to comply, countered, "I know there are several Senators who desire to discuss this question for a short length of time." New Deal Democrat Sheridan Downey of California occupied the floor for the next few hours, provoking an angry retort by the usually quiet Republican Leader McNary. "I wish to vote," McNary interjected, "as quickly as possible. It is amazing to me that there should be continued delay on the part of those who seem to be anxious for the measure to pass."

Assistant Minority Leader Austin, who likewise favored quick Senate action, remarked, "A filibuster is on."[67]

Despite the economy bloc protests, the filibuster continued. On April 8 Lundeen monopolized debate, addressing colleagues on such diverse topics as work relief, the plight of the farmers, international law, and the European situation. When Lundeen took brief respites, Murray of Montana, Harry H. Schwartz of Wyoming, and Pittman of Nevada delivered speeches so as to prevent any WPA vote. Senators met only briefly on April 10 because Democrat J. Hamilton Lewis of Illinois had died, giving the New Dealers time to rally additional members. By April 11 the Pepper camp nearly had doubled in size, alarming fiscal conservatives.

Roosevelt, meanwhile, wholeheartedly supported the filibuster. In an April 11 note to Pepper, the President ruled out making any compromise with Barkley and insisted upon restoration of the $150 million figure. "The sole question of continuing relief to July 1st," he contended, "is one of arithmetic." If the Senate only authorized $100 million, Roosevelt warned that WPA officials would be compelled to drop 300,000 to 400,000 persons from relief rolls and deny employment to 700,000 and 800,000 on the waiting list.[68] Pepper angered both Barkley and the conservative coalition by reading the Roosevelt letter in floor debate and by introducing an amendment to revive the original amount. Public disclosure of the Roosevelt letter hardened resistance by the erstwhile supporter Barkley, who refused to compromise with the White House. "My daily prayer," Barkley confessed, "is not, 'Lord, show me a fight so I can get into it,' nor is it 'Lord, show me a spot so I can put a Democrat on it.'"[69]

Economy forces the same day terminated the filibuster. Seizing control of the floor for the first time, fiscal conservatives presented at length their case for the $100 million amount. In addition, Majority Leader Barkley secured an agreement from Pepper to end floor debate that day and begin taking roll call votes. "Certainly nobody," Barkley asserted, "can contend that the proponents of the amendment have in any way been unfairly dealt with as to time of debate."[70]

In another setback for Roosevelt the bipartisan coalition easily defeated 49–28 the Pepper amendment. Thirty-two of 58 Democrats rejected the Pepper motion, shattering administration dreams of salvaging the $150 million amount. Nearly 20 percent of the New Dealers, who had supported the earlier McKellar amendment, aligned with fiscal conservatives against the administration. Since the Supreme Court controversy in 1937, Roosevelt had not witnessed such widespread revolt among Democrats against his leadership on such an important issue. Forty-two percent of the Democrats, including Pepper and Mead, favored rescuing the original $150 million figure. Delighted over the infighting within Roosevelt's party,

Republicans almost unanimously rejected any increase in WPA appropriations.

Sectional alignments also shifted dramatically from those on the McKellar amendment. Middle Atlantic senators replaced mountain colleagues as chief crusaders for increased WPA monies, although the latter still backed Pepper forces. Great Plains members again led the economy bloc, but found their strongest allies this time in the South rather than in New England. Instead of following New Dealer Pepper, nearly all southerners joined Byrnes and Harrison in refusing to increase agency funding. Mountain, border, southern, and Great Lakes delegations supported the Pepper proposal less than they had the earlier McKellar amendment, while only New Englanders increased their backing this time for the WPA.

Other forces influenced rejection of the Pepper amendment. Since WPA forces came largely from more populous states and the economy bloc attracted its nucleus of support in agrarian areas, urban-rural divisions weighed heavily in the outcome. The conservative coalition had broadened its base immeasurably this time, signaling difficult days ahead for other domestic measures. Widespread defections by New Deal Democrats meant the President no longer could command the complete loyalty of his party members on Capitol Hill. In addition, senators clearly considered economy more important than welfare programs and made sacrifices in relief policy to keep the budget balanced. WPA officials were forced to dismiss at least 300,000 people from relief rolls and deny jobs to over 700,000 other unemployed persons.

New Dealers did not recover from this setback. Senators quickly rejected an amendment by Democrat Lewis P. Schwellenbach, who had insisted that no needy, able WPA workers should be removed from relief rolls without just cause. Without taking a roll call the upper chamber shouted approval of the House resolution allotting the New Deal agency $100 million, or only two-thirds of the original presidential amount. Although liberals had dominated floor debate, the conservative coalition had handed the WPA another severe jolt.

Several forces ultimately had undone the Pepper camp. Nearly all Republicans had aligned with a majority of Democrats to form a powerful bipartisan coalition, thus slashing Roosevelt's initial request. Sectionally, Great Plains and southern senators had formed the foundation of the economy bloc. Adams and Byrnes largely had persuaded the Appropriations Committee to keep the House version intact, while Barkley had made the task easier by putting his liberal influence behind the $100 million figure. Although refusing to demand party consensus, he asserted afterwards, "Common sense dictated that we act in the situation that prevailed." Taking a realistic attitude, Barkley insisted, "Even if we carried this amendment it would go to conference and in the end we would have to adopt a hundred million."[71]

Congressional independence brought hostile response from the White House. For the second time in three months, representatives and senators had rebuffed Roosevelt on WPA funding and had designated $50 million less than the initial $875 million asked by the President. Roosevelt reluctantly signed the act, but on April 27 sent to Capitol Hill another message recommending nearly $1.5 million to sustain WPA over the 1940 fiscal year. Since private industry would increase hiring as economic conditions improved, the President proposed reducing agency rolls 33 percent to 2 million workers. Lauding the economic benefits of the WPA, he stressed that it had constructed roads, streets, bridges, schools, parks, sanitation and health facilities, and conservation projects. "I am impressed," Roosevelt concluded, "with what can be achieved through a program that not only provides jobs for distressed workers but also stimulates purchasing power and tends to induce further recovery."[72]

Congress thus had challenged both the authority of the executive branch and the prestige of the most influential New Deal agency. The legislative branch subsequently prohibited any WPA employer from being on the relief rolls for over 18 months and abolished the Federal Theatre Arts Project. WPA rolls fell below 2 million persons in the next fiscal year, as economy increasingly overshadowed emergency relief on Capitol Hill. The agency came to a standstill in 1943, when draft calls and wartime jobs gave the WPA formal discharge papers. Congressional conservatism, meanwhile, again challenged the power of the White House on reorganization of the executive branch.

5

REORGANIZATION
OF THE EXECUTIVE BRANCH

Another controversy arose over reorganization of the executive branch. The federal government by 1939 had expanded to over 500 bureaus representing 135 departments and independent agencies, encouraging both inefficiency and duplication of functions. President Roosevelt therefore hoped to reduce the number of executive bodies and to exercise tighter reins over national departments. In seeking to accomplish these objectives, however, the President again provoked power struggles between conservatives and liberals and between Capitol Hill and the White House.

The reorganization issue had come to the forefront in the New Deal era. Roosevelt had championed the redistribution of agency functions more than any previous president, arguing chiefly in terms of improving management rather than of reducing expenditures. In 1936 he had appointed a committee of three distinguished public administration experts, including Louis Brownlow, Charles E. Merriam, and Luther Halsey Gulick, to study administrative operations. Within the next year the committee had recommended that Congress enact legislation to reorganize the executive branch and had urged several steps to improve the effectiveness of government bodies. Specific proposals had included appointing six assistants to the White House staff, extending the civil service system, improving fiscal management, and creating a National Resources Planning Board. In addition, the committee had favored establishing two more cabinet positions to cover public works and welfare, renaming the Department of Interior as the Department of Conservation, and authorizing the President to transfer regulatory commissions and agencies.[1]

At the 1938 session Roosevelt had requested comprehensive reorganization legislation. He had recommended that most autonomous agencies and branches be consolidated into cabinet rank departments and had urged the selection of six new administrative assistants. In hopes of modernizing the merit system, he had proposed replacing the three-man Civil Service Commission with one personnel officer and extending the competitive examinations to include all non-policy positions. Roosevelt also had requested the appointment of an auditor general in lieu of a comptroller general, and had urged the transfer of the Budget Bureau from the Treasury Department to the White House.

Congress, already infuriated over Roosevelt's proposal to enlarge the Supreme Court, had attacked such sweeping restructuring of the executive branch. Anti-New Dealers had contended that the Public Administration Committee proposals would make the President a virtual dictator and would diminish legislative control over the White House. The National Committee to Uphold Constitutional Government and other lobbyists had bombarded both Congress and the mass media with opposition literature. Reorganization legislation had barely survived 49-42 in 1938 in the Senate, which had attached several amendments substantially altering the original committee plan. Bipartisan conservatives, including all Republicans and over one-third of the Democrats, had fallen only a few votes short of recommitting the entire bill. The amended measure had deleted any provision for a department of public works, exempted the Interstate Commerce Commission and other regulatory agencies, and made all executive orders subject to disapproval by joint congressional resolution within sixty days. A few days later the House jolted the administration by sending 204-196 the legislation back to committee and, in effect, killing reorganization for the 1938 session. The bipartisan coalition, comprising 88 Republicans, 108 Democrats, and 8 third-party members, had signaled the White House either to make its proposal much less comprehensive or to abandon reorganization plans. Congressional disenchantment with bureaucracy and the growth of presidential power, coupled with the growing conservative mood nationally, had prevented Roosevelt from restructuring the executive branch.[2]

Although disliking major features of the bill, senators and representatives alike still advocated greater efficiency and economy in the executive branch. "Everyone," Senator Hayden remarked, "favors reorganization in principle, but is against it in some particular. This is the chief reason why nothing has ever been done." But it was inevitable that Congress eventually would enact some type of reorganization measure. "Six Presidents," Hayden stressed, "have asked for such authority and it will have to be granted to some President if waste and inefficiency in government are to be prevented."[3]

Roosevelt, meanwhile, refused to concede defeat. Following the vote, the President insisted that most congressmen favored reorganization in principle and supported 90 percent of the legislative details. Although hoping to retain most of the original bill, he was prevailed upon by Democratic Representative Warren to consider making substantial changes. An expert on executive agencies, Warren ruled out the Senate bill as "impossible" and urged overhauling the House version to exempt the comptroller general and the Civil Service Commission. "I," Warren wrote, "am just as strong for it as ever. The practical situation calls for a dropping of some phases of it and a revamping of others."[4]

Democrats Warren and Cochran, a forty-eight-year-old native of Webster Groves, Missouri, directed preliminary reorganization strategy. Cochran, who had attended public schools in Webster Groves, had worked for several years in editorial departments of various St. Louis newspapers, and had then been secretary to Representative William L. Igoe and Senator William J. Stone. After briefly studying law he had served from 1921 to 1926 as secretary to Congressman Harry B. Hawes. Cochran, who replaced Hawes in 1926, had played major roles in opposing Prohibition and in sponsoring a measure making kidnapping a federal crime. A staunch backer of the 1938 reorganization bill, the New Dealer chaired the Accounts Committee and belonged to the Committee on Expenditures in the Executive Departments.

In late 1938 Warren and Cochran began planning legislative strategy. On December 20 at the White House, they warned the President any reorganization measure would face "a serious situation in the House." Both representatives began drafting a milder version designed to meet objections made by party colleagues at the 1938 session. "I am just sick and tired," Warren complained, "of seeing Democrats hammer the hands of other Democrats."[5] During the next two months Warren and Cochran spent countless hours writing a revised version without seeking any advice from the White House. As Cochran explained, "Up to the hour that the bill was introduced no official nor employee of the executive branch of the Government had been consulted."[6]

On February 23 Warren and Cochran introduced a drastically modified measure discarding the most controversial features of the 1938 legislation. Besides exempting many independent regulatory agencies, the revised bill stripped the President of authority to revamp the civil service system, update accounting procedures, and create new government departments. Cochran regretted making so many concessions but later confided, "It was a case of get what we could."[7] In other respects the provisions of the 1938 measure remained intact. The legislation empowered Roosevelt for two years to transfer, consolidate, or abolish government departments and agencies, to select six administrative assistants, and to control budgets of commissions. Specific reorganization plans recommended by the President would become effective sixty days after submission unless rejected by a majority of Congress.

Prestigious representatives directed the legislative battles for the respective sides. Warren and Cochran, both members of the Select Committee on Government Organization, conducted the campaign for those favoring the milder reorganization proposal. "This bill," Warren contended, "is all that we need. . . . This legislation meets all major objections to the bill last year and will permit a thorough job of reorganization of the government under a review by Congress."[8] In the opposition camp sixty-three-year-old anti–New Deal Democrat Hatton W. Sumners of Texas formed strategy. Sumners, the chairman of the Judiciary Committee, had disagreed sharply with Roosevelt over the Supreme Court bill and thereafter had denounced centralization of the federal government. Sumners feared that the Warren-Cochran measure would aggrandize President Roosevelt's already extensive personal power over executive agencies rather than promote any savings in government. Taber of New York, a 58-year-old Republican, was the most vocal advocate of slashing federal government expenditures in the Appropriations Committee. Taber likewise argued that the President held too much authority and charged that "no important bill in recent months has had so little reason for its existence."[9]

Both sides deplored the awesome national budget deficit and favored reducing federal expenditures. Alarmed over the nearly $50 billion debt, liberal and especially conservative representatives supported in principle the restructuring of federal agencies as a means of achieving economy. Democrat Andrew J. May of Kentucky, chairman of the Military Affairs Committee, insisted "there must come a time, and that very quickly, when expenditures of government, both state and federal, must be greatly curtailed. Otherwise we may witness a complete collapse of our economic structure."[10] "If we continue to follow the road and the pace we have been traveling for the past six years," echoed conservative Republican John Shafer of Wisconsin, "Uncle Sam will soon be bankrupt." "We should end the drunken orgy of spending," Shafer declared, "by the New Deal crackpots, brain trusters, and nitwits who are in the Federal administrative payroll."[11]

Opposing forces disagreed over the effectiveness of executive branch operations. If the Warren-Cochran bill were approved, reorganization advocates argued overlapping and duplication of functions would be eliminated and government spending would be reduced. Democrat Eugene Cox protested, "There are too many of these agencies doing work of a similar character and . . . far too much duplication," while Ways and

Means Committee Chairman Doughton predicted that revamping of Presidential agencies "would bring about many economies in the operation of the various agencies of the Federal Government."[12] On the opposition side representatives contended that the reorganization bill would accentuate the already excessive bureaucracy without producing substantial savings. "Be not deceived," Republican Thomas A. Jenkins of Ohio cautioned, "into the belief that great economies will be effected." "Real economy," Republican Dondero charged, "must come through a withdrawal or suspension of many wasteful and expensive activities in which the Government is now engaged."[13]

As on WPA, presidential power became a controversial issue. Republicans, along with some conservative Democrats, especially criticized the legislation for granting so much authority to the White House and feared Roosevelt would use the measure to tighten personal control over federal agencies. Republican Vorys charged, "The President desires the bill not so much to reorganize as to hold the threat over Boards and Bureaus and who do not follow his views," while Republican James W. Mott of Oregon claimed, "The real purpose of this bill is to permit the President to so change and alter the character of the independent agencies that they will become instead the direct agencies of the President, responsible to him for their actions and dependent upon him for their existence."[14] Besides demanding tighter congressional control over reorganization, they insisted any order should be nullified by majority vote of either house rather than by concurrent resolution. "We believe," Republican Fish contended, "that he has an obsession and a passion for power, that he seeks to grab more and more power at every opportunity." A rabid anti–New Dealer, Fish noted, "We have no faith in the President, and we want to take back some of the power already surrendered by Congress instead of giving him additional power."[15]

Reorganization advocates disputed these politically motivated accusations. Denying that the measure usurped legislative prerogatives, the Warren-Cochran forces claimed the President was more knowledgeable than Congress in the operations of executive agencies. "There is nothing in this bill," Democrat Jerry Voorhis of California stressed, "that gives to the President or any other executive officer a single bit of additional power he did not have before." Since Roosevelt "has available all sources of information, as well as having the executive responsibility," Democrat John R. Murdock of Arizona added, "the President is in a better position to suggest changes in administrative machinery than Congress could possibly do."[16] In addition, the Warren camp argued that the President primarily enforced the laws of Congress and maintained that the legislative branch could reject unwise reorganization orders. Democrat J. Hardin

Peterson of Florida predicted the measure would "safeguard the legislative branch of the Government," while Cox reminded colleagues, "We can exercise our right of rejection by concurrent resolution."[17]

Reorganization confronted the first major hurdle in the highly partisan Select Committee on Government Organization. Since Democrats held six of the nine seats, the outcome hinged upon the ability of Chairman Cochran to keep party colleagues in line. Cochran received unanimous backing from the Democrats, who argued that bureaucracy had grown so enormously as to require steps towards greater efficiency and economy. An indefatigable champion of reorganization, Cochran steered the bill through his committee by a 6–3 margin. Taber and two other Republicans angrily left the room after the vote, protesting that Chairman Cochran had refused to permit amendments, had blocked public hearings, and had permitted the committee only 2½ hours to debate the measure. Taber complained, "The hearings on the whole subject were pitiful," while Republican Charles L. Gifford of Massachusetts asserted, "Nothing but shocking is it when a bill of this kind can be railroaded through like this."[18] Congress, they insisted, specifically should approve each plan submitted by the President before any reorganization orders could be implemented.

As on the volatile WPA question, a robust conservative coalition in the House threatened to block the Warren-Cochran bill. Nearly all Republicans, along with three dozen Democrats, favored an alternative plan presented by fifty-one-year-old Senator Harry F. Byrd of Virginia. Byrd denounced the Roosevelt administration as "the most costly, the most wasteful, and most bureaucratic form of government this republic has ever known."[19] Byrd introduced an amendment, which differed in three basic respects from the Warren-Cochran reorganization measure. Since there was nearly a $50 billion national debt, Byrd urged the legislative branch drastically to reduce federal expenditures and make economy the principal consideration in a reorganization order. The Warren-Cochran bill did not make any declaration for thriftiness, but concentrated primarily on rearranging and consolidating existing bureaus and agencies. Byrd's proposal also compelled the President to submit detailed reports explaining how particular plans would decrease government spending. In another contrast, the Byrd measure prevented both the continuation of temporary federal bodies beyond authorized periods and the creation of new agencies. White House officials, Byrd complained, had established between 1933 and 1937 at least thirty-five additional bureaus or agencies.

Republican representatives particularly resisted the Warren-Cochran bill, but pressure groups this time remained on the sidelines. At a caucus called by Minority Leader Martin on March 6, over two-thirds of the

Republican congressmen promised to oppose the reorganization measure unless tighter restrictions were placed upon presidential power. Most Republicans preferred the Byrd proposal, which made economy the paramount consideration of every reorganization order. Although helping reject the 1938 legislation, lobbyists played a more subordinate role this time. The National Committee to Uphold Constitutional Government, an interest group spearheading earlier national campaigns against Roosevelt's plans to enlarge the Supreme Court and to reorganize the executive branch, refrained from challenging the Warren-Cochran measure very much because the most controversial features were eliminated. "I don't think," committee spokesman Amos Pinchot advised, "we ought to go to bat and try to make a big issue of it."[20]

Between March 6 and 8 representatives engaged in floor debate reminiscent of the spirited WPA exchanges. Before a crowded gallery members participated in what was described by participants as "a knock down, drag out battle" and as "the most exhausting and exciting we have had so far."[21] Warren and Cochran defended their measure, arguing chiefly that reorganization of the executive branch would promote greater efficiency and reduce federal expenditures. Opponents, led by Taber and Sumners, charged that the bill granted the President too much power and insisted on increasing congressional control over White House plans.

At the outset on March 6, Warren forthrightly presented the case for reorganization. He noted that the executive branch had ballooned to 150 agencies encompassing 500 bureaus, resulting in enormous cost to taxpayers and promoting wasteful duplication of effort. The vast bureaucracy, he protested, had developed into "a Frankenstein which has become greater than Congress itself, its creator, and which arrogantly and contemptuously flaunts itself and snaps its fingers into our very faces." In regard to overlapping functions, Warren cited that 65 different agencies gathered statistics, 34 acquired land, 29 loaned government funds, and 28 handled welfare. At least 10 separate bureaus performed wildlife preservation, forestry, home and community planning, and government construction. "There are bureaus," he asserted, "for which there is no earthly excuse for their existence." In an effort to attract conservative backing, Warren insisted the 1939 bill would not create a department of welfare and empowered Congress to reject any plan by concurrent resolution.[22]

Taber, who represented the opposition camp, denied reorganization would reduce the $4 billion annual deficit and insisted upon increasing legislative controls. "Are you ready," Taber asked, "to surrender the birthright of the American people to these bureaucrats who would destroy us unless curbed and unless we put the brakes on spending by this

Government?" Besides looking askance upon delegating further power to a President from the opposite political party, he urged that no executive order become effective without the consent of both the Senate and the House.[23]

Numerous efforts were made to change the status of certain New Deal agencies. On March 8 representatives rejected amendments to subject several groups (Civil Service Commission, Coast Guard, National Labor Relations Board, and U.S. Tariff Commission) to reorganization provisions and thwarted other motions to exempt certain agencies (Civil Aeronautics Authority, Rural Electrification Administration, and U.S. Forest Service). On the other hand, congressmen protected the National Mediation Board, the Railroad Retirement Board, and the National Railway Adjustment Board from possible reorganization and removed the National Bituminous Coal Commission from the exempt list.

A Sumners amendment, which struck at the heart of the Warren measure, provoked bitter controversy. Upset that both the Senate and the House had to reject any reorganization order, Sumners instead proposed empowering either chamber to kill particular presidential plans. Congress, he insisted, should be safeguarded in case Roosevelt issued a directive either violating public interest or endangering separation of powers. "For reorganization to be forced through which is against the judgment of one of the two houses," Sumners warned, "gives rise to an element of friction and discord between the Executive and that House that it (sic) is not worth the price paid for it." Several influential representatives, including Speaker Bankhead, Majority Leader Rayburn, Warren, and Cox, argued that the Sumners proposal would prevent meaningful reform efforts. Rayburn claimed, "If this amendment is adopted there is a strong probability that in the future no reorganization may come about."[24]

This highly explosive question followed an erratic course. In a short-lived victory for the conservative coalition, the House endorsed the Sumners motion 176-156 in a teller vote. Cochran, alarmed at granting either congressional wing the power to reject a presidential order, demanded a roll call. In a striking reversal representatives defeated 209-193 the controversial Sumners amendment. Since their tallies were being recorded this time, Democrats resoundingly supported the Warren camp. Republicans unanimously favored increasing legislative control over the President, but lost on this roll call because only one of every six from the majority party followed suit. Blaming the sudden reversal on "the New Deal forces," Vorys charged the Warren forces had prevented "a real provision for congressional review."[25]

Sectionalism, on the other hand, played a subordinate role in the reversal. Southern and mountain delegations mustered at least 75 percent cooperation among their ranks, but four geographical blocs failed to achieve 70 percent backing for either position. Although Sumners came from Texas, southerners supplied nearly one-third of Warren's support and aligned with western and border Democrats to defeat the motion. Great Lakes and Middle Atlantic Republicans furnished the nucleus of forces clamoring for increased congressional control over the President and were joined by New Englanders.

Conservatives never regained the initiative. On the same day representatives decisively (176–139) rejected Texas Democrat Richard Kleberg's amendment making each reorganization request subject to consent by both houses within sixty days. Before the tally Warren had charged that Kleberg at the last minute "comes up with a dagger and tries to strike this whole proposition down."[26] By a much wider 236–163 margin the House defeated Taber's motion to recommit the bill with instructions to attach the Kleberg proposal. Representatives on March 8 easily (246–153) enacted the comprehensive measure paving the way for Senate action.

Politics again influenced voting behavior more than any other single factor. Rayburn and Martin achieved at least 95 percent unity in their respective camps, making party differences among the sharpest at the 1939 session. To the delight of Warren forces, Democrats set aside ideological differences and nearly unanimously backed the final version. His measure, Warren boasted, secured "the largest percentage of Democrats . . . than we have had on any matter in the last eight years." "To continue to compromise with the Republican Minority," Knute Hill of Washington had warned, "would bring utter defeat to the Democratic Party in 1940."[27]

Minority Republicans, though, solidly repudiated the Warren measure, which their party feared granted the President too much authority. Clifford R. Hope of Kansas, one of only eight Republicans supporting the bill, conceded that his party solidly rejected the legislation for "just pure politics . . . because the Democrats are for it." "A good many Republicans told me," Hope confided, "they saw no harm in it, yet they were afraid to vote for it for fear that their constituents would think it was the same Reorganization bill that was defeated last August." Irked by the Republican resistance, Warren deemed it "a great mistake that Reorganization has been more or less a partisan question for the last three years."[28.]

Sectionalism likewise played a more important role on this tally. A majority of delegations achieved consensus among over three-fourths of their ranks. Southern and border representatives provided almost unanimous support for the Warren-Cochran bill and received more assistance this time from western members. On the opposing side New Englanders directed resistance and were joined by Middle Atlantic and midwestern congressmen in a losing cause.

Warren and Roosevelt both welcomed the outcome. Following the vote, Warren commented, "We feel elated that we got such a fine majority and the bill went through without amendments except those offered by us."[29] On the other hand, the North Carolina Democrat feared the formidable conservative coalition in the Senate would resist the reorganization measure. "There is a crowd in the Senate," Warren charged, "that so completely hate the President that they will do anything that they can to defeat this bill." In a more flamboyant mood Roosevelt predicted the Senate would pass the legislation quickly and even began plans to send the first order to Capitol Hill.[30]

Several forces contributed to the House outcome. Warren had co-sponsored the bill, drafted a compromise version acceptable to dissident Democrats, and led floor debate. Reacting in a humble manner to these tributes, Warren remarked, "The members and the papers have been kind enough to say that my handling of the matter put it through."[31] At his side Cochran had been the other coauthor, chaired the committee reporting the measure, and played a prominent role in floor debate. Democrats, with southern and border members at the helm, had easily overcome Republican resistance.

Reorganization had fared better this time because Warren had removed the most controversial features. Several representatives who had opposed the 1938 measure switched allegiances to the Warren camp because the newer version gave Congress veto power over the President and exempted selected major agencies. Peterson, labeling the Warren legislation as "entirely a different type of bill from the one proposed before," contended, "This new bill would give an opportunity to consolidate overlapping bureaus and eliminate useless ones " and "yet keep legislative matters in the legislative branch." As party colleague J. Wilburn Cartwright of Oklahoma remarked, the legislation "was modified and remodeled until it was passed without serious opposition at this session."[32]

The Senate Committee on Government Organization, meanwhile, drastically revised the intent of the Warren-Cochran version. Although Democrats occupied six of nine seats, Chairman Byrnes, Harrison, and Lucas were the only party members favoring the House bill. Six committee members, including Majority Leader Barkley and Minority Leader McNary, succeeded in inserting the controversial Byrd amendment making economy the paramount consideration of any reorganization order. On March 6 the committee sent the thoroughly revised version to the Senate floor.

Senators sharply disagreed over whether to accept the House or Byrd versions. Since only 38 of 81 members favored the Warren bill as of March 17, New Deal forces faced an uphill battle. Forty-three senators insisted upon requiring affirmative congressional action before any executive plan could become effective. Thirteen Democrats, including Connally, Clark, and Key Pittman, and three Republicans, were undecided.[33]

Several distinguished members directed the floor strategy. Democrat Wheeler led the opposition faction, hoping to increase congressional control over executive reorganization, and was assisted by Byrd. James F. Byrnes of South Carolina, a 58-year-old Democrat, stood at the forefront of the members supporting the House bill and was aided by Barkley. Byrnes, whose father had died before he was born, came from a large family. His mother attempted to support the Byrnes children on a meager dressmaker's income in Charleston, South Carolina. James, although a brilliant student, had left public school at age fourteen and worked as an office boy and stenographer. He had taught himself law and in 1910 had won a seat in the U.S. House of Representatives by campaigning on "nothing but gall." Byrnes had belonged to the Appropriations Committee, which dispensed funding during World War 1 to government agencies. After joining the U.S. Senate in 1931, he was elected assistant majority leader within two years and had become keenly aware of the political situation in every state. A quotable, shrewd, and energetic senator, Byrnes was "a small, wiry, neatly made man, with an odd, sharply angular face from which his sharp eyes peer out with an expression of quizzical geniality." Byrnes supported most New Deal programs and favored executive reorganization as a means of promoting greater efficiency and more economy in the federal government. Barkley, who had edged out Finance Committee Chairman Harrison in 1937 for majority leader, nearly always had supported President Roosevelt on important legislative issues.[34]

Byrnes and Wheeler argued the cases for the respective sides. Starting floor debate, Byrnes lauded the bill as a vast improvement over the 1938 measure because several controversial features had been eliminated. Besides abandoning plans to create a welfare department, the House version exempted the General Accounting Office and the Civil Service Commission. The only other significant change, Byrnes noted, was that Congress now could reject any presidential order by majority rather than two-thirds vote.[35] In response, Wheeler denounced the House legislation for granting Roosevelt unconstitutional powers and insisted either house should be authorized to reject specific plans. Capitol Hill, he complained, is "delegating to the executive branch of government the power to abolish functions of office and repeal laws, and then say that if one branch of

Congress approves the President's action and the other branch does not, it should become the law." In a plea for the legislative branch to exercise its constitutional rights, Wheeler asserted, "We ought to have the intestinal stamina to stand up here and say that we can legislate."[36]

Senators stressed the same basic themes as their House counterparts. Byrnes forces principally argued that the Warren-Cochran version would promote more effective bureaucratic machinery and reduce federal spending. Joining debate more than usual, Barkley affirmed that restructuring of the executive branch would assist immeasurably in "eliminating waste and duplication and bringing about greater efficiency in the administration of the government, and making real economies in government expenses." Herring contended, "Economy in government-housekeeping can only be affected by a determination on the part of government not to spend so much money" and predicted that reorganization "would provide certain economies and greater efficiency." In addition the Byrnes camp defended the House measure as constitutional and denied Roosevelt was usurping legislative power. "The only authority that is granted to the President of the United States under this bill," Democrat Allen J. Ellender of Louisiana maintained, "is simply and solely to group, coordinate, and consolidate the executive agencies. That is all."[37]

Opponents likewise resorted to familiar arguments. The Warren-Cochran version, they protested, delegated the President too much authority to group, coordinate, and consolidate executive agencies, and promoted further centralization without substantial savings. Clark of Missouri objected that giving "sweeping grants of power to the President is to make changes under his own authority without review or checks," while Kansas Republican Capper warned, "These same broad powers, if not restrained in some way, could also be used greatly to increase the cost of administration."[38] In a similar vein, the Wheeler forces insisted Congress should increase control over reorganization orders and be required to approve all presidential plans. The House measure, Democrat William H. King of Utah emphasized, "calls for the abdication of authority of the legislative branch and seems to proceed on the theory that Congress is impotent to deal with legislative matters." The Wheeler faction charged no emergency situation existed to warrant surrendering such vast power to Roosevelt. Since there was "no great emergency," Tydings asserted, "the executive branch has no right to become the legislative branch of the Government."[39]

On March 17 Byrd introduced his controversial economy amendment. The federal government, according to Byrd, had spent $9.5 billion in the 1939 fiscal year, nearly 40 percent above the original amount Roosevelt had requested and almost triple the 1933 figure. As the Virginia Democrat warned, "We cannot operate for too long, without disaster, a government costing more than the ability of people to pay." The reorganization measure, he stressed, provided an excellent opportunity for retrenchment and for achieving a balanced budget. In addition, he charged, "We have the largest peacetime expenditures in our history, the second largest taxation in our peacetime history, and the largest debt in the entire history of America." Byrd concluded, it was "imperative to reduce drastically governmental expenditures and other such reductions as may be accomplished in great measure by proceeding immediately under the provisions of this act."[40]

In a victory for the fiscal conservatives, the Senate approved a compromise version of the Byrd amendment. The Byrnes camp on March 20 agreed to support the Byrd economy proposal, provided the Virginia Democrat modified the tone of the original draft. Byrd promptly doctored the language to state, "It is desirable to reduce substantially governmental expenditures and other such reductions as may be accomplished in some measure by proceeding immediately under the provision of this act." Senators unanimously adopted the milder text, insisting frugality should prevail in every reorganization effort. In Byrd's view, the action signified "a clear declaration from the Congress that the expenditures of the National Government today are excessive and should be substantially reduced."[41]

Anti-Roosevelt forces next focused on attaching the Wheeler amendment. Deploring the rapid growth of presidential power, Wheeler introduced a motion requiring both houses to adopt every executive reorganization plan. "Never in my memory," he asserted, "has there been such extravagance and such waste as there has been in the new departments which have been set up in the Government under the emergency acts." Wheeler was afraid an order would become effective automatically if either chamber failed to act, despite the attitude held by the other legislative wing. Wheeler charged it "is reactionary. It is a step backward. It should not be passed . . . unless Congress has a right to say whether or not it wants the plans proposed by the Executive branch of the Government to become law."[42]

By a razor-thin 45–44 margin the Wheeler amendment on March 21 survived its first major test. Democrats largely opposed the motion, but one-third of Roosevelt's party rebelled against the White House. Barkley experienced much more difficulty than House Majority Leader Rayburn in seeking party unity and witnessed almost as many defections as on the McKellar WPA proposal. On the other hand, Martin lined up the Republican minority unanimously behind the Wheeler proposal. Five Democrats, including administration backers T. F. Green, Schwellenbach, and Truman, and two Republicans, missed the roll call.

The coalition of Republicans and conservative Democrats again had haunted the Roosevelt administration. With the exception of Guy M. Gillette of Iowa, every senator on the President's purge list in the 1938 primaries supported the Wheeler motion. Byrd and Glass of Virginia, along with Bailey of North Carolina, continued to lead the ever-increasing number of Democrats rebelling against Roosevelt's leadership. Although 21 Republicans and 15 Democrats rejected both the President's WPA and reorganization plans, the nature of the anti–New Deal coalition changed considerably. A majority of the conservative Democrats supported the White House on one of the two issues. Eleven Democrats, including Byrnes and Harrison, opposed full funding for work relief and favored the Warren-Cochran proposal, while seven members of Roosevelt's party pursued the opposite course.

Sectional alignments, which had shifted considerably, substantiate the fluctuating composition of the conservative coalition. New England senators directed the campaign for wider congressional control over reorganization plans, while Great Plains members conducted the battle for reduced WPA funds. Great Plains and Pacific colleagues also played major supporting roles in combatting the Warren-Cochran version. Border delegations gave the strongest backing for the two Roosevelt measures, but received most assistance this time from southerners rather than the mountain bloc. Several southerners, including all intended purge victims, deserted the White House this time and rallied behind the Wheeler amendment. Middle Atlantic senators wholeheartedly sided with the administration both times, while Great Lakes members remained quite divided.

Sectionalism influenced voting behavior more than on the comparable Sumners amendment. New England and border delegations registered near-unanimity on the Wheeler motion, while two other blocs achieved at least 75 percent unity. On the other hand, regional considerations had negligible effects on the behavior of Great Lakes, mountain, or southern members. Geographic forces loomed larger in the upper chamber, whereas political considerations were more important in the House.

Administration forces sought immediately to reverse the outcome, provoking complex floor maneuvering. Wheeler's amendment meant Congress must consent to restructuring administrative agencies, replacing the original arrangement whereby reorganization plans took effect within sixty days unless vetoed by the Senate and the House. Following the roll call, Byrnes changed his vote to affirmative so that he could move for reconsideration of the Wheeler proposal. Since he had voted with the prevailing side, Byrnes was entitled to make such a request. Clark of Missouri then promptly moved to reconsider the vote and to table his own motion, the latter step designed to prevent further discussion.

Administration leaders protested the Clark tactic would prohibit senators from debating the question of reconsideration and argued the same member could not make both motions. Clark was forced to withdraw the tabling motion, but Wheeler quickly moved to table the Clark proposal to reconsider.[43]

The voting switches, however, made the Wheeler tabling motion end in a 44-44 deadlock. Breaking the tie, Vice President Garner ruled against the tabling maneuver. Borah, who had supported the Wheeler amendment minutes before, followed his usual practice of refusing to vote for a motion restricting floor debate and quietly abstained when his name was called. "Borah," Republican Hiram Johnson recalled, "simply sat in his seat mute and would not vote." Other considerations may have influenced his voting behavior. With the full support of the Idaho Republican, President Roosevelt had appointed the day before William O. Douglas, a Yale University faculty member and chairman of the Securities and Exchange Commission, to a vacant position on the United States Supreme Court. "It happened at the time of the pendency of the matter," Johnson claimed, Borah "was asking for the appointment of Douglas to the Supreme bench, and that [sic] the President acceded to his request."[44] Majority Leader Barkley, confused by the complex maneuvering, misunderstood the Clark motion and momentarily tipped the scales in favor of the conservative forces. Unaware the motion meant tabling the reorganization legislation, Barkley voted affirmatively the first time the clerk called his name. When several members began chuckling, the bewildered Majority Leader quickly inquired of colleagues what had happened and promptly changed his vote to negative. The abstention by Borah and the reversal by Barkley caused the coalition to suffer its first major defeat on reorganization and paved the way for another roll call on the Wheeler amendment. Clark sought to withdraw his motion to reconsider following the tie vote, but Byrnes objected, and presiding officer Garner ruled against the Missouri Democrat.[45] "We made the best fight we could for the Wheeler amendment," Byrd lamented," and would have won in the Senate excepting that Senator Borah declined to vote." "Had Borah then voted to table the motion," Johnson concurred, "the matter would have been ended, and no power could resurrect it."[46]

Administration forces hurriedly worked behind the scenes to round up votes against the Wheeler proposal. Byrnes, O'Mahoney, and other reorganization advocates controlled the floor for the remainder of the day, preventing anti-New Dealers from forcing a roll call on the Wheeler motion. At the request of the President, Truman flew overnight to Washington from Missouri and was prepared to oppose the Wheeler proposal. Roosevelt also persuaded Foreign Relations Committee Chairman Pittman, who earlier had disapproved of reorganization because the Forest Service might be transferred from the Department of Agriculture to Interior, to reject the Wheeler motion to reconsider. The President assured Pittman no such "drastic change in reorganization" was contemplated, thus inducing the Nevada Democrats to align with the Byrnes faction. Pittman previously had written Roosevelt, "The Forestry Service has progressed, improved its service, and reached a perfect understanding with the stock growers while operating under the Department of Agriculture." If the agency was transferred, Pittman vowed, "it will be my duty to the livestock industry of Nevada, which constitutes the second primary industry, to vote against the pending reorganization act."[47]

On the following afternoon the Senate resembled a soap opera. Clark's motion to reconsider barely survived 46-44, thus setting the stage for a climactic vote on the Wheeler amendment. Spectators crowded the galleries, while senators anxiously awaited the outcome not knowing which side would triumph. At one point Senator Austin remarked, "Now it looks as tho' we would have a tie and that the Vice-Pres. would have to break the tie. It is quite exciting." Senators narrowly rejected 46-44 the controversial Wheeler proposal, reversing their decision of the previous day. Democrats Chavez, Miller, and Truman played crucial roles in shifting the momentum against the Wheeler motion. Since the President promised to retain the Forest Service within the Department of Agriculture, Chavez defected to the Byrnes camp.[48] According to Johnson of California, "The administration had bought Chavez, the half-breed from New Mexico, who had voted for the Wheeler amendment orginally, so the fat was in the fire." A supporter of the Montana Democrat's proposal the previous day, Miller skipped the roll call this time. Truman, absent the day before, opposed the amendment made by his close friend and Interstate Commerce Committee colleague. The sudden reversal of tide dampened the enthusiasm of the Wheeler forces. "It was something of a blow to those of us who had been fighting all along," Johnson conceded. "It will take me a little time to get over this."[49]

As in the House, senators made several attempts to alter the status of individual agencies. In the most spirited confrontation senators rejected 41-38 a proposal by Democrat McCarran to exempt the newly created Civil Aeronautics Authority from any reorganization order. A champion of the blossoming aircraft industry, he feared increased federal regulation would place too many restrictions on the independent agency. "I do not want it," McCarran asserted, "to be destroyed. I do not want the United States to go backward a half century in air transportation." Countering this contention, Byrnes stressed the CAA primarily handled administrative duties well and should not be accorded privileged treatment.[50] The Senate, which refused to subject the United Stated Employees Association and United States Tariff Commission to reorganization orders, agreed to exempt the Federal Deposit Insurance Corporation.

On March 22 the Senate ultimately approved 62–23 the emotionally charged political measure. Patching previous disagreements, Democrats rallied overwhelmingly behind the bill. The conservative Tydings, an intended purge victim in the 1938 primaries, Peter G. Gerry of Rhode Island, and King were the only members of Roosevelt's party casting dissenting votes. With the exception of Robert A. Taft of Ohio and Reed of Kansas, all Republicans rejected the final version and still resented granting reorganization authority to a Democratic president. Sectionally, southerners unanimously backed the final bill and aligned with at least 80 percent of border, mountain, and Great Lakes Democrats. New England Republicans still directed the resistance but this time were joined only by the Pacific delegation.

Senators posed greater resistance than representatives to reorganization legislation. The upper chamber initially had approved the Wheeler amendment compelling congressional consent of every presidential order, but the House rejected the comparable Sumners proposal handily. Although Republicans solidly opposed the Warren-Cochran version in both houses, conservative Democrats rebelled more extensively in the Senate. Southern and border members in both chambers favored granting Roosevelt broader powers to restructure the executive branch, while New England and Great Plains delegations consistently demanded wider legislative control. Western representatives and Middle Atlantic senators defended reorganization much more than did their counterparts from the same region, producing the sharpest internal geographical differences.

Administration forces had survived a very severe test in the upper chamber. Byrnes had played the most instrumental role, presenting the case in floor debate for giving the President broader powers to restructure the government bureaucracy and working effectively behind the scenes rounding up votes. New Deal Democrats, especially those from the border and Middle Atlantic delegations, formed the nucleus of the Byrnes camp and helped guide the House version to victory. In addition, Roosevelt supported the Warren-Cochran bill from the outset and played a major role in reversing the tide on the Wheeler amendment. Above all, Congress reflected the desire of most Americans to reform the undisciplined bureaucracy and to reduce budget deficits.

Byrnes forces ultimately had prevailed in the power struggle with the Wheeler camp. Besides granting the President authority to reorganize executive bureaus and agencies, senators had rejected the Wheeler amendment requiring congressional approval of all orders. Conservatives had resisted delegating Roosevelt broad discretionary power to rearrange government bodies and to issue orders which would automatically become operative after sixty days unless rejected by both houses. After the roll call Assistant Minority Leader Austin had protested, "The Senate votes away its power and responsibility over legislation defining functions and setting up agencies to perform them."[51] On the other hand, the Wheeler faction had protected the independence of the General Accounting Office, Civil Service Commission, Federal Communications Commission, National Labor Relations Board, and other major executive agencies. In addition to inserting the Byrd economy amendment, the conservative coalition had granted Congress authority to veto any executive plan within sixty days by simple majority vote. Byrd conceded, "The bill is so greatly modified that most of the objections have been removed," while Austin labeled the measure "less obnoxious than it formerly was."[52]

Reorganization had survived its most formidable hurdle. On March 27 conferees accepted the Senate version making frugality the paramount consideration of each presidential directive. After signing the bill on April 3 without much fanfare, Roosevelt began to reorganize the executive branch. The first order, submitted in late April, established a Federal Security Agency and a Federal Works Agency, and created an Executive Office of the President. In addition, the order placed the White House office, the Bureau of the Budget, and the National Resources Board in the newly established central staff headquarters. Plan 2 abolished some governmental bodies, including the National Bituminous Coal Commission and the National Emergency Council, and transferred several agencies from one department to another. By mid-May Congress approved both directives, offering less resistance than administration forces had anticipated. Democrat John J. Dempsey of New Mexico boasted that both plans made "a very good effect in the House, better than I have seen in the last five years" and urged Roosevelt to issue additional proposals.[53]

The cordial response abruptly terminated in early 1940, when the President contemplated transferring the Forest Service from the Agriculture to Interior Department. Although pledging earlier to keep the status of the Forest Service intact, Roosevelt favored the shift because practically all agency work involved public lands and Secretary Ickes clamored for the change. When word reached Capitol Hill that Roosevelt might make this transfer, senators reacted in a hostile manner. Forestry Committee Chairman Bankhead, who warned that most members opposed this change, predicted such an order would "arouse serious controversy" and face "probable defeat in the Senate."[54] In a sarcastic tone Independent George Norris suggested the "entire matter might be settled satisfactorily by making Mr. Ickes Secretary of War." On the House side Warren expected an intense battle over the status of the agency and claimed "there is most pronounced opposition against its transfer."[55] Since the forestry lobby also posed big resistance, Secretary Ickes and Senator Byrnes prevailed upon Roosevelt in early February to set aside this proposal.

During the 1940 session the President still presented three reorganization proposals. Plan 3, submitted in early April, consolidated the Office of Commissioner of Accounts and Deposits and Public Service into a new Fiscal Service, combined several agencies including the Bureau of Fisheries and Bureau of Biological Survey, and shifted the Federal Alcohol Commission to the Treasury Department. A few days later Roosevelt urged switching the Civil Aeronautics Authority to the Commerce Department and recommended transferring several agencies from the Agriculture Department. In late May he suggested moving the Immigration and Naturalization Service from the Labor to the Justice Department.[56]

Of all official orders, Plan 4 stirred the most controversy. Senator McCarran opposed changing the status of the CAA because the independent agency had helped establish the United States as a world aviation leader. If the CAA was placed under the jurisdiction of the Commerce Department, he argued, its political independence and effectiveness would be limited. The nation, McCarran cautioned, "must not, at the zenith of its effort, take a step backward." Despite the congressional discontent, the Roosevelt administration believed neither the Senate nor House would kill the order. White House Assistant Stephen Early vowed, "We will beat the opposition" and insisted "the reorganization bill will be accepted." He added, "We are getting the facts out to our friends both in the House and Senate."[57]

Administration officials underestimated the degree of dissatisfaction on Capitol Hill. In early May the House decisively rejected Plan 4 and thus for the first time repudiated a presidential order. Since all reorganization directives would take effect unless discarded by both houses, New Dealers sought to save Plan 4 in the Senate. Byrnes and Barkley quickly defended the transfer in floor debates and held numerous cloakroom conferences with conservative Democrats. A few days later the Senate approved 64-34 the plan transferring the CAA to the Commerce Department. Anti-New Deal Democrats, including Bailey, Glass, Harrison, and Tydings, swung the tide in favor of the White House directive. In late May Congress overwhelmingly approved Plan 5 shifting the Immigration Service.[58]

Reorganization afforded major benefits to the Roosevelt administration. For the first time the President had an immediate staff to control the burgeoning bureaucracy. In July, 1939 he selected

Lauchlin Currie, William McReynolds, and James Rowe as assistants to handle the daily White House duties. Besides appointing one assistant as a liaison with the Civil Service Commission, Roosevelt appropriately selected Representative Warren as comptroller general to audit government accounts and to supervise federal expenditures. Above all, Congress had provided a mechanism for reducing the number of independent agencies and eliminating overlapping functions among departments and bureaus. At the same time the legislative branch plunged into one of the most spirited battles since the 1937 Supreme Court controversy.

6

HATCHETING POLITICAL CORRUPTION

Conservatives meanwhile planned a second assault on the Roosevelt administration's WPA programs. The legislative branch, increasingly alarmed about the political involvement of federal employees in primaries and elections, began considering various ways of strictly regulating such activity. In an effort to strike at the heart of such corruption, Democratic Senator Hatch proposed two comprehensive reform measures.

For over a decade there had been several efforts to strengthen the civil service network. Although the number of classified service workers had multiplied from 14,000 in 1883 to 560,000 in 1926, the merit system had not kept up with the pace of bureaucratic growth. More federal job-holders were outside the classified service in 1926 than the entire 1883 national government working force. Between 1928 and 1935 midwestern and western congressmen had introduced several bills designed to outlaw using official federal patronage in elections and to prohibit these office-holders from utilizing their employment for political purposes. The Senate in 1935 had passed one bill, but had rejected several other proposals designed to reform civil service.[1]

A series of malpractices in the 1938 senatorial campaigns had sparked renewed interest on Capitol Hill in preventing corruption. Several New Deal liberals either seeking renomination or attempting to unseat conservative incumbents were accused of manipulating the WPA to enhance their prospects at the polls. In the Kentucky primary work relief authorities had solicited $24,000 in contributions from agency employees to help Democrat Barkley defeat Albert B. "Happy" Chandler. Party officials had raised these funds directly, with WPA personnel being canvassed to ascertain their party affiliations. In neighboring Tennessee WPA administrators had requested numerous donations from relief workers to help insure the triumph in the primary of New Dealer Stewart. Democratic senatorial aspirants also had benefited from political irregularities in the November election against Republican candidates. The Pennsylvania director had manipulated agency finances in a fruitless effort to help Governor George H. Earle unseat incumbent Senator Davis. Besides selling tickets to WPA workers at party gatherings, WPA administrators had ordered many Republican employees to change their registration to Democrat.

Senate Campaign Expenditures Committee disclosures in January, 1939, also had intensified the drive for reform. Under the direction of sixty-three-year-old Democrat Sheppard of Texas, the committee had upheld accusations that agency officials diverted relief funds towards political purposes in Kentucky, Tennessee, and Pennsylvania. On the other hand, they had spiked similar allegations concerning congressional races in Indiana, Maryland, Missouri, New Jersey, New York, and Ohio. In order to tighten the regulation of primary and general elections, the Sheppard committee had requested legislation prohibiting government officials from either soliciting or receiving contributions from relief workers and other federal employees. In addition, they had recommended denying agency administrators access to lists containing names of relief personnel.[2]

The report had a profound impact on the White House. Before committee findings were released, WPA boss Harry L. Hopkins had often warned state political officials not to coerce agency workers. By seeking to unseat the conservative Gillette of Iowa, however, Hopkins had encouraged state administrators to ignore national directives. In January, 1939, the Roosevelt administration insisted upon the punishment of WPA officials engaging in malpractices or pressuring relief employees. On January 5 Roosevelt urged "the imposition of rigid statutory regulations and penalties" to eliminate improper political activities in federal elections. The President did not propose specific ameliorative legislation, preferring to leave the details to Congress.[3]

Senator Hatch of New Mexico, an affable, quiet, tactful, and industrious forty-nine-year-older, seized the initiative in combatting political corruption. The son of a Kirwin, Kansas, hardware merchant, he had moved to Eldorado, Oklahoma, as a youth and dropped out of public school at age sixteen to work for his father. Hatch subsequently became a journalist for the weekly *Eldorado Courier* and was assigned to cover the county courthouse. Finding the lawyers very eloquent, he studied at Cumberland University to become one and joined a firm with Harry Patton and Sam G. Bratton in Clovis, New Mexico. Patton and Bratton already had developed a lucrative practice covering a substantial portion of the state and launched Hatch on a political career. Through their influence Hatch had become an assistant state attorney general and district judge. Hatch was appointed in 1933 to the U.S. Senate to fill the unexpired term of Bratton, who had resigned to become a circuit judge. An ardent New Dealer, the slender, 5-foot 9 inch, 150-pounder remained in the shadow of fellow Democrat Bronson M. Cutting and his successor Dennis Chavez. Once described as "a mild, drawling little man who walks as if he missed his horse," he could puncture a "windbag" so deftly that the victim would "think Hatch [had] done him a favor."[4]

Hatch had crusaded a long time for purifying politics. Rejecting the patronage system, he introduced in 1935 a bill to prohibit WPA contractors and other politicians from making campaign contributions. When colleagues assured him this abuse already was covered by the Corrupt Practices Act of 1925, he then shelved the plan. The Democratic National Committee, Hatch soon realized, still was obtaining gifts from persons and corporations working for the government. Donations were made in proportion to the size of the contract and were in the guise of advertisements in the party's $250 campaign book. In addition, maladministration of the WPA angered Hatch. Besides insisting upon a complete investigation, he in 1937 sought approval of a bill forbidding federal employees from attending party conventions. After disclosure of a scandal in the Kentucky gubernatorial race, Hatch had offered an unsuccessful amendment to the 1938 relief bill prohibiting the use of WPA funds for political purposes.

Hatch also was infuriated over malfeasance by the rival Chavez Democratic faction in New Mexico. In what *Time* described as "the hottest political scandal of the year," seventy-three WPA employees were indicted by an Albuquerque grand jury in October, 1938, for indulging in unethical practices. Former WPA state administrator Fred Healy and the son-in-law, sister, cousin, nephew, and secretary of Senator Chavez were accused of coercing agency relief workers. Although only five convictions resulted, the conscientious Hatch welcomed the opportunity to expose corruption in New Mexico politics and began framing legislation to eliminate such practices.[5]

In early January Hatch introduced the reform measure. Besides preventing the assessment or solicitation of funds from WPA employees, the legislation prohibited the removal of any personnel because of refusal to change political affiliation. Hatch also inserted the little-publicized section 9 preventing federal officials and workers from using their positions to interfere in presidential or congressional elections. Leaving enforcement to department heads, Hatch vowed to punish any violators with a $1,000 fine or one-year imprisonment. In seeking to limit control by federal officeholders or factions over state politics, he probably did not realize his measure merely would magnify the influence of local bosses, rural legislators, and labor unions.

Sheppard and Austin joined Hatch as co-sponsors. Sheppard, who chaired the increasingly important Military Affairs Committee, had supported the Roosevelt administration on most domestic measures until his investigation unearthed extensive WPA interference in the 1938 elections. Sheppard, who was expected by Hatch to rally southern Democrats behind the legislation, lauded the Hatch bill as a means of preventing coercion of WPA relief workers. Assistant Minority Leader Austin, ranking member of the Military Affairs Committee, was enlisted to garner Republican support for the measure. An anti–New Dealer, Austin endorsed the proposal mainly to limit the growth of the executive branch.

In marked contrast to other legislation, this bill saw no organized resistance develop initially. On April 13 senators spent only a few minutes considering one of the most important bills of the 1939 session and devoted only one page of the *Congressional Record* to the evaluation of the issues at stake. Few members either had read the entire text in advance or had realized the proposal challenged the power of President Roosevelt. New Dealers virtually ignored the far-reaching section 9, which banned most federal executive employees from interfering in national elections or actively participating in political campaigns. In addition, liberals made no attempt to refute the Sheppard committee findings concerning the WPA and state officials. Since the Senate acted so quickly, Austin remarked that no member even made "a disclosure of the revolting things that caused the introduction of the bill."

During debate one brief, lively exchange occurred. Democrat Edward R. Burke of Nebraska, an anti–New Dealer, insisted the measure merited fuller consideration and requested the sponsors to explain more fully the provisions and purposes. "It is an important measure," Burke asserted, "of far-reaching effect to our country; and while I favor it, I think there should be a brief explanation." In reply, Hatch retorted, "I took it to be the attitude of the Senate and of Senators generally that that was unnecessary at this time."[6] Without taking a roll call the Senate overwhelmingly shouted approval of the comprehensive proposal reforming primary and election practices.

Several considerations had influenced the hasty action. WPA scandals, coupled with the Sheppard committee disclosures, had made legislation striking at political corruption both very popular and timely. Few senators had understood the full implications of the entire bill and especially section 9. Playing the most instrumental role in the outcome, Hatch had steered the measure through the Senate unchanged without evoking any controversy. Above all, an overwhelming majority of Americans from both major parties had favored the curbing of political abuses. According to fifteen public opinion surveys conducted in 1938, Americans were convinced politics interfered with the handling of relief and demanded prompt congressional action in eliminating malpractices. Seventy-eight percent supported legislation prohibiting WPA workers from making political contributions, while 62 percent even recommended applying these restrictions to all federal government employees.[7]

Some New Dealers, however, soon regretted the hasty Senate action. Democrat Joseph F. Guffey of Pennsylvania, state party head embroiled in one of the 1938 WPA scandals, insisted within twenty-four hours that the upper chamber reconsider the bill. Attacking section 9, Guffey protested that policy-making officials would be denied active participation in either political management or campaigns and argued that the limitations would particularly hinder the maneuverability of the White House. In an attempt to alleviate Guffey's fears, Hatch denied section 9 was intended to include the President, cabinet members, congressmen, and other policy-making officials. "I am so confident," the New Mexico Democrat remarked, "that these extreme criticisms are unwarranted and altogether unfair that I would, if possible, be glad to argue before any court in the land and let a court decision be rendered as to just what was included in the original Section 9." Since that step might entail long delays, Hatch instead promised to draft a clarifying amendment for presentation in the House.[8]

Roosevelt administration officials privately harbored suspicions about section 9, although still backing the bill publicly. Publicity Director Charles Michelson confidentially accused anti–New Dealers on Capitol Hill of designing section 9 "to hit at the President himself," cabinet officials, and liberal legislators, and implored White House aides to "consider it very carefully before any action is taken by the President."[9] In a message to Congress on April 27 Roosevelt belatedly supported the Senate action. Attacking the enforcement mechanism, he insisted the Civil Service Commission should assume responsibility for punishing violators. "Such legislation," the chief executive reminded Congress, "was recommended in my message of Jan. 5, 1939, and has my hearty endorsement." In addition, the President claimed "enforcement would be simpler if the Congress would place such employees within the classified Civil Service."[10]

The House Judiciary Committee, to the dismay of Hatch, pigeonholed the measure for several weeks. Chairman Sumners, who denounced the legislation, deliberately procrastinated in summoning his committee.

In hopes of expediting action, Senator Hatch on May 31 visited the White House to seek more direct presidential intervention. Roosevelt, though, refused to oblige unless Hatch rewrote section 9 so that he, cabinet officials, senators, and representatives still could participate actively in political campaigns. Declining to bargain with the President, Hatch instead preferred to give verbal rather than written assurance about protection for these major officials.

Dogged persistence by Hatch broke the committee impasse. In late June the New Mexico Democrat threatened to attach his legislation as a rider to the annual relief appropriation bill. Fearing a rider might delay financing of relief agencies, Roosevelt quickly summoned Judiciary Committee members Emanuel Celler of New York and Healey of Massachusetts to the White House. The President urged Celler to use his influence as ranking majority member to summon the committee as soon as possible to consider the Hatch measure. In addition, Roosevelt still insisted the highest executive and legislative officials be exempted from the section 9 restrictions. In remarks to reporters afterwards Celler and Healey labeled the legislation as a step in the right direction and urged removal of "monstrosities" and "absurdities" in the controversial section 9.[11]

In an appearance before Healey's judiciary subcommittee, Hatch introduced a clarifying amendment. He urged retaining the substance of section 9 as passed by the Senate, but recommended exempting the president and vice president, members of Congress and their employees, the White House staff, and heads and assistant heads of the executive departments. Healey's subcommittee quickly adopted these changes, leading the New Mexico Democrat to believe the full Judiciary Committee would follow suit. "Congressman Healey," Hatch stated, "favored the legislation with the clarifying provision I had included. The action of his committee in reporting the proposed amendment convinced me that they really desired to enact the substance of Section 9, but only wanted to make certain that it did not apply to the persons exempted."[12]

The Judiciary Committee, to Hatch's chagrin, altered the measure drastically. Chairman Sumners influenced his colleagues to reject the Hatch amendments to section 9, thus reversing the subcommittee recommendations. Far exceeding the intentions of Hatch, the Judiciary Committee deleted the entire section prohibiting officers or employees from participating in political management or campaigns. Along with exempting the president, vice president, cabinet, and Congress, the Sumners version also permitted federal district attorneys, agency directors, and internal revenue and customs collectors to take an active role in political administration, electioneering, primaries, and conventions. The committee on

June 30 unanimously sent the legislation, which had been amended almost beyond recognition, to the House floor. "We labored," Celler remarked, "long and arduously on this bill. We had a rather peculiar bill from the Senate and we tried to straighten it out."[13]

The revised version infuriated Hatch. Besides accusing the committee of having "emasculated" the proposal, he insisted the deleted portion "was the life and substance of Section 9. With it stricken, the entire section might just as well be omitted from the bill."[14] Exempting all policy-making officials and employees, the New Mexico Democrat charged, was "absurd, monstrous, idiotic, and asinine." Under no circumstances, Hatch argued, would federal district attorneys, WPA officials, and internal revenue collectors be permitted to operate as convention delegates, political campaign managers, or campaign speakers.

Hatch moved quickly to remedy the situation. In a letter to the White House he urged the President to endorse unconditionally his version rather than the Judiciary Committee measure. The New Mexico Democrat wrote Roosevelt:

Knowing your record of opposition to "bossism" and machine control of party politics, and believing these reforms to be in keeping with the principles of our party, I have hoped that your influence could be thrown behind the bill in its entirety, and that you and our party might have credit for a very substantial improvement of party and political affairs. I shall continue to hope that this may be accomplished at this session.[15]

Despite this plea, Roosevelt elected to remain on the sidelines in the House battle.

Hatch also began redrafting section 9 as an amendment for Democrat Dempsey to introduce on the House floor. Seeking to restore most of the original version, he proposed that the president, vice president, cabinet, and other policy-making executives be the only personnel excluded from section 9 restrictions. In addition, any officials determining American foreign policy or administering federal laws also would receive exemptions. Through his amendment, Hatch wished "to make it clear that real policy-making officials are not included" among the personnel subject to section 9 limitations. All other executive employees, including federal district attorneys, agency heads, marshals, and postmasters, could no longer use their positions to influence presidential and congressional elections or take an active role in either political management or campaigns. All references to the legislative branch and its workers were deleted.[16]

On July 20 representatives spent thirteen hours debating the Hatch bill. Journalists, commentators, and interested spectators watched the bipartisan conservative coalition clash with the New Dealers. Anti–New Dealers favored restoration of the stricter Senate version so that tighte controls would govern executive officials and administrators. Sixty-year old Dempsey of New Mexico led the battle seeking reinstatement of the original bill. A native of White Haven, Pennsylvania, he had attended grade schools and then began working at age thirteen as a water boy for a railroad contracting crew. After being employed as a telegrapher he became vice president of the Brooklyn, New York, Rapid Transit Company. He was indicted on charges of second degree manslaughter in 1918 when a Brooklyn subway tunnel wreck killed ninety-seven persons and injured one hundred others. Following acquittal by the New York State Supreme Court, Dempsey had moved to Oklahoma to become presiden of the Continental Oil and Asphalt Company. He then settled in Sant Fe, New Mexico, where he was an independent oil operator and assume the presidency of the United States Asphalt Company. During the early New Deal he directed state operations concerning the National Recover Administration, the Federal Housing Administration, and the Nationa Emergency Council. Joining the U.S. House of Representatives in 1935 he had vacillated on New Deal issues and belonged to the highly publicize Un-American Activities Committee. A close friend of Senator Hatch he directed House strategy for campaign reform and was aided by Repub lican Clarence E. Hancock of New York. New Dealers, on the other hand hoped either to prevent floor action on the Hatch measure or to attacl several restrictive amendments. Democrat Claude Parsons of Illinoi managed the campaign for the opposition camp and was assisted b Celler. Celler, 51-year-old ranking member of the Judiciary Com mittee, feared that the Hatch measure might restrict too many politica activities.

Judicial considerations prevailed among the Parsons forces. Restrict ing the right of administrative federal officials to express opinions o political subjects, they argued, violated the First Amendment right c free speech. In addition, the opposition camp charged that denying goverr ment officials the right to engage in politics deprived them of full citizer ship and violated the due process clause of the Fifth Amendment. A Democrat Frank H. Buck of California contended, the measure wen "far beyond what Congress should enact in the way of limiting free speec and the inherent rights of the American citizen's political activity."[1] Furthermore, the Parsons faction denounced the proposal as an undemc cratic move contravening American traditions. Assistant Democrati Whip Lex Green remarked, "This bill is conceived of everything whic is inimical to democratic success and democratic government."[18]

Political considerations likewise were paramount to the oppositio camp. The conservative coalition, ardent New Dealers charged, favored the bill to retaliate against the growing power of the executive branch. Democrat Kent Keller of Illinois asserted the legislation was motivated by "hatred and fear of Frank Roosevelt," while House Labor Committee head Mary T. Norton of New Jersey warned the President the measure was "gotten up to destroy you."[19] Besides alleging that the bill would weaken the party system, the opposition protested that it restricted the right of party members to attend political functions and discouraged campaign contributions. Parsons feared the proposal would bring "the demise of political parties in this country," while Celler tersely remarked, "The bill hurts my party. It goes too far." At the same time, the Parsons forces claimed the 1938 WPA scandals were exaggerated and denied Congress should interfere in state factional squabbles. Charging Hatch with seeking merely to purify New Mexico politics, they argued that the states concerned should settle their own internal problems. "I can see no reason," Democrat Charles I. Faddis of Pennsylvania stated, "why the Congress should have been required to wash the dirty linen of the New Mexico political set-up."[20]

In defending the measure the Dempsey camp relied mainly on moral and political themes interspersed with historical references. Vivid accounts of the WPA scandals, including those in Kentucky, Tennessee, Pennsylvania, and New Mexico, were presented. "There has been going on throughout the length and breadth of this country," Kansas Republican Edward H. Rees charged, "a system of racketeering that is incomprehensible and indefensible." According to the Dempsey forces, the Hatch measure would take considerable strides towards eliminating political graft, corruption, and coercion of WPA workers. "This bill with teeth in it," Republican Fish retorted, "is directed at all political ghouls and vampires who exploit the needy and obtain funds of those on relief."[21] The Dempsey wing also maintained that the legislation was based on civil service rules operating for over one-half century. A former philosophy professor, Democrat Thomas V. Smith of Illinois praised the proposal as "a stroke in the right direction. It will have to be followed up very carefully and very assiduously before it does much (sic) revolutionary." The Dempsey camp also denied that the Hatch measure would unduly restrict the freedom of individuals to express political opinions. Sweeney insisted that the legislation "does not repeal or change in any particular the La Follette Anti-Gag law, which gives you the right to speak on any public questions."[22]

During the thirteen-hour session the Dempsey forces overpowered the Parsons camp. In a move to restore the controversial section 9, the House shouted down the Judiciary Committee version. Representatives solidly approved by 165-55 teller vote a far-reaching amendment by Hancock extending restrictions upon political activity to include primaries and national conventions. Since his side was in firm control, Dempsey seized the opportunity to introduce the Hatch amendment restoring much of section 9. This amendment specifically prohibited all executive officials, except the president, vice president, cabinet, and policy-making officials, from participating actively in primaries and elections.

The Parsons forces, meanwhile, remained on the defensive. Parsons insisted a roll call vote be taken on the Dempsey proposal, but this strategy backfired. Since only sixty-five members supported the Parsons approach, the Illinois Democrat fell considerably short of the 20 percent figure required to force a roll call. In another setback for the Parsons camp, the House decisively approved by a 243-117 teller margin the Dempsey amendment reviving much of the original section 9. Healey moved to recommit the altered bill to the Judiciary Committee, but congressmen solidly rejected (232-146) this attempt to block final floor action. With the midnight hour rapidly approaching, the weary representatives wholeheartedly endorsed (241-134) the modified comprehensive reform measure.[23]

On the final roll call bipartisan conservatives overwhelmed the New Dealers. Although Democrats leaned against the Hatch bill, nearly 40 percent bolted from Majority Leader Rayburn, preventing Roosevelt's party from exercising its vast numerical superiority. Republicans solidly favored this tougher measure and aligned with the rebellious Democrats to override the Parsons wing. As Republican Vorys summed up, "a great deal of pressure was brought by the New Deal forces to defeat the original purpose of the bill. . . . However, Republicans, with the help of some patriotic Democrats, were able to secure the bill's passage."[24] Since six of the eight regional delegations failed to achieve 75 percent unity, geography this time played a very subordinate role. New England members, who cooperated more than any other section, directed the campaign for the Dempsey forces and allied closely with midwestern congressmen. Middle Atlantic, southern, and border state representatives also supported the Hatch measure. Although Dempsey came from New Mexico, westerners provided the core of resistance to the political reform bill.

Politically and sectionally, alignments contrasted sharply with reorganization patterns. Partisanship continued to play a dominant role, but declined in importance on the Hatch measure because Democrats were so divided this time. Republicans supported campaign reform as zealously as they had protested executive reorganization, but were far more effective than earlier. New England and midwestern delegations approved of the Hatch measure to a much greater extent than they had approved reorganization, while southern and border congressmen exhibited the opposite pattern. On the whole, the conservative coalition acted more consistently than New Dealers on the two questions. New England representatives conducted the anti-Roosevelt forces on both reorganization and campaign reform, relying heavily in both instances on midwesterners. In the liberal camp southern and border members stood at the forefront on reorganization, and westerners assumed this role on the Hatch measure.

Dempsey's forces had prevailed in the House. Conservatives had outlawed pernicious political activity by federal district attorneys, agency heads, marshals, and postmasters, and had extended restrictions beyond elections to include primaries and nominating conventions. Anti-New Dealers had prohibited both the intimidation of WPA workers at the polls and the granting of favors for either party activity or voting pledges. In other setbacks for liberals, representatives retained sections outlawing solicited contributions from relief workers, use of agency employee names for political purposes, and designation of WPA funds to interfere with elections. On the other hand, New Dealers found limited consolation in the exemption of the president, vice president, cabinet, and Congress and in weak enforcement apparatus.

Numerous forces had swung the momentum in the House towards campaign reform. Dempsey played a more dynamic role than any other congressman, cooperating closely with Hatch and serving as chief spokesman for the bill on the House floor. Wielding substantial authority once again, the bipartisan coalition of Republicans and conservative Democrats had continually triumphed over the liberal wing. Sectionally, northeastern and midwestern representatives had exhibited more power than the usually influential southern Democrats. Above all, the American public demanded reform of the existing political system so as to avert a repetition of the notorious WPA scandals.

Conservatives, meanwhile, sought quick Senate approval of the revised bill without floor debate. When Hatch called up the House version for concurrence the next day, he received hearty cooperation from Vice President Garner. A long-time critic of the WPA, the sly Garner quickly banged the gavel and uttered, "Without objection, it is so ordered." Majority Whip Minton, who was infuriated with these tactics, moved instead that the Senate send the amended measure to a conference committee. Hatch then stared at Minton and accused the liberals of making "many unwarranted, unfair, unjust and unreasonable criticisms." Besides claiming that the House had "made it better legislation," Hatch contended a conference committee might kill the measure. "Let there be no hiding place," the New Mexico Democrat maintained, "behind pious intentions that we favor the bill and then send it to conference to die." Since the New

Dealers lacked the numerical forces to sustain resistance, Minton quickly dropped his motion. "I have no intention," he insisted, "to knife my friend in the back. So far as I am concerned, the Senator may have his bill and God bless him."[25] After resistance by liberals had subsided, the Senate unanimously approved the House amendments and sent the legislation to the White House.

Roosevelt was placed under considerable pressure from liberals to veto the measure. Following the House action, fourteen angry Democratic senators and representatives sent letters or telegrams to the White House denouncing the bill in such terms as "outrageous" and "vicious."[26] These irate Democrats, who represented a broad geographical spectrum, argued the legislation would infringe upon individual constitutional liberties and would be detrimental to the administration party. "In the name of protecting civil rights of the citizens," Cox claimed, "Congress by this act, violates them." "I feel so badly over the political demonstration," Representative Guy L. Moser of Pennsylvania remarked, "with such deep feeling of resentment as an old fashioned dyed-in-the-wool Democrat."[27] Furthermore, several Democrats insisted the Hatch forces lacked the numbers to override a presidential rejection. Celler, who had canvassed party members, argued "a veto of the Hatch bill would be sustained beyond question," while Faddis assured the President "the bill can never be passed over your veto."[28]

In response, the President even drafted a veto message. Roosevelt refused to delegate enforcement powers to department heads, who still might order their employees to participate actively in election campaigns. Restricting political involvement by federal officials, he warned, merely would increase the influence of state and municipal machines over the political process. Backers of state and local political machines, the President protested, "already greatly outnumber the federal officeholders" and give priority to "local rather than national" considerations.[29]

Attorney General Frank Murphy and Senator Hatch, however, both prevailed upon the President to sign the measure. Murphy conceded the bill was "open to a good many political objections," singling out those sections prohibiting federal employees from either preparing or delivering speeches and from engaging in other campaign activities. On the other hand, Murphy feared a veto might encourage Congress to charge the Roosevelt administration with politicizing relief and deliberately subordinating the importance of the WPA scandals. "I doubt the advisability," Murphy counseled the President, "to veto or, if the Bill is signed, of any statement." Murphy advised Roosevelt to approve the measure quietly, thus conveying to Congress that he had reservations about the legislation.[30] In a letter to Roosevelt on July 28, Hatch stressed that federal employees still could attend Jackson Day dinners, make voluntary political contributions, and engage in all other campaign activities except delivering campaign speeches. The legislative branch, he claimed, merely intended "to make exactly the same rules which now apply to employees under the classified service applicable to those in the non-classified service."[31]

On August 2 the President reluctantly signed the comprehensive Hatch bill. Roosevelt issued a brief statement supporting campaign reform and gave assurance that the measure would not infringe upon individual liberties. "I have striven in public life and in private life," the President stated, "for decency in political campaigns. I regard this new legislation as at least a step in the right direction." Besides cautioning judges not to make the bill a "gag" act, Roosevelt insisted federal employees should retain the freedom to speak publicly on party issues and candidates, to make voluntary contributions, and to attend political meetings. Congress, he urged, should expand the scope to include state and local government workers, who outnumbered national jobholders by nearly 4 to 1 and who were "vastly more influential in determining the results of both federal and state elections."[32]

Following the August adjournment of Congress, Hatch drafted an amendment broadening the range of the original measure. He proposed prohibiting pernicious political activity by 300,000 state employees paid wholly or partially from federal funds. Since the President had protested granting enforcement authority to departmental heads, Hatch instead empowered the Civil Service Commission to define illegal campaign action and investigate alleged violations. Any non-elected, non-policy-making state administrative official found interfering with national elections would be fined $1,000 and be imprisoned for one year. On January 8 Hatch introduced the amendment and argued that failure to widen the original act would signify that the legislative branch had "decided to go back to the spoils system."[33]

Roosevelt, along with the American people, welcomed the amendment. At a press conference on March 5 he heartily endorsed extending the initial terms to include workers partially paid by the federal government. In addition, the President lauded the section stripping departmental directors of enforcement authority and designating the Civil Service Commission instead as overseers. A Gallup poll in late February showed 77 percent of Americans favored extending the 1939 act to include state employees.[34]

Democrats directed the spirited floor debate for the respective sides. Between March 4 and March 18 senators filled around 300 pages of the *Congressional Record* arguing over the Hatch amendment and devoted more time in 1940 to this measure than to any other legislative issue except selective service. Complex floor maneuvering and eighteen roll calls awaited the media and interested spectators, who crowded galleries throughout the tense, two-week period. Hatch led the drive to regulate state and municipal employees, assisted by Majority Leader Barkley and Chandler of Kentucky. Unlikely candidates for helping direct campaign reform measures, they had been bitter rivals in the scandal-tainted 1938 senatorial primary. Although opposing the 1939 measure, Barkley supported the Hatch amendment this time because President Roosevelt wholeheartedly backed the legislation. Democrat Scott W. Lucas of Illinois conducted the campaign against extension of the Hatch Act and was aided by Majority Whip Minton and Pepper. Lucas, although an ardent supporter of New Deal agricultural and labor legislation, frequently placed principle above political party loyalty. Minton and Pepper disagreed sharply with the Roosevelt administration this time and were formidable foes for the Hatch camp.

Reformers defended the measure mainly on moral grounds. Above all, they argued the amendment would help to eliminate the manipulation and coercion of federally funded agency employees. "Extorting money from employees for corrupt political purposes," Democrat Matthew M. Neely of West Virginia protested, "is one of the most indefensible outrages of modern times."[35] "The real purpose of the law," Democrat O'Mahoney contended, "was to prevent the use of government office for purely partisan purposes. As long as a public official discharges his official duties in a perfectly impartial manner and refrains from active leadership in political campaigns, he is within the law." The Hatch forces insisted federally funded state jobholders should be compelled to follow the same regulations as federal workers. "I do not think it is fair," Barkley remarked, "to tie every Federal employee to a tree and allow every State employee who draws his pay from Washington to roam at large over the wood lot, play politics," and "exercise his influence."[36]

Historical and constitutional arguments were made by the reformers. Denying allegations that the legislation was revolutionary, they argued that the measure followed traditional merit system guidelines and noted that the Civil Service Commission since 1887 had imposed similar regulations upon classified workers. Hatch had used "exactly the same language which now applies to thousands and thousands of employees under civil service," while Chandler indicated, "I would much prefer to deal with the Civil Service Commission or some unbiased, non-partisan, honest agency that undertook to decide on the merits." In addition, the Hatch forces denied extension of the 1939 act would infringe upon the individual liberties of federally funded employees. "We could have drafted a more drastic bill," Hatch claimed, "and still have been within the Constitution."[37]

Political ramifications of the amendment, meanwhile, upset opponents. Besides warning that the measure would hurt their party, New Deal Democrats favored far less punitive legislation. Senator Guffey predicted, "This is going to be the most destructive piece of legislation for the two party system of government—in which I am a firm believer—that has ever been put on the legislative books of our country," while Minton accused Republicans of seeking to "hatchet the Democratic Party out of Washington."[38] Since Republicans did not occupy the White House or control Congress, the Lucas camp charged they sought to limit the influence of the Democrats by supporting the Hatch bill. "When the Republicans get into power," Pittman asserted, "they won't permit anything like the Hatch Act to break up their organization."[39] The Hatch measure, opponents objected, made states the pawns of the highly centralized federal bureaucracy. "Our State," Bailey of North Carolina affirmed, "is fully competent to attend to its business. . . . I do not intend to turn our State over to a crowd of politicians from the North and West." "This is," Pepper asserted, "the most monstrous effort to extend the Federal power, the most outrageous attempt to impose the Federal will upon every beneficiary of the Federal bounty, which to my knowledge has ever been proposed in the American Congress."[40]

The Lucas faction also denounced the measure as discriminatory. The Hatch amendment, opponents maintained, favored major policy-making officials at the expense of less prestigious state workers. Miller of Arkansas protested that the legislation unfairly exempted department heads and deputies from restrictions upon political activities. "Yet the man who pushes the wheelbarrow," Miller pointed out, "the engineer, the janitor, the clerk, the stenographer, and others, can only vote, they must not open their mouths, they must not exercise their rights of citizenship." Although the bill eliminated minor campaign abuses, the Lucas forces contended it would not eliminate larger violations by wealthier contributors. Democrats particularly resented the enormous donations made by the Pews, DuPonts, Rockefellers, and other prominent families to Republican candidates. Bankhead angrily queried, "Are we to permit the big fellows like Pew, the DuPonts, and others to continue to make great contributions to political campaigns and to political committees . . . , to flood the country with advertising, to put speakers on national radio chains and local stations without limit, to engage in all the pernicious activities which the use of money in elections can make possible?" "Until we effectively restrain or control huge contributions by beneficiaries of certain policies," Herring declared, "I am not in favor of restricting the average citizen from expressing his opinion as to the principles, party, or candidate which he believes is best for his own and his country's interest." Herring claimed that "we have already gone too far in invading the right to political expression of the citizens in the states."[41]

Judicial considerations also prompted the Lucas forces to attack the measure. The Hatch amendment, they warned, would infringe unduly upon freedom of speech and other liberties guaranteed in the Bill of Rights. Alarmed by the legal ramifications of the bill, Lucas argued, "We are invading the right of an American citizen to participate freely and openly in the election of men to public office." In a similar vein they complained that the proposal granted excessive legislative and judicial authority to the Civil Service Commission and invaded states' rights. "I do not think that we have the right," McKellar asserted, "to turn over to the Civil Service Commission or to any other Commission the right to legislate." Herring disapproved of "placing in the hands of a little commission of bureaucrats here in Washington the power to determine what is punishable as pernicious political activity" and protested that the legislation "proposes to dictate to the states their behavior."[42]

Shortly after floor debate began, Democrats feuded over strategy. Since approximately two-thirds of Roosevelt's party opposed extending the 1939 act, Minton insisted Barkley call a caucus binding all members to support the position taken by the majority. Fearful the Lucas camp would control a caucus, Barkley rejected Minton's plea and threatened to resign if the opposition forced the issue. Barkley maintained, "When I must stifle my views . . . because I happen to be majority leader of the Senate, I will call a conference of the Democratic members of the Senate and tender my resignation as majority leader." "For seven years," he recalled, "we have never found need to call a caucus on a major piece of legislation, and I would not call one on a simple bill to put a little purity into politics."[43] The Minton faction, tempered by Barkley's candid comments, dropped their demand for a caucus and spared the majority leader from resigning.

Democratic dissenters instead revived the filibuster, a tactic effectively used on other issues. Since they could not defeat the amendment outright, Lucas, Minton, Pepper, and around three dozen other Democrats monopolized floor debate beginning March 9 to prevent a final vote. "Every damn Republican in the Senate," the flamboyant Bilbo remarked, "is joining with the few Democrats and it looks now like they will pass the bill." On March 9 Josh Lee of Oklahoma filled 11 pages of the *Congressional Record* with an impassioned plea for more assistance to farmers.[44] Richard B. Russell of Georgia two days later moved that the Senate begin consideration of the Agriculture Appropriations measure, but the diversionary proposal was rejected by nine votes. Continuing the filibuster, Minton, Wagner of New York, and other opponents gave lengthy speeches either denouncing the amendments or digressing on unrelated topics. "I know they are for the Hatch Act," Minton charged, "because they have fights in their States with the Governor or the road commissioner who might run against them."[45]

For several days Hatch forces could not break the impasse. On March 11 and 14 Lucas, Minton, and other opponents shouted down attempts by Barkley to halt the stalling tactics. Hatch angrily retorted, "It seems as if they are using every conceivable means to block a vote on the measure." "I am perfectly confident," he contended, "that we have debated the bill from every angle, and that Senators have made up their minds how they will vote."[46] In a similar vein Austin of Vermont commented, "They claim that this is not a filibuster! It has all the disagreeable features of one without benefit of legs to take them to the goal. We are numb with the impact of sound." As one participant in the stalling strategy remarked, opponents still intended "to filibuster the Hell out of the Hatch bill."[47]

Republicans, meanwhile, rarely joined the debate. Utilizing a strategy of divide and conquer, Minority Leader McNary preferred to let Democrats battle among themselves and concentrated on rounding up solid Republican support for the Hatch amendment. Behind the scenes Republicans criticized the New Deal Democrats for resorting to filibuster tactics. The opposition Lucas camp resented that members of their party were cooperating with Republicans in favoring the legislation. Bailey noted, "Unfortunately, while the Republicans see its significance and rejoice to support it, many Democrats are beguiled into thinking it is a clean politics bill."[48] In addition, the Lucas forces warned Republicans the Democratic infighting would not extend to other issues. "Just because I happen to be on the other side of (sic) my leader in this fight," Minton explained, "doesn't mean we won't be together on the vital issues. We'll be fighting for those things the New Deal is interested in."[49]

The filibuster subsided in mid-March. Besides facing mounting pressure from the irate Hatch forces to halt the delaying tactics, the Lucas forces did not receive any cooperation from Roosevelt. In hopes of prolonging the filibuster, Minton on March 13 lunched with the President at the White House and urged him to cease supporting the Hatch amendment. State political machines, backed by workers benefiting from patronage, he argued, were preferable to party organizations dominated by wealthy individuals. Roosevelt, though, still insisted upon applying restrictions for both federal and state officials. Upon leaving the White House Minton conceded to reporters that his faction would lose the floor battle and denied charges his camp was engaging in a filibuster.[50] Within 48 hours the Senate began acting on amendments.

Dissident Democrats made numerous attempts to weaken the measure with amendments. On March 5 Miller proposed the removal of restrictions on political activity of state jobholders beneath the rank of policy makers so that they could enjoy the same privileges accorded to governors and other elected officials. Miller labeled the Hatch version as "the most pernicious provision found in any statute I have ever seen" because the bill "exempted the policy formers, the bureaucrats, the men in Washington."[51] By a narrow 44–41 margin the Hatch camp succeeded in rejecting the Miller motion.

Politics played a more influential role than sectionalism in the outcome. With the exception of J. Chandler Gurney of South Dakota, minority Republicans aligned with twenty-two Democrats to reject the Miller proposal. Around two-thirds of the Democrats supported the Miller amendment, but widespread defections within the party destroyed any existing numerical advantage. Third parties played a major role because a shift of votes by two of the three senators would have reversed the outcome. The Pacific, New England, and southern delegations registered over 80 percent solidarity, while all other regional blocs were divided sharply. New England and Pacific members led the resistance to the Miller motion, assisted by midwestern and Middle Atlantic senators. Miller rallied the most enthusiastic backing for his plan from southern colleagues, who allied with mountain and border state Democrats. Despite holding enormous numerical power, the southerners could not overcome the formidable northeastern-midwestern combination.

Between March 8 and 13 the Minton forces suffered more setbacks. Democrats Francis T. Maloney of Connecticut, Prentiss M. Brown of Michigan, and Bankhead introduced amendments designed to weaken the Hatch measure. These senators proposed allowing relief workers to attend party meetings and deliver campaign speeches, prohibiting very wealthy corporation stockholders from indulging in political activities or making contributions, and limiting campaign donations by any person or corporation to $1,000 annually. The Hatch forces easily defeated each amendment, never allowing the Lucas faction more than thirty-six votes.

Dogged persistence, though, eventually paid dividends for the indefatigable Lucas camp. Bankhead introduced a controversial amendment limiting contributions by any person or corporation to $5,000 and punishing violators with $5,000 fines and five-year prison terms. In the first major setback for the Hatch coalition, the Senate narrowly approved (40–38) the Bankhead proposal, significantly changing the complexion of the campaign reform measure. Shipstead temporarily jolted the Lucas forces by switching his vote to produce a 39–39 deadlock, but O'Mahoney countered the move, rescuing the Bankhead proposal.[52]

Political considerations easily overshadowed sectionalism this time. Although still divided sharply, Democrats cooperated slightly more on this roll call to enable adoption of the Bankhead amendment. Three influential Democrats, including Education and Labor Committee Chairman Thomas, purge target Tydings, and Interstate Commerce Committee head Wheeler, deserted the Hatch camp and joined the majority segment of their party. Farmer-Laborite Lundeen and Progessive LaFollette supported the Bankhead motion, giving third parties the balance of power. With the exception of Frazier of North Dakota, Republicans rejected limiting political contributions. Two sections registered at least 75 percent co-operation, but the remaining six blocs split sharply over limiting campaign expenditures. Southerners continued to lead the fight for the Lucas forces, aligning again with mountain members to help provide the slim margin for Bankhead. On the losing side, the New England delegation unani-mously repudiated the amendment and aligned with Pacific and Middle Atlantic colleagues.

The Lucas forces, however, found their victory short-lived. By a deci-sive 52–31 margin, the Senate the next day rejected an attempt by Lucas to recommit the bill. Lucas insisted the Privileges and Elections Committee study the constitutionality of granting the executive Civil Service Com-mission legislative and judicial authority. Republicans unanimously op-posed recommittal and combined with nearly one-half of the Democratic members to thwart the Lucas motion. "Our Republicans," Assistant Minority Leader Austin boasted, "have hung together better than before during my experience here."[53] As on previous roll calls, New Englanders stood at the forefront of the Hatch coalition and continued to receive strong backing from Pacific and Great Plains members. Although numerically powerful most of the time, southerners found few allies in seeking to recommit the measure.

The recommittal motion produced a spirited clash between floor managers Hatch and Lucas. In an attempt to downplay the significance of the Lucas amendment, Hatch claimed section 15 defining Civil Service Commission powers "has never been, to me, an important part of the bill." Lucas responded by challenging Hatch to accept a compromise solution. "If he will send the bill back to the committee and bring back Section 15 in line with what the majority of members believe is constitutional," Lucas pledged, "I will vote for the bill." Spurning this offer, Hatch re-torted, "That is too high a price to pay for Section 15" and protested that "the undoubted effect would be to kill the bill." Hatch lamented, "Almost every move that is possible to be made to kill the bill has been made against this bill. We would get no legislation, and that is what is wanted."[54]

Hatch forces continued to prevail on remaining votes. By a decisive 47-30 tally, the Senate approved a Hatch amendment preventing state employees from engaging in pernicious political activities already denied to national workers. In addition, they also accepted 42-34 another proposal by the New Mexico Democrat applying Civil Service restrictions to all federally owned state jobholders. On March 18 the Hatch measure was adopted by a commanding 52-28 margin.

A broader political and sectional consensus developed on the final vote. Despite being sharply divided, a majority of Democrats joined a solid Republican phalanx to insure a smooth pathway for campaign reform. Sectionally, five of eight blocs registered at least 70 percent cooperation. As on earlier roll calls, New England, Pacific, and Great Plains delegations formed the nucleus of the Hatch forces. Mountain and border members joined the bipartisan coalition this time, turning the outcome into a rout. On this tally the Hatch camp even attracted limited backing from southerners.

Political and sectional patterns differed markedly from the reorganization issue. Since Democrats were disunited, politics assumed a less dominant role on the Hatch measure. Republicans, who followed McNary's leadership quite closely, solidified their ranks slightly on campaign reform. On the two issues regional alignments differed strikingly. New England, border, and mountain senators supported executive reorganization to a much greater extent than political reform, while southern, Pacific, and midwestern members responded in opposite fashion. Leadership, though, fluctuated little on the two issues. Southerners usually directed the New Deal forces, while New Englanders consistently conducted the bipartisan coalition. The border and mountain blocs had played prominent supportive roles in the reorganization matter, but the Great Plains and Pacific delegations performed this function on the Hatch bill.

Campaign reform had survived a very formidable challenge. Republican solidarity, as reflected in the New England-Midwestern alliance, had helped guide the controversial legislation to ultimate victory. In seeking tighter restrictions on political activity, Hatch had contributed more than any other individual to the triumph of campaign reform. Besides spearheading the drive to extend the 1939 act, he had labored diligently in the Privileges and Elections Committee, managed floor strategy, and defended the amendment in debates. "Senator Hatch," a Kansas representative acknowledged, "is to be especially commended for the fight he has made for this bill."[55] Majority Leader Barkley had resisted attempts by party insurgents to force a caucus and had participated much more than usual in floor debates. In addition, public opinion had solidly favored regulating the political involvement of nationally funded state employees.

Congressional reaction to the Senate outcome varied. Representatives disagreed sharply over the extent of damage inflicted by the Lucas faction to the measure. Despite the formidable opposition Republican Clifford R. Hope of Kansas contended the senators had not attached "any particularly bad amendments." On the other hand, Democrat Lyle H. Boren of Oklahoma argued, "The original bill has been so emasculated by amendments that the original is hardly recognizable."[56] If the bill had not had moral overtones, senators would have opposed the legislation. "This measure," admitted Hiram Johnson, "leaves me rather cold. It is one of that sort that is honored more in the breach than in the observance, but it presents a moral issue, and long ago, I learned that even though only presented as a moral issue, it is the duty of one who passes upon it to favor it." The Senate, according to opponents of the Hatch amendment, had loosened the restrictions contained in the original version. Besides boasting, "We have done a good job of crippling it," Bailey remarked, "I do not think this bill will get through the Congress."[57]

From the outset House Democratic leaders achieved much stronger party loyalty. Speaker Bankhead and Majority Leader Rayburn, who both rejected any extension of the 1939 measure, avoided the type of bickering experienced by Barkley and Minton and quietly averted participating in the House battle. Since Roosevelt already had endorsed the measure publicly, Bankhead and Rayburn refused to pressure Democratic representatives to reject the Senate version. "I certainly cannot tell the Judiciary Committee," Bankhead told reporters on March 18, "what to do. I am opposed to it, but despite that the committee may report it."[58]

House Judiciary Committee Chairman Sumners sought to block further congressional action on the Hatch measure. Inasmuch as the legislation infringed upon states rights, he did not summon his committee for nearly a month and then quickly disposed of the bill. At one meeting in early May Sumners handed committee members little pieces of paper marked with the words "Yes" and "No" and asked each member to indicate if they favored tabling the measure. After collecting the ballots in his Stetson hat, he announced 14 of 24 congressmen favored postponing the matter indefinitely. Thirteen of the committee members later claimed they had voted to send the bill to the House floor, indicating Sumners may not have counted the votes accurately.[59]

Dempsey, who was upset over the Sumners straw poll, quickly sought to revive the measure. "I recognize," Dempsey admitted, "that there are members of the House against this bill and that some members would like to see it scuttled in committee. But the country is for the bill." The New Mexico Democrat posted on Speaker Bankhead's desk a petition to discharge the bill from the Judiciary Committee. "This," he assured reporters, "is not an ordinary petition. It is rather a bill of honor showing the people of this nation who are for clean politics."[60] By May 7 Dempsey secured 123 of the requisite 218 names on the petition and received direct assistance from the White House.

On May 6 Roosevelt wholeheartedly endorsed the controversial legislation. Welcoming this intervention, Dempsey argued the committee would extend the Hatch Act and predicted Democratic resistance would weaken. "It seems to me," Dempsey concluded, "that the President's public demand for passage of the bill clinches the case for us. Those Democrats who have claimed that the bill was being used by Republicans to harrass them politically ought now to apologize."[61]

The discharge petition, coupled with Roosevelt's statement, encouraged a Judiciary Committee rebellion against Sumners. By a 14-11 margin on May 7, a bipartisan coalition transcending sectional lines forced the committee to reconsider the legislation. Seven Democrats, led by Celler and Healey, aligned with a like number of Republicans to revive the Hatch amendment. Although three Republicans opposed reopening the question, Democrats furnished the principal resistance. Northeastern and midwestern committee members supplied the nucleus of representatives rescuing the legislation, while southern and border congressmen still preferred postponing the amendment indefinitely.

During the next three weeks the House Judiciary Committee attached four major amendments sponsored by Democrat Francis E. Walter of Pennsylvania. One proposal limited annual spending by national party committees to $3 million, at least 50 percent less than the amount used up by either Republicans or Democrats in the 1936 elections. In addition, the committee broadened coverage to include officials and employees of of state educational, religious, and philanthropic institutions receiving federal assistance and prevented nationally funded employees from taking leaves of absence to seek elective office. The effective date for implementing the measure also was changed to October 1, so the measure would not apply to the 1940 primaries.

Sumners suffered other setbacks in committee deliberations. Republican Albert L. Vreeland of New Jersey steered through twin proposals limiting political contributions by social, economic, and labor organizations to $5,000 and stripping parties of authority to issue and sell campaign books. During the 1936 presidential election Democrats had raised substantial sums through selling campaign books. During the middle of May the committee twice rejected motions by Democrat Edward W. Creal of Kentucky to table the measure.

Despite the continued opposition of Chairman Sumners, the Judiciary Committee on May 29 easily approved (16-8) sending the campaign reform measure to the House floor. Republicans Chauncey W. Reed, Louis E. Graham of Pennsylvania, and Vreeland, who had favored tabling the question earlier, joined the group seeking House action. Although Democrats controlled the committee, they divided very sharply on the bill. Of the 14 Democrats, 6 rebelled against Chairman Sumners and aligned instead with all 10 Republicans to report the legislation. Northeasterners directed the drive for sending the measure to the House floor and were assisted by midwestern colleagues. A more homogeneous group politically and sectionally, opponents belonged to the Democratic Party and came from southern states.[62]

Buoyed by the committee action, Dempsey reentered the scene. The New Mexico Democrat, along with Abe Murdock of Utah, persuaded the Rules Committee on June 6 to permit the House to consider the Hatch measure. The legislation, Dempsey told committee members, signified "a new bill of rights for Federal employees." Floor debate was limited to four hours, divided equally between the two sides, and a five-minute restriction was placed on each amendment. In letters to signers of the earlier discharge petition a month later, Dempsey urged their continued backing of the amended Hatch bill. Besides praising these signers for playing "a vital part in support of this legislation," he requested their presence on July 9 for the beginning of floor debate. "There are," Dempsey stressed, "some extremely important amendments to be offered. Your further support at this time is vitally necessary."[63]

On July 9 and 10 congressmen considered the controversial measure. Before crowded galleries and anxious reporters representatives filled the *Congressional Record* with the colorful language reminiscent of the 1939 debate. Dempsey again managed floor strategy for extending the amendment and delivered several timely speeches. Judiciary Committee member Hancock played a valuable supporting role, often joining floor discussions and rallying solid Republican backing. Sumners led the resistance to campaign reform, assisted by states rightist Sam Hobbs of Alabama.

At the outset of debate Dempsey wholeheartedly endorsed the Hatch measure. "I do not know of one employee," he contended, "in the Federal Service who would give up the protection afforded him by the Hatch Act and go back to the chaotic and oppressive condition that has existed in many States for many years." In order to make standards equitable, Dempsey argued that federally subsidized state workers should receive the same protection and be subject to identical restrictions as national government employees. Taxpayers' money, he vowed, would no longer be diverted arbitrarily towards supporting spoils-oriented state political machines.[64]

On the following day Sumners countered with spirit. He labeled the

Hatch measure "perhaps the most important bill that has been considered by this Congress in 25 years." A strict interpreter of the Constitution, Sumners particularly condemned the growth of federal powers and argued that extension of the 1939 act would unduly violate states' rights. "This bill," he warned, "is the farthest reach of bureaucratic powers into the vitals of democratic institutions and in favor of bureaucracy that has been proposed in this Government." The Judiciary Committee chairman charged, "You are bribing them, and browbeating them, saying to the States that if you do not come across here in accordance with the views of somebody in Washington, we will make you regret it."[65] Following the emotional presentation, Sumners received a solid round of applause from many colleagues.

Defenders of the Hatch proposal echoed common themes. Above all, they insisted the measure would diminish the spoils system by helping to curb political malpractices. Representative Fish argued, "We are striking a blow in defense of free institutions, the ballot box [and] of democracy itself," while Smith of Illinois remarked, "For the party in power to use jobs publicly paid for to prosper its partisan advantage is clearly outrageous to any general conscience."[66] Considering legal ramifications beneficial, the Dempsey camp claimed campaign reform would protect more fully the constitutional rights of individual workers and would discourage the intimidation of voters. Besides denying the revolutionary nature of the legislation, they predicted the Civil Service Commission would enforce the provisions effectively. Hancock counseled, "What we are trying to do here is nothing new, strange, or startling," while Smith lauded the Civil Service Commission as the "standard Federal agency to save the most skilled Federal workers from political domination and to prevent them in turn from officially influencing political outcomes."[67]

Familiar arguments likewise were used by opponents. Giving priority to the judicial ramifications, they insisted the measure would infringe on trial by jury, freedom of speech, and other personal liberties. Republican Donald L. O'Toole of New Jersey accused Congress of trying to "legislate people out of their constitutional rights." In addition, the faction complained the bill threatened states' rights by designating too much power to the federal government. The legislation, Hobbs charged, was "an attempt to overthrow our dual system of government by restraining the States from exercising their indisputable right to control their own elections and to make their own laws" and was an "outrageous rape of the sovereign powers of the State." Opponents also feared the measure would stifle the desire of state employees to participate in the election process. "If you destroy the incentive of the American people to take part in politics," Democrat Butler B. Hare of South Carolina claimed, "then you destroy democracy as a whole."[68]

Representatives made three major changes in the bill. At the insistence of Dempsey the House on July 10 adopted proposals making the legislation effective immediately rather than on October 1 and forcing persons accused of violations to appear before the Civil Service Commission. In addition, congressmen easily approved Georgia Democrat Robert Ramspeck's amendment empowering the commission to subpoena persons and documents when violations were charged. An expert on the merit system, Ramspeck argued, "If you want them to do the job under this act they must have the power."[69]

Dempsey forces thwarted several attempts by the Sumners camp to weaken the legislation. By a 120–84 teller vote representatives rejected a motion by Democrat John E. Rankin of Mississippi preventing utility holding companies from affecting the outcome of primaries or elections. Rankin had hoped to diminish the influence of Republican presidential nominee Wendell Willkie, who had directed a public utilities company. By a wider 109–59 margin congressmen defeated a rider by New Deal Democrat Lee Geyer of California to outlaw the controversial poll tax. A last-minute effort by Republican Thomas Ball of Connecticut to recommit the Hatch measure to the Judiciary Committee also was rejected (182-103).

On July 10 representatives easily approved the Hatch bill (243-122). In comparison to the Senate, politics figured more prominently in the outcome. Republicans backed the reform legislation almost unanimously and capitalized on widespread division among Roosevelt's party. Since Majority Leader Rayburn did not exhibit dynamic leadership, Democrats split more sharply on this issue than on the other five domestic questions.

Sectionalism likewise played a more dynamic role than in the upper chamber. Five delegations achieved at least 75 percent cooperation, while two others followed close behind. Mountain and New England congressmen spearheaded the drive to extend the 1939 measure and rallied formidable backing except in the highly Democratic regions. Although less unified than usual, southerners followed their Senate counterparts in leading resistance to broadening campaign reform. The Hatch bill also caused a cleavage among the border Democrats, who were much less enthusiastic than their Senate mates about applying the restrictions to state workers. By contrast, mountain and Great Lakes members endorsed the legislation with much more vigor than their comparable Senate colleagues.

Party alignments in the House resembled the final vote in 1939, but sectional blocs changed dramatically. With the exception of Representative Ball, Republicans unanimously supported the two Hatch proposals. Democrats leaned against both measures, but were slightly more receptive to the 1940 amendment. Since the two major parties shifted less than 5 percent on the two bills, political sentiments had remained remarkably steady. Northeastern and especially western representatives were far more enthusiastic about the amendment extending campaign reform, while southern states rightists attacked the 1940 legislation much more than the original proposal.

Dempsey had played the most crucial House role in broadening the scope of the 1939 act. A close friend of Hatch, he had sponsored the House measure, posted the discharge petition, expedited the Judiciary Committee action, and ardently defended the amendment on the House floor. In a congratulatory wire to Dempsey Senator Norris commended "the splendid work you did in pushing the Hatch-Dempsey measure through the House. I believe the country owes to you, more than any other one man, the result obtained."[70]

Within two weeks the Hatch measure became law. Senators quickly concurred in the House amendments and sent the legislation to the White House. On July 20 Roosevelt quietly signed the bill, making the restrictions applicable to 250,000 federally funded state workers. At a press conference in mid-August Republican candidate Willkie likewise wholeheartedly backed the 1940 act.[71]

Congress had revamped the electoral system. Above all, political restrictions already placed on national government employees were broadened to include state jobholders receiving pay checks from the nation's capital. In an effort to control the influence of very wealthy donors, contributions made by individuals or organizations to national committees were limited to $5,000. Since the Republican and Democratic committees had spent lavishly on the 1936 election, a $3 million ceiling was placed on annual party expenditures. Congress also prevented the purchase of goods, commodities, or advertisements to support political campaigns, thus prohibiting Roosevelt's party from selling the very popular campaign books.

On the other hand, the Hatch measure had several weaknesses. The legislation did not apply either to political bosses or to a vast cadre of jobholders, who could continue indulging freely in campaign malpractices. Although a ceiling of $5,000 was placed on donations to national committees, state and municipal organizations still could receive and dispense contributions in excess of that amount. In addition, the bill discouraged federally subsidized employees from exercising freedom of speech and other constitutional rights guaranteed to American citizens. Any person accused of violating the Hatch Act could request court proceedings but was not guaranteed a trial by jury. Bans made on the purchase of goods, commodities, or advertising for campaign coffers jeopardized the future of Jackson and Jefferson Day dinners and other political gatherings. Finally, the Civil Service Commission was granted questionable quasi-judicial authority and lacked the personnel to enforce the legislation.

The Hatch Act of 1940 fell short of original expectations. Instead of reducing expenditures, candidates in 1940 spent $45 million for pamphlets, posters, and radio broadcasts for national, state, and local campaigns. Both political parties accused opponents of exceeding limitations on disbursements and of violating other sections. To the chagrin of Roosevelt's party, Republicans doled out $20 million on national campaign elections. Representative Celler, who originally backed the 1940 measure, complained that "abuses by the other side were as astounding as they were contemptible. This act," he insisted, "must be amended and I should like to be in the forefront of the fight to bring about some amendments to it."[72] Despite these weaknesses, the Hatch Act constituted a significant step towards eradicating political corruption.

7

EPILOGUE

The New Deal had entered in January 1939 a third stage characterized by a vigorous battle between the New Dealers and the conservative bipartisan coalition. During this stage, Congress had continued several New Deal programs and enacted a few pioneering domestic measures. On the other hand, the legislative branch had increased its own independent authority in relation to the executive branch, scrutinized New Deal measures more carefully, and reduced federal spending.

New Deal Democrats and the bipartisan conservative coalition had disagreed sharply in 1939 and 1940 on domestic economic and political measures. New Deal Democrats had favored the continuation of Roosevelt's existing policies, including the monetary, trade, and work relief programs. Besides supporting the growth of executive power under Roosevelt, they had favored granting the President authority to reorganize the executive branch. New Deal Democrats largely had opposed the Hatch Acts regulating political activity by federal officials and had rejected slashing expenditures for the Works Progress Administration and other agencies. By contrast, the bipartisan conservative coalition was comprised of nearly all Republicans and a varying group of anti-New Deal Democrats. These conservatives had opposed extending the monetary, trade, work relief, and other New Deal programs. In addition, they had disapproved of delegating increased authority to Roosevelt to reorganize the executive branch and supported the Hatch Acts restricting campaign involvement by executive officials. Fiscal conservatives, they had sought to balance the budget and championed slicing allocations for the WPA and other New Deal agencies.

Congress had extended several significant New Deal programs. Historians usually have stressed that Congress concentrated very little on the New Deal after 1938 and shifted attention to foreign policy and defense legislation.

As indicated in earlier chapters, however, the legislative branch was more reform-minded than previously thought. Congress, after considerable debate, had renewed for two years the President's power to devalue the dollar, purchase foreign silver, and utilize the $2 billion Stabilization Fund. In addition, the legislative branch had extended for three years the chief executive's authority to negotiate trade agreements without Senate ratification and had permitted Roosevelt to lower tariff rates by 50 percent. Although allocating $50 million less than the President desired, the Senate and House had appropriated $825 million to enable the WPA to continue hiring unemployed workers on public works and cultural projects.

Contrary to traditional stereotypes, Congress also had enacted a few pioneer legislative measures in the 1939-1940 period. The legislative branch had approved a national transportation policy placing inland shippers under federal jurisdiction for the first time and bringing rail, motor, and water carriers under uniform, centralized control. In order to reduce the number of government agencies and overlapping functions, the Senate and House had granted the chief executive authority to issue orders reorganizing national bureaus and agencies. Although the Hatch Acts encountered resistance from New Dealers, Congress had restricted considerably the political activity of national government and federally-paid state employees.

On the other hand, Congress had exhibited considerable independence of the executive branch on New Deal questions. The bipartisan coalition had furnished considerable opposition to the extension of New Deal economic programs. Conservatives nearly had terminated the President's prerogatives to devalue the currency and buy foreign silver. In addition, the bipartisan coalition almost had prevented the continuation of the reciprocal trade program and nearly had required Senate approval of all commercial agreements. Representatives belonging to the waterway, agricultural, or railway blocs had demonstrated considerable independence on the transportation measure.

Congress likewise had not acted as a rubberstamp for the President on the three political questions.[1] The bipartisan coalition had declined to authorize Roosevelt the entire $875 million he requested for the WPA, compelling the President to drop some workers from the relief program. Although Roosevelt preferred a comprehensive reorganization measure, the legislative branch had restricted the Presidential authority to revamp the executive branch and had exempted several independent agencies from orders. The bipartisan coalition, despite strong reservations by Roosevelt and New Dealers, had adopted the Hatch Act of 1939 placing restrictions on national political campaign activity.

In the House, New Deal alignments had fluctuated much more than those of the bipartisan conservative coalition. Democrats solidly had supported both New Deal economic and political legislation, but had received much more Republican support on political than economic measures. Southern and border representatives had directed the campaign for New Dealers on economic questions, joined by the mountain bloc on monetary issues and by the Middle Atlantic members on reciprocal trade. The border delegation usually had commanded floor strategy on political subjects, assisted by Pacific representatives on the WPA and by southerners on reorganization. On the other hand, the conservative coalition had remained quite consistent on economic and political legislation. Republican congressmen had supplied the nucleus of resistance to the New Deal monetary, trade, and reorganization bills. Usually aligning with midwesterners, New England representatives had directed the conservative onslaught against most New Deal financial and political measures.

The opposite pattern had occurred in the Senate, where New Dealers were more consistent than the bipartisan conservative coalition. Democrats had directed and dominated the New Deal forces advocating both economic and political bills. The border delegation constantly had shared leadership roles for the New Dealers, aligning with the southerners on financial issues and with the Middle Atlantic bloc on political issues. By contrast, the conservative coalition had fluctuated considerably on economic and political questions. Republicans consistently had opposed New Deal currency, trade, work relief, and reorganization bills, but had found more Democratic sympathies on political rather than financial measures. New Englanders continually had directed the conservative opposition to the New Deal, joined by westerners on economic issues and by the midwesterners and southerners on political matters.

These alignments did not apply, however, to the transportation and campaign restriction legislation. Although usually endorsing the other domestic programs, Democrats had resisted openly both the railroad and election practices legislation. Majority party members serving water, labor, and agricultural districts had disapproved of making major changes in national transportation policy. Westerners had led the barrage in the House against the 1939 Hatch bill, while the southern and border blocs had conducted the drive to defeat the 1940 amendments.

Some unexpected alignments occurred. Republicans allied with western rather than southern Democrats on economic measures.[2] Conforming to their historical tradition, Republicans insisted upon the abandonment of the bimetallic standard and urged a return to gold as the exclusive standard. They also attacked the monetary measure because it granted excessive authority to the President, who belonged to the opposite party and who had not ruled out running for a third term. Granting Roosevelt too much control over monetary subjects, they warned, might induce him further to augment executive power. Western Democrats protested domestic mines were being undersold by foreign competitors, forcing widespread layoffs in American silver plants. Besides urging an increase in rates for domestic metals, western Democrats requested the federal government to stop purchasing silver abroad.

This unusual marriage also appeared on reciprocal trade. Republicans and western Democrats both represented geographical regions suffering some detrimental effects from the administration's low tariff policies.

In order to protect their industrial and agricultural products from over-seas competitors, Republicans customarily had supported high duties. Reciprocity, the minority party argued, had permitted importers to under-sell American grain and dairy products and had made it more difficult for domestic farm producers to market their goods. According to the Republicans, the chief executive was exercising authority specifically designated to Congress by the Constitution. Trade agreements, they insisted, were revenue measures that should originate in the House and treaties that should require Senate ratification. Since 1940 was a presi-dential election year, Republicans also hoped to capitalize on this issue in their campaign to wrest control of the White House from Roosevelt's party. Western Democrats likewise objected that the tariff reductions had encouraged agricultural and mining importers to swamp American markets with lower priced goods. Producers from west of the Mississippi River, including copper, silver, lead, and zinc mines, livestock, fruit, and vegetable farmers, could not compete on an equitable basis with foreign traders.

Southerners, on the other hand, supported the President whole-heartedly on economic issues. Dominating this bloc, Democrats tradi-tionally had endorsed a bimetallic currency and low tariff program. Since the Constitution delegated the chief executive with principal authority over international monetary and trade questions, they argued Congress should accede to Roosevelt's wishes on such matters. Administration commercial programs also had boosted their economy. The bimetallic standard had promoted inflation, giving the farmers more money with which to pay their debts, and had enabled southerners to purchase silver from abroad at cheaper rates. Under the reciprocal trade policy southern tillers exported more agricultural products to Latin American nations and bought at more economical prices the manufacturing products their section needed. Roosevelt's monetary and trade programs helped stabilize Latin American finances, enhancing the prospects for maintaining peace in the Western Hemisphere.

New England members usually opposed legislation even more adamantly than did midwesterners, who are often considered the leading critics of Roosevelt's domestic policies.[3] Comprising the highest propor-tion of Republicans in Congress, New Englanders hoped to use these economic and political measures as campaign issues in the upcoming 1940 presidential election. The extension of presidential powers to devalue the dollar and to negotiate trade agreements, they contended, infringed upon legislative revenue and treaty-making powers. On the reorganization sub-ject, they complained the President really intended to tighten White House reins over independent agencies. The Democratic Party, they objected, had dominated the administration of relief programs and had manipulated WPA workers in state primaries and elections. Economic determinism also dictated New England opposition to monetary and trade measures. Serving a variety of manufacturing companies favoring a return to the gold standard, these legislators disliked the inflationary tendencies inherent in a bimetallic system. Since reciprocity programs had resulted in declining markets for northeastern producers, they demanded the United States restore more protectionist rates.

Western Democrats, surprisingly, wielded more authority than their southern political colleagues on economic issues in the Senate. Nearly crippling the reciprocal trade program, they also prevented adoption of monetary legislation until prices were raised for domestic silver. The mountain delegation controlled an unusually high proportion of seats in the upper chamber for one section, belonged almost exclusively to one political party, accumulated an impressive amount of seniority, and chaired several major committees. Historians usually have labeled southern Democrats the most powerful bloc in Congress, but those senators clearly did not control the balance of power on either the currency or trade measures.[4]

By contrast, southerners held substantial authority on political questions and clashed sharply with the chief executive over the WPA and Hatch bills. Roosevelt, they charged, had used his landslide victory in the 1936 presidential elections to aggrandize his personal influence at the expense of the legislative branch. Southern grievances included Roosevelt's attempt to alter the size of the Supreme Court, his desire to purge conservative party members in the 1938 primaries, and his intervention enabling Alben W. Barkley to upset Pat Harrison for the majority leader post. Besides favoring decentralization of relief programs, these anti–New Dealers accused the chief executive of seeking to augment his personal influence by reorganizing the executive branch. Federal expenditures for domestic policies, they protested, made it virtually impossible to balance the budget, thus burdening further the American taxpayer.

Political considerations prevailed on most legislation. On the WPA, reorganization, and campaign reform measures, there were fiery exchanges between New Dealers and anti-Roosevelt forces. Republicans and conservative Democrats charged work relief policies were too centralized and asserted Roosevelt sought reorganization primarily to strengthen his personal control over the executive branch. With the campaign reform bill of 1939, the coalition attempted to retard the growth of presidential power. Party interests were less evident on economic questions because western Democrats bolted Barkley's leadership on monetary and trade legislation.

Sectionalism served as a dominant force on financial measures. On the monetary and reciprocal trade bills, supporters represented regions relying upon both stable international currencies and extensive foreign markets. Transportation reformers claimed federal assistance to railroads would improve services to farmers in their geographical areas. On the other hand, midwestern and mountain delegations protested that the continuation of low tariff rates would hurt both miners and grain farmers and warned that federal regulation of inland water carriers would increase transportation costs. With the exception of the WPA bill, regionalism had much less impact on political legislation. Rural legislators complained that WPA officials habitually favored urban geographical areas both in hiring practices and in wage scales.

Congressional leadership played dynamic roles on both economic and political questions. Party chiefs typically operated more effectively in the House and especially among minority Republicans. Adhering closely to the directives of Joseph W. Martin, Jr., of Massachusetts, Republican representatives displayed at least 95 percent unity on the reorganization, campaign reform, monetary, and trade measures and divided noticeably only on work relief appropriations. Majority Leader Rayburn commanded 90 percent loyalty or better from his forces on the WPA, reorganization, monetary, and trade bills, but at least one-third of the Democrats repudiated his direction on the transportation and campaign reform legislation. On the Senate side, Republican head Charles L. McNary secured at least 95 percent backing on all political bills and received wholehearted cooperation on economic measures. Democrats, however, encountered more obstacles in rallying party solidarity. Inasmuch as at least 30 percent rebelled on each proposal except transportation reform, Majority Leader Barkley wielded less effective control over his own party. Democrats separated most sharply on the work relief and campaign reform questions, both being major sources of disagreement between party chieftains and the Roosevelt administration. Barkley in April, 1939, split with the President by accepting the $100 million compromise figure for the WPA, while Democratic Whip Minton led resistance in 1940 to amending the Hatch Act.[5]

The legislative behavior of the members of the Seventy-sixth Congress was determined largely by party interests and economic blocs. Political and sectional loyalties governed policy decisions so markedly that individuals seldom had much freedom of choice on roll calls. In contrast to the minority Republicans, Democrats played maverick roles far more often in the House and especially in the Senate. Carter Glass followed the dictates of his conscience in opposing the President's monetary and trade programs, while Tydings of Maryland followed neither political party nor geographical considerations in opposing reorganization of the executive branch. Truman, who represented numerous farmers, defied the wishes of the Roosevelt administration by favoring reductions in WPA funding.

On the three economic issues, the executive branch had used different approaches. Roosevelt administration personnel, particularly the State Department, participated most actively in the battle for reciprocal trade extension. White House forces deserved less credit for the enactment of the monetary measure, although Roosevelt eventually intervened in the struggle. The President's initial refusal to make any concessions on the silver issue hampered considerably the effectiveness of the executive branch. If the chief executive had compromised with the silver bloc earlier, the expiration of the monetary legislation on June 30 might have been averted. The administration, though, made relatively little impact on the transportation bill. After helping salvage the Wheeler-Lea proposal in the House, the President remained on the sidelines and even kept silent on the eventual conference report. A railroad reformer at the outset, he eventually shifted to a neutral position because of the controversial nature of the issue.

Political questions likewise generated a variety of responses from the White House. The executive branch wholeheartedly endorsed emergency funding for work relief programs to cover the remainder of the 1939 fiscal year. Besides recommending the initial $875 million amount for WPA, Roosevelt discussed legislative strategy with the Appropriations Committee and party leadership and continually expounded on the subject. When Congress contemplated reducing the supplemental WPA appropriations in April, 1939, the President sent to Senator Pepper a note urging adoption of the entire $150 million amount. Roosevelt pursued an erratic course on campaign reform, initially favoring the principles embodied in the legislation. After realizing the bill was designed to reduce the power of the executive branch, he nearly vetoed the proposal. In 1940 the President enthusiastically supported the Hatch amendment and even issued a statement expediting Judiciary Committee action. Roosevelt played a relatively passive role on the reorganization question, leaving legislative strategy in 1939 almost entirely to Congressmen Warren and Cochran.

Pressure groups, meanwhile, held varying degrees of influence, depending on the economic issue at stake. On transportation legislation, waterway, labor, and agricultural organizations deluged Congress with correspondence urging removal of restrictions on inland water carriers, deletion of consolidation provisions, and protection for farmers exporting products. Lobbyists also protested the reciprocal trade bill, but could not block extension of the administration program. Agricultural and mining groups bombarded Congress with mail and testified at committee hearings about the dangers of continuing a low tariff policy. From inception to enactment, though, lobbyists made little noise on the monetary measure.

In regard to political questions, interest groups also made a mixed impact. The anti–New Deal Committee to Uphold Constitutional Government influenced Congress to drop several controversial features of the 1938 reorganization proposal, including exemption of several federal bureaus and agencies and strengthening of legislative control over executive actions. On work relief and campaign reform, lobbyists played subordinate roles. The National Conference of Mayors, the Workers Alliance, and other liberal organizations made fervent pleas for increasing WPA appropriations, but an economy-minded Congress instead sliced both presidential requests. Since the Hatch proposals contained very complex language, campaign reform evoked the least comment from lobbyists on Capitol Hill.[6]

In the final analysis, the significance of both the economic and political measures enacted by Congress has been underplayed in the literature of the Roosevelt period.[7] Until being overshadowed by the outbreak in Europe of World War 2, these issues held the limelight. Neutrality revision, selective service, and other foreign policy questions received much more attention after Germany attacked Poland.[8] Economic measures, which historians have largely neglected, played a vital role in helping the United States to stabilize internal financial conditions and to bolster foreign countries against possible aggression. Political legislation, likewise given scant treatment by academia, assisted in alleviating unemployment, promoting government efficiency, and striking at political corruption.

This study has been an initial attempt to analyze congressional action on selected economic and political issues before World War 2. Further examination will be required to determine whether or not these trends and patterns applied to other legislation submitted to the Seventy-sixth Congress. In 1939 the legislative branch considered a farm parity plan, National Labor Relations Act amendments, self-liquidating public works projects, a national housing measure, and other controversial proposals. At the 1940 session Congress acted on another agricultural subsidies bill, appropriations for the National Youth Administration, a federal food stamp plan, and other significant domestic legislation. An investigation of these and other major internal issues handled by the Senate and House could provide further illumination on the period characterized by the waning of the New Deal.

APPENDIX

Table

TABLE 1: Political Party Affiliation by Region, 1940

Region	Senate			House		
	Democrat	Republic.	Other[a]	Democrat	Republic.	Other[b]
New England	4	9	0	7	23	0
Middle Atlantic	5	3	0	46	52	1
Great Lakes	7	4	1	36	55	2
Great Plains	6	6	3	18	30	1
South	20	0	0	99	0	0
Border	11	0	0	40	5	0
Mountain	16	2	0	12	3	0
Pacific	4	3	0	19	10	0

a - Third party senators included two Farmer-Laborites, one Progressive, and one Independent.

b - Third party representatives included two Progressives, one Farmer-Laborite, and one American-Laborite.

Source for Tables 1-5 - Roll Call Data, Seventy-sixth Congress, Inter-University Consortium for Political Research, University of Michigan, Ann Arbor, Michigan

TABLE 2: Political Party Alignments on Major Roll Calls, House

Roll Call Issue	Dem. Yes	Dem. No	Rep. Yes	Rep. No	Others Yes	Others No	Total Yes	Total No
Reed Amend. on Money 4/21/39	4	221	153	0	1	4	158	225
Wadsworth Amendment on Transportation 7/26/39	73	144	22	127	4	2	99	273
Wadsworth Amendment on Transportation 8/12/40	83	95	27	114	2	3	112	212
Reciprocal Trade 2/23/40	211	20	5	146	2	2	218	168
Work Relief 1/13/39	236	6	155	10	6	0	397	16
Work Relief 3/31/39	219	23	67	88	6	0	292	110
Sumners Amendment on Reorganization 3/8/39	34	206	156	0	3	3	193	209
Reorganization 3/8/39	233	5	8	147	5	1	246	153
Hatch Act of 1939 7/20/39	82	133	156	0	3	1	241	134
Hatch Act of 1940 7/10/40	88	120	151	1	4	1	243	122

TABLE 3: Political Party Alignments on Major Roll Calls, Senate

Roll Call Issue	Dem. Yes	Dem. No	Rep. Yes	Rep. No	Others Yes	Others No	Total Yes	Total No
Adams Silver Amendment on Money 6/26/39	31	27	15	2	2	1	48	30
Adams Devaluation Amendment on Money 6/26/39	30	28	16	1	1	2	47	31
Conference Report on Money 7/5/39	40	19	1	18	2	2	43	39
Bailey Amendment on Transportation 5/25/39	15	40	6	14	1	3	22	57
Transportation Act 9/9/40	43	11	15	3	1	1	59	15
Pittman Amendment on Reciprocal Trade 3/29/40	19	43	20	0	2	1	41	44
Reciprocal Trade Act 4/5/40	38	19	3	16	1	2	42	37
McKellar Amendment on Work Relief 1/27/39	42	26	1	20	3	1	46	47
Pepper Amendment on Work Relief 4/11/39	24	32	1	17	3	1	28	49
Wheeler Amendment on Reorganization 3/21/39	21	43	21	0	2	2	44	45
Reorganization Act 3/22/39	58	4	2	18	3	1	63	23
Miller Amendment on Hatch Act 3/6/40	40	22	1	19	0	3	41	44
Bankhead Amendment on Hatch Act 3/14/40	36	19	1	18	3	1	40	38
Hatch Act of 1940 3/18/40	35	27	21	0	2	1	58	28

TABLE 4: Sectional Alignments on Major Roll Calls, House

Roll Call Issues	New England		Middle Atlantic		Great Lakes		Great Plains		South		Border		Mountain		Pacific	
	y	n	y	n	y	n	y	n	y	n	y	n	y	n	y	n
Reed Amendment on Money 4/21/39	18	5	45	38	47	34	28	17	4	76	4	29	3	11	9	15
Wadsworth Amendment on Transportation 7/26/39	5	21	27	47	9	69	8	36	29	50	7	27	2	10	12	13
Wadsworth Amendment on Transportation 8/12/40	8	10	15	47	14	57	15	29	35	34	13	16	1	8	11	11
Reciprocal Trade 2/23/40	6	22	40	38	32	50	16	28	76	4	31	5	4	7	13	14
Work Relief 1/13/39	29	6	82	2	86	2	44	6	81	0	33	0	13	0	29	0
Work Relief 3/31/39	14	11	56	29	53	32	33	14	64	21	33	1	12	2	27	1
Sumners Amendment on Reorganization 3/8/39	19	7	49	37	56	32	30	14	17	67	10	24	3	10	9	18
Reorganization Act 3/8/39	7	19	42	43	37	51	19	25	79	3	31	3	10	3	21	6
Hatch Act 7/20/39	23	4	49	31	62	23	34	10	41	34	18	10	4	6	5	12
Hatch Act 7/10/40	25	1	58	23	61	15	33	10	22	54	17	17	6	0	21	2

TABLE 5: Sectional Alignments on Major Roll Calls, Senate

Roll Call Issues	New England		Middle Atlantic		Great Lakes		Great Plains		South		Border		Mountain		Pacific	
	y	n	y	n	y	n	y	n	y	n	y	n	y	n	y	n
Adams Silver Amendment on Money 6/26/39	5	5	2	5	4	4	8	3	6	8	5	5	13	0	5	0
Adams Devaluation Amendment on Money 6/26/39	8	2	3	4	4	4	9	2	4	10	3	7	11	2	5	0
Conference Report on Money 7/5/39	1	10	5	3	5	4	3	8	10	5	8	2	9	5	2	2
Bailey Amendment on Transportation 5/25/39	4	7	0	8	0	7	3	11	6	9	5	2	2	12	2	1
Transportation Act 9/9/40	6	4	7	0	7	0	6	4	8	7	8	0	14	0	3	0
Pittman Amendment on Reciprocal Trade 3/29/40	10	2	3	5	3	5	6	5	2	15	1	7	11	4	5	1
Reciprocal Trade Act 4/5/40	1	10	3	3	5	2	4	7	15	1	9	1	4	9	1	4
McKellar Amendment on Work Relief 1/27/39	3	8	5	3	5	5	3	11	10	10	7	3	10	4	3	3
Pepper Amendment on Work Relief 4/11/39	4	6	5	3	2	5	2	11	2	11	3	5	7	6	3	3
Wheeler Amendment on Reorganization 3/21/39	9	1	3	5	5	5	9	3	6	13	1	8	8	8	4	1
Reorganization Act 3/22/39	2	8	4	2	8	2	9	5	16	0	8	1	13	2	3	3
Miller Amendment on Hatch Act 3/6/40	1	9	3	4	4	5	4	8	15	3	5	4	9	6	0	5
Bankhead Amendment on Hatch Act 3/14/40	0	9	3	5	4	4	5	7	13	3	4	3	10	4	1	3
Hatch Act of 1940 3/18/40	11	1	5	3	4	4	9	2	6	10	7	3	11	4	5	1

NOTES

PREFACE

1. A typical early work on the New Deal is Basil Rauch, *The History of the New Deal 1933-1938* (New York, 1944).

2. Joseph Alsop and Turner Catledge, *The 168 Days* (New York, 1938), describes the Supreme Court controversy, while Joseph Boskin, "Politics of an Opposition Party: The Republican Party in the New Deal Period" (Ph.D. dissertation, 1959), assesses Republican problems.

3. Justus D. Doenecke, *The Literature of Isolationism: A Guide to Non-Interventionist Scholarship, 1930-1972* (Colorado Springs, 1972), surveys the voluminous works on foreign policy and defense.

4. Samuel Lubell, *The Future of American Politics* (New York, 1952); James MacGregor Burns, *Roosevelt: The Lion and the Fox* (New York, 1956); and William E. Leuchtenburg, *Franklin D. Roosevelt and the New Deal, 1932-1940* (New York, 1963). Other fundamental works include Arthur M. Schlesinger, Jr., *The Age of Roosevelt,* vols. 2, 3 (Boston, 1958, 1960), and Frank Freidel, *Franklin D. Roosevelt: Launching the New Deal* (Boston, 1973).

5. Richard Polenberg, *Reorganizing Roosevelt's Government: The Controversy over Executive Reorganization, 1936-1939* (Cambridge, Mass., 1966); James T. Patterson, *Congressional Conservatism and the New Deal* (Lexington, Ky., 1967).

6. Revisionist works on the role of reform in the Republican period from 1921 to 1933 include: Ellis W. Hawley, *The Great War and the Search for Modern Order: A History of the American People and Their Institutions, 1917-1933* (New York, 1979); Robert K. Murray, *The Harding Era: Warren G. Harding and His Administration* (Minneapolis, 1969); Donald R. McCoy, *Calvin Coolidge: The Quiet President* (New York, 1967); Joan Hoff Wilson, *Herbert Hoover: Forgotten Progressive* (Boston, 1975); David Burner, *Herbert Hoover: A Public Life* (New York, 1978); Jordan A. Schwarz, *The Interregnum of Despair: Hoover, Congress, and the Depression* (Urbana, 1970); and Martin L. Fausold and George T. Mazuzan (eds.), *The Hoover Presidency: A Reappraisal* (Albany, N.Y., 1974).

7. Allan Seymour Everest, *Morgenthau, the New Deal, and Silver* (New York, 1950); Fred L. Israel, *Nevada's Key Pittman* (Lincoln, 1963).

8. Ralph L. Dewey, "Transportation Act of 1940," *American Economic Review* 31 (March, 1941): 15-26; Robert W. Harbeson, "The Transportation Act of 1940,"

The Journal of Land and Public Utility Economics 17 (August, 1941): 291-302; Claude Moore Fuess, *Joseph B. Eastman: Servant of the People* (New York, 1952); Ari and Olive Hoogenboom, *A History of the ICC* (New York, 1975).

9.   James C. Pearson, *The Reciprocal Trade Agreements Program* (Washington, 1942); Lloyd C. Gardner, *Economic Aspects of New Deal Diplomacy* (Madison, 1964); Samuel Flagg Bemis, *The Latin-American Policy of the United States* (New York, 1943); Richard N. Kottman, *Reciprocity and the North Atlantic Triangle, 1932-1938* (Ithaca, 1968).

10.   Searle F. Charles, *Minister of Relief: Harry Hopkins and the Depression* (Syracuse, 1963); Donald S. Howard, *The WPA and Federal Relief Policy* (New York, 1943); Jane De Hart Mathews, *The Federal Theater, 1935-1939: Plays, Relief, and Politics* (Princeton, 1967); Richard D. McKinzie, *The New Deal for Artists* (Princeton, 1973).

11.   Barry Dean Karl, *Executive Reorganization and Reform in the New Deal* (Cambridge, Mass., 1963); Polenberg; A. J. Wann, *The President As Chief Administrator: A Study of Franklin D. Roosevelt* (Washington, 1968).

12.   Dorothy Ganfield Fowler, "Precursors of the Hatch Act," *Mississippi Valley Historical Review* 47 (September, 1960): 247-62; C. Vann Woodward (ed.), *Responses of the Presidents to Charges of Misconduct* (New York, 1974).

13.   The fourteen significant Senate roll calls are the Adams Silver and Devaluation amendments, the conference report on the Monetary Act of 1939, the Bailey amendment on transportation, the Transportation Act of 1940, the Pittman amendment on reciprocal trade, the Reciprocal Trade Act of 1940, the McKellar and Pepper amendments on work relief, the Wheeler amendment on reorganization, the Reorganization Act of 1939, the Miller and Bankhead amendments on political reform, and the Hatch Act of 1940. The ten major House roll calls are the Reed amendment to the Monetary Act of 1939, the Wadsworth amendments on transportation, the Reciprocal Trade Act of 1940, the Work Relief Act of 1939, the supplementary Work Relief Act of 1939, the Sumners amendment on reorganization, the Reorganization Act of 1939, and the Hatch Acts of 1939 and 1940.

14.   The regional breakdown is as follows: *New England*: Connecticut, Maine, Massachusetts, New Hampshire, Rhode Island, Vermont; *Middle Atlantic*: Delaware, New Jersey, New York, Pennsylvania; *Great Lakes*: Illinois, Indiana, Michigan, Ohio, Wisconsin; *Great Plains*: Iowa, Kansas, Minnesota, Missouri, Nebraska, North Dakota, South Dakota: *South*: Alabama, Arkansas, Florida, Georgia, Louisiana, Mississippi, North Carolina, South Carolina, Texas, Virginia; *Border*: Kentucky, Maryland, Oklahoma, Tennessee, West Virginia; *Mountain*: Arizona, Colorado, Idaho, Montana, Nevada, New Mexico, Utah, Wyoming; *Pacific*: California, Oregon, Washington.

1. THE EXTENSION OF THE MONETARY PROGRAM

1.   Milton Plesur, "The Republican Comeback of 1938," *Review of Politics* 24 (October, 1962): 525-62; Raymond Clapper, "Return of the Two Party System," *Current History* 49 (December, 1938): 13-15; Ernest K. Lindley, "The New Congress," *Current History* 50 (February, 1939): 15-17.

2.   The historical background is described in Jordan A. Schwarz, *1933: Roosevelt's Decision: The United States Leaves the Gold Standard* (New York, 1969), John A. Brennan, *Silver and the First New Deal* (Reno, 1969), and Everest.

3.   Franklin D. Roosevelt (hereafter abbreviated FDR) to William B. Bankhead, January 19, 1939, National Archives, Legislative Division, (hereafter abbreviated Nat. Arch., Leg. Div.) folder on H.R. 3325; Henry Morgenthau, Jr., memorandum for FDR, January 17, 1939, FDR Library, official file (hereafter abbreviated OF) 21.

4.   *Congressional Record*, 76th Congress, 1st Session, vol. 84, April 18, 20, 1939, pp. 4413, 4610; U.S. Congress, House, Committee on Coinage, Weights, and Measures, rpt. no. 406, "Extending the Time within Which the Powers Relating to

the Stabilization Fund and Alteration of the Dollar May Be Exercised," April 13, 1939 (Washington, 1939).

5. *Congressional Record,* April 20, 1939, pp. 4570, 4574, 4601.

6. House Coinage Com., rpt. no. 406, "Stabilization Fund"; *Congressional Record,* April 18, 1939, p. 4407.

7. *Congressional Record,* April 18, 1939, pp. 4408–09; W. Sterling Cole to Hiel Gorey, January 14, 1939, Cole MSS, box 20; House Coinage Com., rpt. no. 406, "Stabilization Fund."

8. *New York Times,* April 19, 1939.

9. Schwarz, Brennan, Everest, Israel, and James T. Patterson, *Congressional Conservatism and the New Deal* (Lexington, Ky., 1967), have stressed the economic or sectional aspects of monetary legislation.

10. V. O. Key, Jr., *Southern Politics in State and Nation* (New York, 1949), Lubell, and Frank Freidel, *F.D.R. and the South* (Baton Rouge, 1965), have emphasized the coalition of Republicans and conservative Democrats.

11. FDR to Andrew L. Somers, April 24, 1939, FDR MSS, President's Personal File (hereafter abbreviated PPF) 5947; memorandum for General Watson, undated, FDR MSS, OF 229, box 12; *Current Biography*, 1941, pp. 892-94.

12. Key Pittman to FDR, December 17, 1938, FDR MSS, OF 229, box 12; David L. Porter, "Key Pittman and the Monetary Act of 1939," *Nevada Historical Society Quarterly* 21 (Fall, 1978), p. 206; *Congressional Record,* June 21, 1939, p. 7608; *Richmond Times Dispatch*, June 18, 1939.

13. *Congressional Record*, June 15, 23, 1939, pp. 7209, 7763; William E. Borah to Irvin Rockwell, June 23, 1939, Borah MSS, box 433; Elmer Thomas to Ellison D. Smith, March 14, 1939, Thomas MSS, money legislation, box C; U.S. Congress, Senate, Committee on Banking and Currency, rpt. no. 591, "Devaluation of Dollar and Stabilization Fund," June 13, 1939 (Washington, 1939).

14. *Congressional Record*, June 30, 1939, p. 8415; *Richmond Times Dispatch*, June 18, 1939.

15. Clyde M. Reed to William Allen White, July 7, 1939, White MSS, box 222; Robert F. Wagner, speech, Washington, June 19, 1939, Wagner MSS, speeches.

16. Key Pittman to Alva Adams et al., April 24, 1939, Borah MSS, box 433; Porter, "Pittman," pp. 206–07; "Silver Conference Held at Reno," *Mining Congress Journal* (May, 1939), p. 566; Carl Hayden to Key Pittman, April 29, 1939, Hayden MSS, 633/18; William E. Borah to Key Pittman, April 26, 1939, Borah MSS, box 433; Carl Hayden to Fred Noon, April 29, 1939, Hayden MSS, 633/18.

17. Carl Hayden to Gov. R. T. Jones, June 16, 1939, Hayden MSS, 633/18.

18. *New York Times*, June 22, 28, 1939; *Congressional Record*, June 21, 1939, pp. 7591–627; Key Pittman to FDR, June 24, 1939, FDR MSS, PPF 745.

19. Reed to White, July 7, 1939.

20. "Congressional Poll on Neutrality," *Congresssional Intelligence* Magazine (April 7, 1939), p. 4; Israel, p. 167; Porter, "Pittman," p. 209.

21. Elliott Roosevelt (ed.), *FDR: His Personal Letters, 1928-1945,* 2 (New York, 1950): 898; Everest, pp. 72–73.

22. Key, Lubell, and Freidel all have stressed the power of southern delegations in Congress and the anti–New Deal coalition. Schwarz, Brennan, Everest, Israel, and Patterson have described the role of western Democrats on economic issues.

23. Sherman Minton to William Allen White, undated, White MSS, box 222.

24. Key Pittman, press release, June 30, 1939, Pittman MSS, box 162; Porter, "Pittman," p. 210.

25. *Congressional Record*, June 30, 1939, pp. 8412, 8415.

26. Carl Hayden to Kean St. Charles, July 3, 1939, Hayden MSS, 633/18.

27. Reed to White, July 7, 1939; Reed to William Allen White and twenty-five Kansas newspaper friends, July 13, 1939, White MSS, box 222.

28. Hiram W. Johnson to Hiram W. Johnson, Jr., July 1, 1939, Johnson MSS, pt. 6, box 7.

29. Johnson to Johnson, Jr. July 1, 1939; Johnson to Johnson, Jr., July 2, 1939, Johnson MSS, pt. 6, box 7.
30. Key Pittman to FDR, June 30, 1939, FDR MSS, PPF 745.
31. Key Pittman to Zeb Kendall, July, 1939, Pittman MSS, box 38; Porter, "Pittman," pp. 210–11; Carl Hayden to Miss Alma Dungan, July 14, 1939, Hayden MSS, 633/18.
32. Johnson to Johnson, Jr., July 8, 1939, Johnson MSS, pt. 6, box 7.

2. THE BROADENING OF TRANSPORTATION REGULATION

1. Railroad problems are assessed in Earl Latham, *The Politics of Railroad Coordination* (Cambridge, Mass., 1939); John F. Stover, *American Railroads* (Chicago, 1961); and John F. Stover, *The Life and Decline of the American Railroad* (New York, 1970).
2. I. L. Sharfman, *The Interstate Commerce Commission: A Study in Administrative Law and Procedure*, 5 vols. (New York, 1931–37), Ari and Olive Hoogenboom, *A History of the ICC* (New York, 1975), and Claude Moore Fuess, *Joseph B. Eastman: Servant of the People* (New York, 1952), describe the federal regulation of transportation. Inland waterway problems are analyzed in Stuart Daggett, *Principles of Inland Transportation*, 2nd ed. (New York, 1934); and William J. and Robert W. Hull, *The Origin and Development of the Waterways Policy of the United States* (Washington, 1967).
3. Burton K. Wheeler, *Yankee from the West* (Garden City, 1962); *Current Biography*, 1940, pp. 857–60.
4. Clyde M. Reed to William Allen White, May 17, 1939, White MSS, box 219; Lindsay C. Warren et al. to Burton K. Wheeler, June 21, 1939, Nat. Arch., Leg. Div., folder on S. 2009.
5. Memorandum for General Watson, April 20, 1939, FDR MSS, OF 31, box 9.
6. U.S. Congress, Senate Committee on Interstate Commerce, rpt. no. 433, "Transportation Act of 1939," May 16, 1939 (Washington, 1939); Harry S. Truman to W. J. Thomure, May 16, 1939, Truman MSS, senatorial file (hereafter abbreviated sen.), box 152.
7. Reed to White, May 17, 1939.
8. Wheeler, p. 350.
9. *Current Biography*, 1945, pp. 28–30.
10. *New York Times*, May 29, 1939; Truman to L. W. Childress, August 21, 1940, Truman MSS, sen., box 153; Truman to R. K. Keas, May 23, 1939, Truman MSS, sen., box 152.
11. A. Victor Donahey to Burton K. Wheeler, April 8, 1939, Nat. Arch., Leg. Div., sen. 76A-E1, box 60; U.S. Congress, Senate, Committee on Interstate Commerce, rpt. no. 433, pt. 2, "Transportation Act of 1939," May 17, 1939 (Washington, 1939).
12. Eugene F. Schmidtlein, "Truman the Senator" (Ph.D. dissertation, 1962), p. 192; *Dallas News*, March 22, 1940; Reed to White, May 17, 1939; Clyde L. Herring, C B S radio address, Washington, D.C., February 21, 1939, Herring MSS, box 2.
13. Sen. Inter. Comm. Comm., rpt. no. 433, pt. 2, "Transportation Act of 1939," May 17, 1939; Clyde M. Reed to John Vesecky, July 19, 1939, Clifford R. Hope MSS, legislative correspondence (hereafter abbreviated leg. corr.), box 151.
14. William E. Borah to W. H. Cowles, June 2, 1939, Borah MSS, box 431; *New York Times*, May 25, 1939; Reed to Vesecky, July 19, 1939.
15. *New York Times*, May 25, 26, 1939; *Congressional Record*, 76th Congress, 1st Session, vol. 84, May 25, 1939, p. 6066.
16. Clyde M. Reed to William Lambertson et al., May 7, 1940, Hope MSS, leg. corr., box 182.
17. Borah to Cowles, June 2, 1939.

18.　Theodore G. Bilbo to Milton Smith, February 19, 1940, Bilbo MSS, file R; Borah to Cowles, June 2, 1939.

19.　Wheeler, p. 350; Truman to Burton K. Wheeler, June 6, 1939, Nat. Arch., Leg. Div., sen. 76A-E1, box 60; Truman to Powell Groner, May 27, 1939, Truman MSS, sen., box 152.

20.　Clyde M. Reed to William Allen White, November 17, 1939, White MSS, box 226.

21.　James W. Wadsworth, Jr., to R. C. Watson, May 9, 1939, Wadsworth Family MSS, box 24; Clifford R. Hope to I. J. Carter, July 21, 1939, Hope MSS, leg. corr., box 151.

22.　Warren to Wheeler, June 21, 1939; Henry A. Wallace, Jr., to John H. Bankhead, July, 1939, FDR MSS, OF 31, box 9; A. F. Whitney to Railway Labor Lodges, April 26, 1939, Nat. Arch., Leg. Div., sen. 76A-E1, box 60.

23.　Truman to Robert Lund, February 28, 1940, Truman MSS, sen., box 153.

24.　Clarence F. Lea to FDR, July 19, 1939, FDR MSS, OF 173, box 1.

25.　John M. Vorys to constituents, July 31, 1939, Vorys MSS, box 3; John H. Kerr to R. C. Holland, May 9, 1940, Kerr MSS, box 15.

26.　J. J. Mansfield to Lindsay C. Warren, June 6, 1939, Warren MSS, box 21-A; *Congressional Record*, July 22, 1939, p. 9753.

27.　Warren to Zeb Norman, July 28, 1939, Warren MSS, box 21-B; Warren to H. M. Thompson, June 9, 1939, Warren MSS, box 21-A; Mansfield to Warren, June 6, 1939.

28.　Clifford R. Hope to J. P. Fengel, May 8, 1940, Hope MSS, leg. corr., box 182; Vorys to John Davis, July 31, 1939, Vorys MSS, box 4; George H. Bender, speech, Washington, D. C., April, 1939, Bender MSS, container 3.

29.　Warren to Wheeler, June 21, 1939; Vincent F. Harrington to Warren, April 1, 1940, Warren MSS, box 22-C.

30.　Clifford R. Hope to Jess Denious, May 18, 1940, Hope MSS, leg. corr., box 182; Vorys to constituents, May 14, 1940, Vorys MSS, box 3.

31.　Mansfield to Warren, June 6, 1939; Wadsworth to Watson, May 9, 1939.

32.　Vorys to A. F. Whitney, July 31, 1939, Vorys MSS, box 4; Hope to A. R. Turner, December 26, 1939, Hope MSS, leg. corr., box 182.

33.　Wadsworth to Watson, May 9, 1939; John Taber to Mrs. William McIntosh, January 3, 1940, Taber MSS, box 67; *Congressional Record*, July 22, 1939, p. 9753.

34.　Warren to W. S. Creighton, June 15, 1939, Warren MSS, box 21-A; Hope to Carter, July 21, 1939.

35.　Warren to Thompson, June 9, 1939.

36.　Warren to H. E. Boyd, July 20, 1939, Warren MSS, box 21-B; Mansfield et al. to House of Representatives, July 15, 1939, Warren MSS, box 21-B; Mansfield et al. to House of Representatives, July 22, 1939, W. Sterling Cole MSS, box 21.

37.　Marvin Jones to Burton K. Wheeler, July 29, 1939, Nat. Arch., Leg. Div., sen. 76A-E1, box 60; Vincent F. Harrington to House of Representatives, April 1, 1940, Warren MSS, box 22-C.

38.　*New York Times*, July 26, 1939.

39.　Lea to FDR, July 19, 1939.

40.　Walter Splawn to FDR, July 29, 1939, FDR MSS, OF 31, box 9; Edwin Watson, memorandum for FDR, July 18, 1939, FDR MSS, OF 31, box 9.

41.　Clyde M. Reed to William Allen White, July 27, 1939, White MSS, box 222; Splawn to FDR, July 29, 1939.

42.　Warren to T. D. Parish, July 27, 1939, Warren MSS, box 21-B; Warren to Norman, July 28, 1939.

43.　Truman to P. N. Coburn, November 8, 1939, Truman MSS, sen., box 152.

44.　Lachlan Macleay to Burton K. Wheeler, January 20, 1940, Nat. Arch., Leg. Div., sen. 76A-E1, box 61; Warren Estes to Wheeler, December 2, 1939, Nat. Arch., Leg. Div., sen. 76A-E1, box 59.

45.　A. F. Whitney to Wheeler, January 26, 1940, Nat. Arch., Leg. Div., sen.

76A-E1, box 61; Edward O'Neal to Wheeler, December 21, 1939, Nat. Arch., Leg. Div., Sen. 76A-E1, box 61.

46. Joseph Eastman to Wheeler, January 29, 1940, Nat. Arch., Leg. Div., sen. 76A-E1, box 61; Edwin Watson, memorandum for FDR, March 6, 1940, FDR MSS, OF 173, box 2.

47. Truman to Lund, February 28, 1940; Edwin Watson, memorandums for FDR, March 5, 6, 1940, FDR MSS, OF 173, box 2; memo, March 8, 1940, Nat. Arch., Leg. Div., sen. 75A-E1, box 59.

48. Harrington to House, April 1, 1940; Jones to Wheeler, July 29, 1939.

49. Reed to Lambertson, May 7, 1940; Clarence F. Lea to A. F. Whitney, May 2, 1940, Nat. Arch., sen. 76A-E1, box 59.

50. Reed to Lambertson, May 7, 1940; Truman to Childress, August 16, 1940.

51. Frederick Brenckman et al. to FDR, May 2, 1940, Nat. Arch., Leg. Div., 76A-E1, box 59.

52. Lindsay C. Warren to Col. George Gillette, May 4, 1940, Warren MSS, box 22-C; Warren to Herbert Peele, March 14, 1940, Warren MSS, box 22-B; Kerr to Holland, May 9, 1940.

53. Clarence F. Lea to FDR, May 1, 1940, FDR MSS, OF 173, box 2; Edwin Watson, memorandums for FDR, May 2, 3, 1940, FDR MSS, OF 173, box 2.

54. Herbert R. Eberharter to Lindsay C. Warren, May 17, 1940, Warren MSS, box 22-C; Vorys to constituents, May 14, 1940.

55. Clifford R. Hope to E. L. Beard, May 10, 1940, Hope MSS, leg. corr., box 182; John Taber to B. L. Voorhis, June 3, 1940, Taber MSS, box 67.

56. Clarence F. Lea to Lindsay C. Warren et al., June 7, 1940, Warren MSS, box 23; Vorys to constituents, May 14, 1940; Alfred Steinberg, *The Man from Missouri* (New York, 1962), p. 150.

57. Eberharter to Warren, May 17, 1940; Warren to S. Otis Bland, August 15, 1940, Warren MSS, box 23.

58. Walter Splawn to FDR, May 15, 1940, FDR MSS, OF 173, box 2.

59. Truman to Dr. W. L. Brandon, August 19, 1940, Truman MSS, sen., box 153; Burton K. Wheeler, press release, August, 1940, Nat. Arch., Leg. Div., sen. 76A-E1, box 61.

60. Vincent F. Harrington to House of Representatives, August 6, 1940, Warren MSS, box 23; James W. Wadsworth, Jr., to House of Representatives, August 7, 1940, Warren MSS, box 23; Gilbert Y. Steiner, *The Congressional Conference Committee* (Champaign-Urbana, 1951), p. 105.

61. Warren to Bland, August 15, 1940.

62. J. J. Mansfield et al. to House of Representatives, August 10, 1940, Nat. Arch., Leg. Div., folder on S. 2009.

63. Steiner, pp. 105–06.

64. Wheeler, p. 351.

65. Thurman Arnold to Edwin Watson, September 5, 1940, FDR MSS, OF 173, box 2.

66. Clyde M. Reed to Claude Gray, October 8, 1940, Nat. Arch., Leg. Div., sen. 76A-E1, box 59.

67. Wheeler, p. 351.

68. Truman to T. J. Davis, September 13, 1940, Truman MSS, sen., box 153; Truman to J. M. Flesch, September 5, 1940, Truman MSS, sen., box 153. The provisions and impact of the Transportation Act are described in Ralph L. Dewey, "Transportation Act of 1940," *American Economic Review* 31 (March, 1941): 15-26; Truman C. Bigham, "The Transportation Act of 1940," *Southern Economic Journal* 8 (July, 1941): 1-21; Robert W. Harbeson, "The Transportation Act of 1940," *Journal of Land and Public Utility Economics* 17 (August, 1941): 291-302; and Hoogenboom.

3. THE CONTINUATION OF RECIPROCAL TRADE

1.   High tariff policies are outlined in Frank W. Taussig, *The Tariff History of the United States,* 8th ed. (New York, 1931), and Joseph M. Jones, Jr., *Tariff Retaliation* (Philadelphia, 1934).

2.   The historical background of reciprocal trade is examined in James C. Pearson, *The Reciprocal Trade Agreements Program* (Washington, 1942); Grace Beckett, *The Reciprocal Trade Agreements Program* (New York, 1941); Samuel Flagg Bemis, *The Latin-American Policy of the United States* (New York, 1943); Power Yung-Chao-Chu, "A History of the Hull Trade Program, 1934–1939" (Ph.D. dissertation, 1957); and Richard N. Kottman, *Reciprocity and the North Atlantic Triangle, 1932-1938* (Ithaca, 1968).

3.   *New York Times,* January 5, 30, 1940; U.S. Congress, House, Committee on Ways and Means, hearings, "Extending the Authority of the President under Section 350 of the Tariff Act of 1930, as Amended," January 11, 12, 1940 (Washington, 1940); U.S. Congress, Senate, Committee on Finance, hearings, "Extending the Authority of the President under Section 350 of the Tariff Act of 1930, as Amended," February 26, 27, 1940 (Washington, 1940). For a concise statement of the secretary of state's views, see Cordell Hull to Charles L. McNary, December 16, 1939, McNary Papers, box 44.

4.   *New York Times,* January 4, 1940.

5.   *Current Biography,* 1942, pp. 213-15.

6.   Karl M. Le Compte to George Mills, December 15, 1939, Le Compte MSS, box 17; *Congressional Record,* 76th Congress, 3rd Session, vol. 86, February 20, 1940, p. 1691; February 21, 1940, p. 1782.

7.   *Congressional Record,* February 19, 1940, pp. 1631-34; February 20, 1940, pp. 1699, 1701.

8.   Clifford R. Hope to D. S. Ray, February 3, 1940, Hope MSS, leg. corr., box 182; Benton F. Jensen, speech, Washington, D. C., November 3, 1939, Jensen MSS, box 16.

9.   Robert L. Doughton to Agnew Bahnson, undated, Doughton MSS, drawer 12.

10.   *Congressional Record,* February 20, 1940, p. 1678; James W. Wadsworth, Jr., to Mrs. Walter Campbell, March 5, 1940, Wadsworth Family MSS, box 25.

11.   Roy O. Woodruff to George N. Peek, November 20, 1939, Peek MSS, box 34; Allen T. Treadway to George N. Peek, November 27, 1939, Peek MSS, box 34.

12.   *New York Times,* January 30, 1940; Henry Carter to Roy O. Woodruff, January 29, 1940, Peek MSS, box 35.

13.   U.S. House, Ways and Means Committee, hearings, "Reciprocal Trade," January 24, 31, February 3, 1940 (Washington, 1940).

14.   Robert L. Doughton to C. H. Turner, March 1, 1940, Doughton MSS, drawer 12.

15.   Roy O. Woodruff to George N. Peek, February 22, 1940, Peek MSS, box 35; Clifford R. Hope to C. H. Brilhart, February 20, 1940, Hope MSS, leg. corr., box 176.

16.   Division of Trade Agreements, memorandum for Mr. Gray, February 12, 1940, FDR MSS, OF 66; Fred L. Israel (ed.), *The War Diary of Breckinridge Long* (Lincoln, 1966), pp. 45-57.

17.   Henry Carter to George N. Peek, March 22, 1940, Peek MSS, box 35.

18.   Clifford R. Hope to Albert Weaver, March 22, 1940, Hope MSS, leg. corr., box 182; Arthur H. Vandenberg to Joseph Doyle, Jr., December 26, 1939, Vandenberg MSS, July, 1939–July, 1940.

19.   *Congressional Record,* April 2, 1940, p. 3807; Key Pittman to Henry F. Grady, November 24, 1939, Pittman MSS, box 157; Arthur Capper, press release, February 29, 1940, Cordell Hull MSS, box 86.

20.   Joseph C. O'Mahoney to D. F. Logan, April 5, 1940, O'Mahoney MSS, box 54; Guy M. Gillette, C B S radio address, Washington, D. C., March 25, 1938, in

Congressional Record, 75th Congress, Appendix, March 25, 1938, p. 1180; Pat Harrison, speech, Washington, D. C., March 25, 1940, Harrison MSS, speeches; Truman, statement, March, 1940, Truman MSS, sec. file, box 168.

21. Key Pittman to Edwin C. Johnson, March 7, 1940, Pittman MSS, box 158; Pittman to Joe McDonald, March 8, 1940, Pittman MSS, box 158; Joseph C. O'Mahoney to Rev. Charles Bream, April 27, 1940, O'Mahoney MSS, box 54.

22. Vandenberg to Doyle, December 26, 1939; Hiram W. Johnson to Frank Doherty, January 13, 1940, Johnson MSS, pt. 3, box 19.

23. Truman statement, March, 1940; Carl Hayden to George Hay, April 10, 1940, Hayden MSS, 632/5.

24. Charles L. McNary to Mrs. Helen Laughlin, January 26, 1940, McNary MSS, box 45; Pat Harrison, press release, February 21, 1940, Harrison MSS, file 2; Hayden to Hay, April 10, 1940.

25. Arthur Capper to William Allen White, January 30, 1940, White MSS, box 231; Charles L. McNary to Cordell Hull, December 12, 1939, McNary MSS, box 44.

26. Theodore F. Green to Milton Sapinsley, February 9, 1940, Green MSS, box 148.

27. Pittman to Boudinot Atterbury, January 3, 1940, Pittman MSS, box 157; Carter Glass to Wallace Tiffany, May 15, 1940, Glass MSS, box 385; Glass to W. F. Maginis, March 13, 1940, Glass MSS, box 391.

28. Pittman to Lee Ellsworth, January 9, 1940, Pittman MSS, box 157; Carter to Peek, March 22, 1940.

29. *New York Times*, March 27, 1940; Israel, pp. 48, 51–52.

30. *New York Times*, March 28, 1940; Sherman Minton to Robert F. Wagner, March 25, 1940, Wagner MSS, file B-3.

31. Pittman to Burton K. Wheeler, March 28, 1940, Pittman MSS, box 158; *New York Times,* March 29, 1940.

32. *New York Times*, April 6, 1940; Harold L. Ickes, *The Secret Diary of Harold L. Ickes* 3 (New York, 1954): 161.

33. FDR to Pat Harrison, April 6, 1940, Harrison MSS, file 2; Cordell Hull to Harrison, April 5, 1940, Harrison MSS, file 2.

34. Pittman to John Robbins, April 8, 1940, Pittman MSS, box 158. Democrats Harry H. Schwartz of Wyoming and Lewis P. Schwellenbach of Washington defected from the dissenting coalition hours before the final roll call.

35. Joseph C. O'Mahoney to Kenneth Cox, April 6, 1940, O'Mahoney MSS, box 54; O'Mahoney to H. J. King, April 9, 1940, O'Mahoney MSS, box 54.

36. Hiram W. Johnson to Hiram W. Johnson, Jr., April 6, 1940, Johnson MSS, pt. 6, box 8.

37. Samuel I. Rosenman (ed.), *The Public Papers and Addresses of Franklin D. Roosevelt* 9 (New York, 1941): 154–55; *New York Times*, April 13, 1940.

4. MAINTAINING WORK RELIEF PROGRAMS

1. Lester V. Chandler, *America's Greatest Depression, 1929-1941* (New York, 1970); Edward Robb Ellis, *A Nation in Torment: The Great American Depression, 1929-1939* (New York, 1971), Irving Bernstein, *Turbulent Years: A History of the American Worker, 1933-1941* (New York, 1970), and John A. Garraty, *Unemployment in History: Economic Thought and Public Relief* (New York, 1978) describe economic conditions. New Deal relief programs are treated in Josephine Chapin Brown, *Public Relief, 1929-1939* (New York, 1940); Arthur W. MacMahon, J. D. Millett, and Gladys Ogden, *The Administration of Federal Work Relief* (Chicago, 1941); and William Bremer, "Along the 'American Way': The New Deal's Work Relief Programs for the Unemployed," *Journal of American History* 62 (December, 1975): 643–46.

2. Donald S. Howard, *The WPA and Federal Relief Policy* (New York, 1943),

Robert E. Sherwood, *Roosevelt and Hopkins: An Intimate History* (New York, 1948), and Searle F. Charles, *Minister of Relief: Harry Hopkins and the Depression* (Syracuse, 1963) provide the historical background of the WPA.

3. *Washington Post*, January 4, 1939; Escal F. Duke, "The Political Career of Morris Sheppard, 1875–1941" (Ph.D. dissertation, 1958), pp. 477–84; C. Vann Woodward (ed.), *Responses of the Presidents to Charges of Misconduct* (New York, 1974), pp. 267–68.

4. *New York Times*, January 1, 1939; Bascom N. Timmons, *Garner of Texas* (New York, 1948), pp. 240–42.

5. Corrington Gill to Morris Sheppard, August 24, 1939, Sheppard MSS, A/14/120; FDR to Congress, January 5, 1939, Nat. Arch., Leg. Div., HR 76A-F2.1.

6. U.S. Congress, House, Committee on Appropriations, "Additional Work Relief and Relief, Fiscal Year, 1939," hearings, January 6, 1939 (Washington, 1939).

7. *Congressional Record*, 76th Congress, 1st Session, vol. 84, January 12, 1939, p. 266; January 13, 1939, p. 288; Martin L. Sweeney, speech, Cleveland, Ohio, October 22, 1939, Sweeney MSS, container 1.

8. John Taber, press release, January 12, 1939, Taber MSS, box 63.

9. *Congressional Record*, January 13, 1939, pp. 290, 296; John M. Vorys to J. F. Thoelcke, February 1, 1939, Vorys MSS, box 5.

10. *Congressional Record*, January 12, 1939, p. 251; Sweeney, speech, October 22, 1939.

11. *Congressional Record*, January 12, 1939, p. 257; Karl Stefan to Edgar Howard, January 30, 1939, Stefan MSS, box 24; George H. Bender, speech, Washington, D.C., March 22, 1939, Bender MSS, container 3.

12. Robert L. Doughton to R. B. Cooke, January 14, 1939, Doughton MSS, drawer 11; *Congressional Record*, January 13, 1939, p. 310.

13. *Congressional Record*, January 12, 1939, p. 260; January 13, 1939, p. 305; George H. Bender, speech, Washington, D.C., 1940, Bender MSS, container 3.

14. *Congressional Record*, January 12, 1939, p. 257.

15. *Congressional Record*, January 12, 1939, p. 263; Frank Horton to John Taber, April 17, 1939, Taber MSS, box 49.

16. *New York Times*, January 13, 1939; Taber, press release, January 12, 1939; Cary S. Henderson, "Congressman John Taber of Auburn: Politics and Federal Appropriations, 1923–1962" (Ph.D. dissertation, 1964). pp. 194–95.

17. Stephen Early, memorandum for Grace Tully, January 13, 1939, FDR MSS, OF 444-C; Early to Lewis Berne, January 14, 1939, FDR MSS, OF 444-C.

18. *Congressional Record*, January 12, 1939, p. 249; *New York Times*, January 12, 1939.

19. *Congressional Record*, January 12, 1939, pp. 241–45.

20. *Congressional Record*, January 12, 1939, pp. 249–50.

21. *Congressional Record*, January 12, 1939, pp. 246–47.

22. *Congressional Record*, January 12, 1939, pp. 267–70; January 13, 1939, pp. 308–9.

23. *New York Times*, January 14, 1939; Lex Green to T. P. Chairis, February 10, 1939, Green MSS, box 45.

24. *Congressional Record*, January 13, 1939, p. 318; James W. Wadsworth, Jr., to Jerry Wadsworth, January 26, 1939, Wadsworth Family MSS, box 33.

25. George H. Bender, speech, Washington, D.C., March 1, 1939, Bender MSS, container 3; Wadsworth to Wadsworth, January 26, 1939.

26. *New York Times*, January 18, 19, 1939.

27. *New York Times*, January 18, 1939; U.S. Congress, Senate, Committee on Appropriations, "Additional Work Relief and Relief, Fiscal Year, 1939," hearings, January 17, 1939 (Washington, 1939).

28. *New York Times*, December 1, 1941.

29. James T. Patterson, *Congressional Conservatism and the New Deal* (Lexington, Ky. 1967), p. 295; U.S. Congress, Senate, Committee on Appropriations, rpt. no. 4,

"Additional Appropriations for Work Relief and Relief for the Fiscal Year Ending June 30, 1939," January 23, 1939 (Washington, 1939).

30. *Newsweek* 13 (February 6, 1939): 15; *Washington Star*, January 24, 1939; Walter K. Roberts, "The Political Career of Charles Linza McNary, 1924–1944" (Ph.D. dissertation, 1953), p. 257.

31. *Congressional Record*, January 24, 1939, p. 671.

32. *Congressional Record*, January 24, 1939, pp. 685–87.

33. William E. Borah to W. R. Wolfe, January 17, 1939, Borah MSS, box 425; *Congressional Record*, January 25, 1939, p. 771.

34. *Congressional Record*, January 24, 1939, p. 690.

35. *Congressional Record*, January 24, 1939, p. 698; May René Lorentz, "Henrik Shipstead: Minnesota Independent, 1923–1946" (Ph.D. dissertation, 1963), p. 81.

36. Robert F. Wagner, press release, January 23, 1939, Wagner MSS, shelf; *Congressional Record*, January 26, 1939, p. 815.

37. Joseph C. O'Mahoney to R. H. MacPherson, April 27, 1939, O'Mahoney MSS, box 52; O'Mahoney to W. M. Jeffers, April 27, 1939, O'Mahoney MSS, box 52.

38. Rush Dew Holt, press release, January 20, 1939, Holt MSS, A&M 1701, box 102; *Congressional Record*, January 25, 1939, p. 767.

39. FDR, memorandum for Alben W. Barkley and Sam Rayburn, January 24, 1939, FDR MSS, OF 444-C; *New York Times*, January 24–26, 1939; *Congressional Record*, January 27, 1939, pp. 863–79, 887.

40. Hiram W. Johnson to Hiram W. Johnson, Jr., January 29, 1939, Johnson MSS, pt. 6, box 7.

41. James J. Davis to Cornelius Scully, January 28, 1939, Davis MSS, box 23.

42. Johnson to Johnson, January 28, 1939: Johnson MSS, pt. 6, box 7.

43. Harold L. Ickes (ed.), *The Secret Diary of Harold L. Ickes*, 2 (New York, 1954): 570; *New York Times*, February 3, 1939; FDR to Congress, February 7, 1939, Nat. Arch., Leg. Div., HR76A-F2.1.

44. Johnson to Johnson, January 28, 1939.

45. Hiram W. Johnson to Frank Doherty, January 30, 1939, Johnson MSS, pt. 3, box 18.

46. FDR to Congress, February 7, 1939.

47. *Time* 33 (March 27, 1939): 13–14; *New York Times*, February 8, 1939.

48. Annette T. Rubinstein (ed.), *I Vote My Conscience: Debates, Speeches, and Writings of Vito Marcantonio* (New York, 1956), pp. 96–97; William Nelson to FDR, March 9, 1939, FDR MSS, OF 444-C.

49. *New York Times*, March 10, 1939; FDR to William Nelson, March 11, 1939, FDR MSS, OF 444-C.

50. *New York Times*, March 11, 1939.

51. FDR to Congress, March 14, 1939, Nat. Arch., Leg. Div., HR76A-F2.1; *New York Times*, March 15, 1939.

52. *New York Times*, March 17, 23, 28, 1939.

53. Patterson, p. 303; *New York Times*, March 25, 1939.

54. U.S. Congress, House, Committee on Appropriations, "Further Additional Appropriations for Work Relief, Fiscal Year 1939," hearings, March 15–21, 1939 (Washington, 1939); John Taber, press release, March 29, 1939, Taber MSS, box 55; Henderson, pp. 198–200.

55. *Congressional Record*, March 30, 1939, pp. 3563, 3570–73.

56. *Congressional Record*, March 31, 1939, pp. 3663, 3667.

57. *Congressional Record*, March 31, 1939, pp. 3636, 3641.

58. *Congressional Record*, March 30, 1939, p. 3558; March 31, 1939, p. 3641.

59. *Congressional Record*, March 31, 1939, p. 3659.

60. *New York Times*, April 12, 1939.

61. Patterson, p. 304; Ickes, 2: 612.

62. *Congressional Record*, April 6, 1939, pp. 3880, 3886.

63. *Congressional Record*, April 11, 1939, p. 4887.

64. *Congressional Record*, April 6, 1939, p. 3902.

65. *Congressional Record*, April 6, 1939, p. 3906; April 7, 1939, p. 3960.

66. *Congressional Record*, April 6, 1939, p. 3892; April 11, 1939, p. 4073.

67. *Congressional Record*, April 7, 1939, p. 3961, 3969; *New York Times*, April 8, 1939; *Washington Post*, April 11, 1939.

68. FDR to Claude Pepper, April 11, 1939, Pepper MSS, 66-A-82, box 112.

69. *New York Herald Tribune*, April 12, 1939.

70. *Congressional Record*, April 11, 1939, p. 4099.

71. *New York Times*, April 12, 1939.

72. FDR to Congress, April 27, 1939, Nat. Arch., Leg. Div., HR 76A-F2.1; Samuel I. Rosenman (ed.), *The Public Papers and Addresses of Franklin D. Roosevelt*, 8 (New York, 1941): 303–04.

5. THE REORGANIZATION OF THE EXECUTIVE BRANCH

1. The historical background of executive reorganization is described in *Report of the President's Committee on Administrative Management* (Washington, 1937); Barry Dean Karl, *Executive Reorganization and Reform in the New Deal* (Cambridge, Mass., 1963); Richard Polenberg, *Reorganizing Roosevelt's Government: The Controversy over Executive Reorganization, 1936-1939* (Cambridge, Mass., 1966); and A. J. Wann, *The President As Chief Administrator: A Study of Franklin D. Roosevelt* (Washington, 1968).

2. Polenberg, pp. 125–80; James T. Patterson, *Congressional Conservatism and the New Deal* (Lexington, 1967), pp. 214–29; Louis Brownlow, *A Passion for Anonymity: The Autobiography of Louis Brownlow* (Chicago, 1958), pp. 343–86; J. M. Ray, "Defeat of the Administration Reorganization Bill," *Southwestern Social Science Quarterly* 20 (September, 1939): 115–24.

3. Carl Hayden to J. Early Craig, April 12, 1938, Hayden MSS, 590/4.

4. Lindsay C. Warren to FDR, November 14, 1938, Warren MSS, box 20-A; Warren to John J. Cochran, November 23, 1938, Warren MSS, box 20-A.

5. Warren to James F. Byrnes, December 22, 1938, Warren MSS, box 20-A; Warren to E. C. Flanagan, March 18, 1939, Warren MSS, box 20-B.

6. *Congressional Record*, 76th Congress, 1st Session, vol. 84, March 6, 1939, p. 3505.

7. Polenberg, p. 186; *New York Times*, February 24, 1939. The exempted bodies included all cabinet agencies, the Coast Guard, Engineer Corps of the Army, Federal Communications Commission, Federal Power Commission, Federal Trade Commission, Interstate Commerce Commission, National Labor Relations Board, Securities and Exchange Commission, Board of Tax Appeals, Employees Compensation Commission, Maritime Commission, Tariff Commission, Veterans Administration, and the National Bituminous Coal Commission.

8. *New York Times*, February 24, 1939.

9. John Taber to Miss Kathleen Mc Cullough, April 14, 1939, Taber MSS, box 63.

10. *Congressional Record*, March 7, 1939, p. 2398.

11. *Congressional Record*, March 8, 1939, p. 2476.

12. *Congressional Record*, March 8, 1939, p. 2476; Robert L. Doughton to A. J. Carney, March 25, 1939, Doughton MSS, drawer 11.

13. *Congressional Record*, March 7, 1939, pp. 2388, 2397.

14. John M. Vorys to George Chandler, March 10, 1939, Vorys MSS, box 4; *Congressional Record*, March 7, 1939, p. 2401.

15. *Congressional Record*, March 7, 1939, p. 2399.

16. *Congressional Record*, March 7, 1939, pp. 2392, 2408.

17. J. Hardin Peterson, Washington newsletter, March 16, 1939, Peterson MSS, box 20; *Congressional Record*, March 7, 1939, p. 2379.

18. *New York Times*, March 3, 4, 1939; Taber to McCullough, April 14, 1939; *Congressional Record*, March 6, 1939, p. 2315.

19. *Current Biography*, 1942, pp. 117-20.

20. *New York Times*, March 7, 1939; Polenberg, p. 186; Amos Pinchot to Frank Gannett, March 17, 1939, Pinchot MSS, box 66.

21. Lindsay C. Warren to William Bragaw, March 11, 1939, Warren MSS, box 20-B; Vorys to Chandler, March 10, 1939.

22. *Congressional Record*, March 6, 1939, pp. 2311-13.

23. *Congressional Record*, March 6, 1939, pp. 2307-8.

24. *Congressional Record*, March 8, 1939, pp. 2498-500.

25. *New York Times*, March 9, 1939; Vorys to Chandler, March 10, 1939.

26. *Congressional Record*, March 8, 1939, p. 2501.

27. Warren to Edwin Gill, March 10, 1939, Warren MSS, box 20-B; Knute Hill to P. H. Drewry, March 13, 1939, FDR MSS, OF, 285, box 8.

28. Clifford R. Hope to S. R. Stebbins, March 14, 1939, Hope MSS, leg. corr., box 151; Warren to O. K. LaRoque, May 4, 1939, Warren MSS, box 21-A.

29. Warren to Harry McMullen, March 11, 1939, Warren MSS, box 20-B.

30. Warren to Flanagan, March 18, 1939; Harold L. Ickes (ed.), *The Secret Diary of Harold L. Ickes*, 2 (New York, 1954): 594-95.

31. Warren to Flanagan, March 18, 1939.

32. J. Hardin Peterson, Washington newsletter, undated, Peterson MSS, box 20; J. Wilburn Cartwright, newsletter, April 1, 1939, Cartwright MSS, box 168.

33. "Congressional Poll on Reorganization," *Congressional Intelligence* 7 (March 18, 1939): 4.

34. *Current Biography*, 1941, pp. 125-27; James F. Byrnes, *All in One Lifetime* (New York, 1958); Alben W. Barkley, *That Reminds Me* (Garden City, 1954); Martha Swain, *Pat Harrison: The New Deal Years* (University, Miss., 1978).

35. *Congressional Record*, March 16, 1939, pp. 2808, 2815.

36. *Congressional Record*, March 16, 1939, p. 2943.

37. Barkley, CBS radio address, August 12, 1939, Barkley MSS, box 5; Clyde L. Herring, speech, Des Moines, Iowa, May 11, 1939, Herring MSS, box 4; *Congressional Record*, March 21, 1939, p. 3024.

38. Bennett Champ Clark to Lindsay C. Warren, November 21, 1938, Warren MSS, box 20-A; *Congressional Record*, March 20, 1939, p. 2954.

39. *Congressional Record*, March 20, 1939, p. 2952; March 22, 1939, p. 3086.

40. *Congressional Record*, March 17, 1939, pp. 2905-6; *New York Times*, March 17, 1939.

41. *Congressional Record*, March 20, 1939, p. 2949; *New York Times*, March 21, 1939.

42. *Congressional Record*, March 20, 1939, pp. 2957, 2968.

43. *New York Times*, March 22, 1939; Hiram W. Johnson to Hiram W. Johnson, Jr., March 26, 1939, Johnson MSS, pt. 6, box 7.

44. Johnson to Johnson, March 26, 1939.

45. *New York Times*, March 22, 1939.

46. Harry F. Byrd to Amos Pinchot, March 28, 1939, Pinchot MSS, box 66; Johnson to Johnson, March 26, 1939.

47. FDR to Key Pittman, March 21, 1939, Pittman MSS, box 15; Pittman to FDR, March 21, 1939, Pittman MSS, box 15.

48. Warren R. Austin to Mrs. Chauncey Austin, March 22, 1939, Austin MSS, general correspondence; Ickes, 2: 602-3.

49. Johnson to Johnson, March 26, 1939.

50. *Congressional Record*, March 21, 1939, pp. 3100, 3102.

51. Austin to Austin, March 22, 1939.

52. Byrd to Pinchot, March 28, 1939; Warren R. Austin to Mrs. Chauncey Austin, March 17, 1939, Austin MSS, correspondence with mother.

53. FDR to Congress, April 25, 1939, FDR MSS, OF 285C, box 8; FDR to

Congress, May 9, 1939, FDR MSS, OF 285C, box 8; Polenberg, pp. 187–88; Kannee, memorandum for Edwin Watson, May 10, 1939, FDR MSS, OF 285C, box 8.

54.   FDR, memorandum for director of the budget, January 24, 1940, FDR MSS, OF 285-C, box 9; Edwin Watson, memorandum for FDR, January 29, 1940, FDR MSS, OF 1-C.

55.   George W. Norris to FDR, January 25, 1940, Norris MSS, package 111, box 2; Lindsay C. Warren to John J. Cochran, February 7, 1940, FDR MSS, OF 1-C.

56.   FDR to Congress, April 2, 11, 1940, FDR MSS, OF 285-C, box 9; FDR to Congress, May 22, 1940, FDR MSS, OF 285-C, box 9.

57.   *New York Times*, May 2, 1940; Stephen Early, memorandum for FDR, April 26, 1940, FDR MSS, OF 285, box 9.

58.   *New York Times*, May 9, 15, 28, 1940, June 1, 1940; Polenberg, p. 188.

6. THE HATCHETING OF POLITICAL CORRUPTION

1.   Dorothy Ganfield Fowler, "Precursors of the Hatch Act," *Mississippi Valley Historical Review* 47 (September, 1960): 247–62.

2.   Escal F. Duke, "The Political Career of Morris Sheppard, 1875-1941" (Ph.D. dissertation, 1958), pp. 477–84; C. Vann Woodward (ed.), *Responses of the Presidents to Charges of Misconduct* (New York, 1974), pp. 267–68; *Washington Post*, January 4, 1939.

3.   Searle F. Charles, *Minister of Relief: Harry Hopkins and the Depression* (Syracuse, 1963), p. 181; FDR to Congress, January 5, 1939, Nat. Arch., Leg. Div., HR76A-F2.1.

4.   *Current Biography*, 1944, pp. 277–81.

5.   Charles, pp. 196-98; *Time* 32 (October 31, 1938): 11; *Santa Fe New Mexican*, October 20, 21, 1938.

6.   *Congressional Record*, 76th Congress, 1st Session, vol. 84, April 13, 1939, pp. 4191–92.

7.   *New York Times*, January 22, 1939.

8.   *New York Times*, April 15, 1939; Carl A. Hatch to Joseph C. O'Mahoney, July 18, 1939, O'Mahoney MSS, box 45.

9.   Stephen Early, memorandum for Rudolph Forster, April 17, 1939, FDR MSS, OF 252.

10.   *New York Times*, April 28, 1939.

11.   *Time* 33 (June 26, 1939): 16–17.

12.   Hatch to Edwin Watson, June 17, 1939, FDR MSS, President's secretary's files, box 54.

13.   Hatch to O'Mahoney, July 18, 1939; *Congressional Record*, July 20, 1939, p. 9597.

14.   *New York Times*, July 6, 1939; Hatch to O'Mahoney, July 18, 1939.

15.   Hatch to O'Mahoney, July 18, 1939.

16.   Ibid.

17.   Frank H. Buck to FDR, July 27, 1939, FDR MSS, OF 252.

18.   Lex Green to FDR, July 26, 1939, FDR MSS, OF 252.

19.   Kent Keller to FDR, August 1, 1939, FDR MSS, OF 252, box 4; *Congressional Record*, July 20, 1939, pp. 9594–96; *New York Times*, July 21, 1939.

20.   *Congressional Record*, July 20, 1939, pp. 9594–96; Charles I. Faddis to FDR, July 26, 1939, FDR MSS, OF 252.

21.   *Congressional Record*, July 20, 1939, pp. 9603, 9611.

22.   Thomas V. Smith to Lee Hills, August 2, 1939, Smith MSS, box 8; Martin L. Sweeney, speech, Cleveland, Ohio, October 22, 1939, Sweeney MSS, container 1.

23.   *New York Times*, July 21, 1939; *Time* 34 (July 31, 1939): 10.

24.   John M. Vorys to Miss Dorothy Coppock, July 21, 1939, Vorys MSS, box 3.

25.   *New York Times*, July 22, 1939; *Time* 34 (July 31, 1939): 10.

26.   Keller to FDR, August 1, 1939; William L. Nelson to FDR, July 22, 1939, FDR MSS, OF 252.

27.   Eugene Cox to FDR, July 28, 1939, FDR MSS, OF 252; Guy L. Moser to FDR, August 1, 1939, FDR MSS, OF 252.

28.   Emanuel Celler to Edwin Watson, July 31, 1939, FDR MSS, OF 252; Faddis to FDR, July 26, 1939. Representatives Frank H. Buck of California, John M. Coffee of Washington, Richard M. Duncan of Missouri, Thomas F. Ford of California, Lex Green of Florida, Frank E. Hook of Michigan, James F. O'Connor of Montana, and Joseph B. Shannon of Missouri also urged the President to veto the Hatch bill.

29.   Draft of proposed veto message, July 29, 1939, FDR MSS, PSF, box 54.

30.   Frank Murphy to FDR, July 26, 1939, FDR MSS, PSF, box 54.

31.   Hatch to FDR, July 28, 1939, FDR MSS, PSF, box 54.

32.   Samuel I. Rosenman (ed.), *The Public Papers and Addresses of Franklin D. Roosevelt*, 8 (New York, 1941): 410-15. Hatch, who feared the President might veto the bill, praised Roosevelt's final action and wired the White House "THANK YOU!" Hatch to FDR, August 2, 1939, FDR MSS, 1938-1939, box 61.

33.   *New York Times*, January 9, 1940; *Congressional Record*, 76th Congress, 3rd Session, vol. 86, March 5, 1940, pp. 2338-43.

34.   *New York Times*, February 28, 1940, March 6, 1940.

35.   *Congressional Record*, March 8, 1940, p. 2574.

36.   Joseph C. O'Mahoney to Arthur Jett, May 4, 1940, O'Mahoney MSS, box 50; *Congressional Record*, March 6, 1940, p. 2438.

37.   *Congressional Record*, March 5, 1940, pp. 2339, 2351, 2361.

38.   *Congressional Record*, March 9, 1940, p. 2594; March 11, 1940, p. 2634.

39.   Key Pittman to James Farley, January 15, 1940, Pittman MSS, box 13.

40.   Josiah W. Bailey to H. B. Caldwell, March 18, 1940, Bailey MSS, political file, 1940; *Congressional Record*, March 13, 1940, p. 2801.

41.   *Congressional Record*, March 26, 1940, p. 2436; March 13, 1940, p. 2773; Clyde L. Herring, press release, March 14, 1940, Herring MSS, box 2.

42.   *Congressional Record*, March 5, 1940, p. 2351; March 6, 1940, p. 2427; Herring, press release, March 14, 1940.

43.   *Congressional Record*, March 6, 1940, p. 2438; *Time* 35 (March 18, 1940): 15.

44.   Theodore G. Bilbo to John L. Smith, March 11, 1940, Bilbo MSS, file O; *Congressional Record*, March 9, 1940, pp. 2599-610.

45.   *Congressional Record*, March 11, 1940, p. 2633.

46.   *Congressional Record*, March 11, 1940, p. 2638.

47.   Warren R. Austin to Mrs. Chauncey Austin, March 13, 1940, Austin MSS, general correspondence, 1939-1940; Bilbo to Smith, March 11, 1940.

48.   Austin to Austin, March 9, 1940, Austin MSS, Corr. with mother; Bailey to J. H. Folger, March 21, 1940, Bailey MSS, pol. file, 1940.

49.   *New York Times*, March 14, 1940; *Time* 35 (March 25, 1940): 19.

50.   *New York Times*, March 14, 1940.

51.   *Congressional Record*, March 5, 1940, p. 2358.

52.   *New York Times*, March 15, 1940.

53.   Austin to Austin, March 14, 1940, Austin MSS, corr. with mother.

54.   *Congressional Record*, March 15, 1940, pp. 2931-32.

55.   Clifford R. Hope to William Washburn, March 15, 1940, Hope MSS, leg. corr., box 178

56.   Hope to Washburn, March 15, 1940; Lyle H. Boren to Wade George, March 14, 1940, Boren MSS, box 74.

57.   Hiram W. Johnson to Hiram W. Johnson, Jr., March 17, 1940, Johnson MSS, pt. 6, box 8; Bailey to T. L. Kirkpatrick, March 16, 1940, Bailey MSS, pol. file, 1940.

58.   *New York Times*, March 19, 1940.

59.   *New York Times*, May 4, 1940; *Time* 35 (May 13, 1940): 20.

60.   *New York Times*, May 2, 4, 1940.

61. *New York Times*, May 7, 1940.

62. *New York Times*, May 8, 15, 24, 30, 1940; U.S. Congress, House, Committee on Judiciary, rpt. no. 2376, "Extension of Act to Prevent Pernicious Political Activities," June 4, 1940 (Washington, 1940).

63. *New York Times*, June 7, 1940; John J. Dempsey to Thomas V. Smith, July 7, 1940, Smith MSS, box 5.

64. *Time* 36 (July 22, 1940): 17; *Congressional Record*, July 9, 1940. p. 9361.

65. *Congressional Record*, July 10, 1940, pp. 9434–35, 9439.

66. *Congressional Record*, July 9, 1940, pp. 9365, 9367.

67. *Congressional Record*, July 9, 1940, pp. 9366, 9379.

68. *Congressional Record*, July 9, 1940, p. 9374; July 10, 1940, pp. 9429, 9455.

69. *Congressional Record*, July 10, 1940, p. 9463.

70. George W. Norris to John Dempsey, July 11, 1940, Norris MSS, package 111, box 1.

71. *New York Times*, July 21, 1940; *Vital Speeches* 6 (September 1, 1940): 676–79.

72. Ferrel Heady, "The Hatch Decisions," *American Political Science Review* 41 (August, 1947): 687–99; Emanuel Celler to FDR, November 13, 1940, FDR MSS, PPF 2748.

7. EPILOGUE

1. James T. Patterson, *Congressional Conservatism and the New Deal* (Lexington, 1967), Richard Polenberg, *Reorganizing Roosevelt's Government: The Controversy over Executive Reorganization, 1936–1939* (Cambridge, Mass., 1966), and other works describe how Congress acted very independently of the President on domestic issues in Roosevelt's second term.

2. V. O. Key, Jr., *Southern Politics in State and Nation* (New York, 1949), Samuel Lubell, *The Future of American Politics* (New York, 1952), Frank Freidel, *F.D.R. and the South* (Baton Rouge, 1965), and James T. Patterson III, "The Failure of Party Realignment in the South, 1937–1939," *Journal of Politics* 27 (August, 1965): 602–17, stress the anti–New Deal coalition between Republicans and conservative Democrats.

3. Julius Turner, *Party and Constituency: Pressures on Congress* (Baltimore, 1951), Lubell, and Patterson emphasize the role of midwesterners as leading the Republicans criticizing Roosevelt's domestic policies. Biographies particularly concentrate on midwestern Republicans in this period. Biographical subjects include Arthur Capper, Robert M. LaFollette, Jr., William Lemke, Gerald P. Nye, Robert A. Taft, and Arthur H. Vandenberg.

4. Key, Lubell, Freidel, Patterson, and others describe the enormous power before World War 2 of southern senators and representatives. James F. Byrnes, *All in One Lifetime* (New York, 1958), Tom Connally, *My Name Is Tom Connally* (New York, 1954), C. Dwight Dorough, *Mr. Sam* (New York, 1962), and other works show the power of individual southern members.

5. Pertinent memoirs include Joseph W. Martin, Jr., *My First Fifty Years in Politics* (New York, 1960), and Alben W. Barkley, *That Reminds Me* (Garden City, 1954). Dorough, Dwayne L. Little, "Man in the Middle: Sam Rayburn as Majority Leader, 1937–1940," *Proceedings of the Florida College Teachers of History* (1971), Walter J. Heacock, "William Brockman Bankhead: A Biography" (Ph. D. dissertation, 1952), and Walter K. Roberts, "The Political Career of Charles Linza McNary, 1924–1944" (Ph.D. dissertation, 1954), assess the role of congressional leaders.

6. Polenberg, pp. 55–78, shows the effectiveness of pressure groups on reorganization legislation. The unsuccessful attempt of lobbyists to secure increased appropriations for the WPA is described in U.S. Congress, House, Committee on Appropriations, "Additional Work Relief and Relief, Fiscal Year, 1939," hearings, January, 1939 (Washington, 1939).

7.   The principal published works discussing the role of Congress in the 1937–39 period on domestic issues are Patterson and Polenberg.

8.   Historical studies assessing the congressional response on foreign policy issues include Robert A. Divine, *The Illusion of Neutrality* (Chicago, 1962); Manfred Jonas, *Isolationism in America, 1935–1941* (Ithaca, 1966); and Robert Sobel, *The Origins of Interventionism: The United States and the Russo-Finnish War* (New York, 1960).

BIBLIOGRAPHY

The notes include the most important sources for this study. The following sources were also consulted and provided helpful background information:

MANUSCRIPT COLLECTIONS

Barkley, Alben W., MSS, Margaret I. King Library, University of Kentucky.
Bloom, Sol, MSS, New York Public Library.
Cannon, Clarence, Jr., MSS, Western Historical Manuscripts Collection, University of Missouri.
Keogh, Eugene J., MSS, George Arents Research Library, Syracuse University.
Nichols, Jack, MSS, Western History Collections, University of Oklahoma Library.
Norton, Mary T., MSS, Rutgers University Library.
Nye, Gerald P., MSS, Herbert Hoover Presidential Library, West Branch, Iowa.
Schwellenbach, Lewis P., MSS, Library of Congress.
Thomas, Elbert D., MSS, Franklin D. Roosevelt Library, Hyde Park, New York.
Tobey, Charles W., MSS, Baker Memorial Library, Dartmouth College.

GOVERNMENT PUBLICATIONS

Biographical Directory of the American Congress, 1774-1971. Washington: U. S. Government Printing Office, 1971.
Immediate Relief for Railroads, House Document No. 583, 75th Congress, 3rd Session. Washington: U. S. Government Printing Office, 1938.
Report of the Committee Appointed September 20, 1938 by the President of the United States to Submit Recommendations upon the General Transportation Situation. Washington: U. S. Government Printing Office, 1938.

BIOGRAPHIES AND AUTOBIOGRAPHIES

Blackorby, Edward C., *Prairie Rebel: The Public Life of William Lemke.* Lincoln: University of Nebraska Press, 1963.
Burns, James MacGregor, *Roosevelt: The Lion and the Fox.* New York: Harcourt Brace, 1956.
Burns, James MacGregor, *Roosevelt: The Soldier of Freedom.* New York: Harcourt Brace Jovanovich, 1970.

Cole, Wayne S., *Senator Gerald P. Nye and American Foreign Relations*. Minneapolis: University of Minnesota Press, 1962.

Fausold, Martin L., *James W. Wadsworth, Jr.: The Gentleman from New York*. Syracuse: Syracuse University Press, 1975.

Hull, Cordell, *The Memoirs of Cordell Hull*, 2 Vols. New York: Macmillan, 1948.

Huthmacher, J. Joseph, *Senator Robert F. Wagner and the Rise of Urban Liberalism*. New York: Atheneum, 1968.

Levine, Ervin, *Theodore Francis Green; the Washington Years, 1937–1960*. Providence: Brown University Press, 1971.

Libbey, James K., *Dear Alben: Mr. Barkley of Kentucky*. Lexington: University Press of Kentucky, 1979.

Lowitt, Richard, *George W. Norris: The Triumph of a Progressive, 1933–1944*. Urbana: University of Illinois Press, 1978.

Maney, Patrick J., *'Young Bob' La Follette: A Biography of Robert M. La Follette, Jr., 1895–1953*. Columbia: University of Missouri Press, 1978.

McKenna, Marian C., *Borah*. Ann Arbor: University of Michigan Press, 1961.

Miller, Merle, *Plain Speaking: An Oral Biography of Harry S. Truman*. New York: Putnam's, 1974.

Moley, Raymond, *After Seven Years*. New York: Harper, 1939.

Moore, John Robert, *Senator Josiah William Bailey of North Carolina*. Durham: Duke University Press, 1968.

Patterson, James T., *Mr. Republican: A Biography of Robert A. Taft*. Boston: Houghton Mifflin, 1972.

Perkins, Frances, *The Roosevelt I Knew*. New York: Viking, 1946.

Socolofsky, Homer E., *Arthur Capper: Publisher, Politician, and Philanthropist*. Lawrence: University of Kansas Press, 1962.

Schaffer, Alan, *Vito Marcantonio: Radical in Congress*. Syracuse: Syracuse University Press, 1966.

Steinberg, Alfred, *Sam Rayburn: A Biography*. New York: Hawthorn Books, 1975.

Tompkins, C. David, *Senator Arthur H. Vandenberg: The Evolution of a Modern Republican, 1884–1945*. East Lansing: Michigan State University Press, 1970.

Tugwell, Rexford, *The Democratic Roosevelt*. Garden City: Doubleday, 1957.

BOOKS

Bigham, Truman C., and Merrill J. Roberts, *Transportation: Principles and Problems*. New York: McGraw-Hill, 1952.

Conkin, Paul, *The New Deal*, 2nd Ed. New York: Thomas Y. Crowell, 1975.

Crawford, Arthur Whipple, *Monetary Management under the New Deal: The Evolution of a Managed Currency System*. Washington: American Council on Public Affairs, 1940.

Donahoe, Bernard F., *Private Plans and Public Dangers: The Story of FDR's Third Term Nomination*. Notre Dame: University of Notre Dame Press, 1965.

Emmerich, Herbert, *Essays on Federal Reorganization*. Birmingham: University of Alabama Press, 1950.

Flanagan, Hallie, *Arena: The History of the Federal Theatre*. New York: Russell Sage Foundation, 1940.

Friedman, Milton and Anna Jacobsen Schwartz, *A Monetary History of the United States*. Princeton: Princeton University Press, 1963.

Gill, Corrington, *Wasted Manpower*. New York: Norton, 1939.

Hawley, Ellis W., *The New Deal and the Problem of Monopoly, 1933–39*. Princeton: Princeton University Press, 1966.

Hobbs, Edward H., *Executive Reorganization in the National Government*. University, Miss.: University of Mississippi Press, 1953.

Hobbs, S. Huntington, Jr., *North Carolina: An Economic and Social Profile*. Chapel Hill: University of North Carolina Press, 1958.

Hopkins, Harry L., *Spending to Save*. New York: Norton, 1936.

Johnson, G. Griffith, *The Treasury and Monetary Policy, 1933–1938*. Cambridge, Mass.: Harvard University Press, 1939.

Letiche, John H., *Reciprocal Trade Agreements in the World Economy*. New York: King's Crown Press, 1948.

Mangione, Jerre, *The Dream and the Deal: The Federal Writers' Project, 1935–1943*. Boston: Little, Brown, 1972.

Meriam, Lewis and Laurence F. Schmeckebeir, *Reorganization of the National Government: What Does It Involve?* Washington: Brookings Institution, 1939.

Paris, James Daniel, *Monetary Policies of the United States, 1932–1938*. New York: Columbia University Press, 1938.

Perkins, Dexter, *The New Age of Franklin Roosevelt 1932–45*. Chicago: University of Chicago Press, 1957.

Schwarz, Jordan A., *The Interregnum of Despair: Hoover, Congress, and the Depression*. Urbana: University of Illinois Press, 1970.

Wecter, Dixon, *Age of the Great Depression*. New York: Macmillan, 1948.

ARTICLES AND UNPUBLISHED SOURCES

Boskin, Joseph, "Politics of an Opposition Party: The Republican Party in the New Deal Period." Diss. University of Minnesota, 1959.

Cooley, Everett L., "Silver Politics in the United States, 1918–1946." Diss. University of California, Berkeley, 1951.

Coombs, F. Alan, "Joseph Christopher O'Mahoney: The New Deal Years." Diss. University of Illinois, 1968.

Gordon, Lester J., "John McCormack and the Roosevelt Era." Diss. Boston University Graduate School, 1976.

Grady, Henry F., "Reciprocal Trade Agreements for Trade Extension," *Annals of the American Academy of Political and Social Science*, 211 (September, 1940), 58–64.

McGinnis, Patrick, "Republican Party Resurgence in Congress, 1936–1946." Diss. Tulane University, 1967.

Moore, Winfred B., Jr., "New Southern Statesman: The Political Career of James Francis Byrnes, 1911–1941." Diss. Duke University, 1976.

Pope, Robert D., "Senatorial Baron: The Long Political Career of Kenneth D. McKellar." Diss. Yale University, 1976.

Porter, David, "Senator Carl Hatch and the Hatch Act of 1939," *New Mexico Historical Review*, XLVIII (April, 1973), 151–164.

Porter, David, "Senator Pat Harrison of Mississippi and the Reciprocal Trade Act of 1940," *Journal of Mississippi History*, XXXVI (November, 1974), 363–376.

Porter, David L., "The Congressional Battle Over the Reciprocal Trade Extension in 1940," *Midwest Review*, 2 (Spring, 1977), 35–52.

Porter, David L., "Representative Lindsay Warren, the Water Bloc, and the Transportation Act of 1940," *North Carolina Historical Review*, L (Summer, 1973), 273–288.

Price, Charles M. and Joseph Boskin, "The Roosevelt 'Purge': A Reappraisal," *Journal of Politics*, XXVIII (August, 1966), 660–670.

Riddick, Floyd M., "First Session of the Seventy-sixth Congress," *American Political Science Review*, XXXIII (December, 1939), 1022–1043.

Riddick, Floyd M., "Third Session of the Seventy-sixth Congress," *American Political Science Review*, XXV (April, 1941), 284–303.

Rogers, Lindsay, "Reorganization: Post Mortem Notes," *Political Science Quarterly*, 53 (June, 1938), 161–172.

Ruetten, Richard T., "Burton K. Wheeler of Montana: A Progressive Between the Wars." Diss. University of Oregon, 1961.

Smyrl, Frank H., "Tom Connally and the New Deal." Diss. University of Oklahoma, 1968.

Stoesen, Alexander R., "The Senatorial Career of Claude D. Pepper." Diss. University of North Carolina, 1965.

Sullivan, Lawrence, "Relief and the Election," *Atlantic Monthly,* CLXII (November, 1938), 607–615.

Thomas Eugene P., "Has the Trade Agreements Program Succeeded?," *Annals of the American Academy of Political and Social Science,* 211 (September, 1940), 72–75.

HISTORIOGRAPHICAL GAPS

Despite the extensive literature, there still are several gaps in the congressional literature of the New Deal period. Using Patterson's adroit study as a model, historians should examine the role of liberal coalitions on Capitol Hill. Such a work would clarify who the New Dealers were, what characteristics they shared, when and how they formed as a coalition, and the effectiveness of their organization. Most legislative leaders unfortunately did not write personal memoirs or reminiscences. There are no published biographies yet of Senators Alva B. Adams, Carl A. Hatch, Scott W. Lucas, Kenneth D. McKellar, Sherman Minton, Claude Pepper, or Morris Sheppard. On the House side, no historian has published biographies of Clarence Cannon, Jr., Emanuel Celler, John J. Cochran, Hatton W. Sumners, John Taber, or Lindsay C. Warren. With the exception of reorganization and possibly transportation, each issue warrants further study. No monograph describes the entire legislative history of the Hatch Acts or the WPA. In addition, historians should devote more attention to monetary and trade legislation in the second term of President Roosevelt. The literature on the New Deal is voluminous, but much remains to be done on Congress in that era.

INDEX